The Divine Lawmaker

The Divine Lawmaker

LECTURES ON

Induction, Laws of Nature, And the Existence of God

John Foster

CLARENDON PRESS · OXFORD

OXFORD
UNIVERSITY PRESS

Great Clarendon Street, Oxford OX2 6DP

Oxford University Press is a department of the University of Oxford.
It furthers the University's objective of excellence in research, scholarship,
and education by publishing worldwide in

Oxford New York

Auckland Bangkok Buenos Aires Cape Town Chennai
Dar es Salaam Delhi Hong Kong Istanbul Karachi Kolkata
Kuala Lumpur Madrid Melbourne Mexico City Mumbai Nairobi
São Paulo Shanghai Taipei Tokyo Toronto

Oxford is a registered trade mark of Oxford University Press
in the UK and in certain other countries

Published in the United States
by Oxford University Press Inc., New York

© John Foster 2004

The moral rights of the author have been asserted
Database right Oxford University Press (maker)

First published 2004

All rights reserved. No part of this publication may be reproduced,
stored in a retrieval system, or transmitted, in any form or by any means,
without the prior permission in writing of Oxford University Press,
or as expressly permitted by law, or under terms agreed with the appropriate
reprographics rights organization. Enquiries concerning reproduction
outside the scope of the above should be sent to the Rights Department,
Oxford University Press, at the address above

You must not circulate this book in any other binding or cover
and you must impose the same condition on any acquirer

British Library Cataloguing in Publication Data

Data available

Library of Congress Cataloging in Publication Data

Data available

ISBN 0-19-925059-6

1 3 5 7 9 10 8 6 4 2

Typeset by Newgen Imaging Systems (P) Ltd., Chennai, India
Printed in Great Britain
on acid-free paper by
T. J. International Ltd., Padstow, Cornwall

To
Howard Robinson

Preface

The Divine Lawmaker is a slightly revised version of a series of lectures that I recently gave at the University of Oxford under the title of 'Induction, Laws of Nature, and the Existence of God'—a title that explicitly indicates the topics that form their subject matter. Needless to say, I have not, in the space of ten lectures, tried to cover all aspects of these topics, though I have tried to deal in some depth with the specific issues on which I focus. Nor, in pursuing these issues, have I tried to provide anything approaching a comprehensive review of the extensive relevant literature. Indeed, apart from the detailed discussion of Armstrong's views on the nature of laws in Lecture 6, I have, for the most part, preferred to focus on the issues in the abstract, rather than in the context of what others have said about them. I have preferred this because I think I can cover the philosophical ground that I want to cover more simply and more clearly by proceeding in this way.

Even with respect to the issues on which I focus, I have not tried to take account of all the considerations that bear on them. This must be especially borne in mind in the case of the issue over the existence of God. As I mention at the outset of the lectures, one of my aims is to provide an argument for the existence of God—a God of a broadly Judaeo-Christian type. I think that the particular argument I present is a powerful one, but it is only one argument, not a wide-ranging general defence. If I were aiming to construct the strongest overall case for Judaeo-Christian theism, I would want to deploy other arguments as well. The reason why I have restricted my attention to this one argument is that, in the context of these lectures, my dialectical concern with the issue of theism is narrowly circumscribed. In effect, I am only concerned with the possibility of theism as a way of responding to two other issues, namely, how we should account for the presence of natural regularities, and how, if at all, we can make sense of the notion of a natural law. And it is in relation to these issues that the relevant argument emerges.

In preparing the final version of the book, I was greatly helped by the detailed comments of two OUP readers—Richard Swinburne and an anonymous reader—who looked at an earlier draft. I am grateful to

Peter Momtchiloff of the Press for organizing this, and to the readers themselves, who took considerable trouble.

Lectures 2 and 4 contain passages that are drawn, sometimes with slight changes, from my paper 'Induction, Explanation, and Natural Necessity', in *Proceedings of the Aristotelian Society*, 83 (1982–3), and from my book *Ayer*, Part III, sections 1–5 (London: Routledge & Kegan Paul, 1985). I am grateful to the editor of the Aristotelian Society *Proceedings* and to the publishers of the book for permission to re-use the relevant material here.

J. F.

Oxford, July 2003

Contents

Lecture 1.	The Problem of Induction	1
Lecture 2.	Some Attempted Solutions	17
Lecture 3.	The Nomological-Explanatory Solution	37
Lecture 4.	Two Objections to NES	57
Lecture 5.	The Problem of Laws	77
Lecture 6.	Armstrong's Theory	94
Lecture 7.	The Scenario without Laws	111
Lecture 8.	The Theistic Account	128
Lecture 9.	God and Laws	149
Lecture 10.	Completing the Picture	167

Bibliography   185
Index   189

LECTURE I
The Problem of Induction

I

I have called these lectures 'Induction, Laws of Nature, and the Existence of God', and it is already clear from the title that I am intending to cover quite a lot of ground. And, on the face of it, *diverse* ground. But there is a connection between the different topics. One of my main aims is to provide an argument for the existence of God—a personal God of a broadly Judaeo-Christian type. But I want to get there in four stages, and it is in these stages that the topics of induction and laws of nature feature.

I want to begin by looking at the familiar problem of induction and trying to show that certain ways of attempting to solve it do not work. This will occupy our attention for the first two lectures. After that—at stage two—I want to introduce and defend what I think is, in its core, the right solution to the problem. It is a solution which the Australian philosopher David Armstrong and I independently hit upon at virtually the same time—Armstrong presenting it in his 1983 book *What is a Law of Nature?*, I in my 1983 paper to the Aristotelian Society entitled 'Induction, Explanation, and Natural Necessity'. Armstrong and I are at opposite ends of the metaphysical spectrum. Armstrong is the foremost modern champion of total materialism. I am one of the few modern defenders of a Cartesian conception of the mind; and, more exotically, I combine this with an idealist view of the physical world (though this is something best ignored in the context of these lectures). Both of us found it amusing, and in a sense reassuring, that, with such contrasting metaphysical outlooks, we managed to converge on the same view in this one area.

Now this solution to the problem of induction involves accepting the existence of laws of nature, and it involves recognizing these laws not just as regularities in the behaviour of things (consistencies in how the world works in different places and times), but as forms of natural necessity—as laws whose obtaining *ensures* that things behave and interact in certain regular ways. It is this that brings the discussion to its third stage. For I want, in this next stage, to show that accepting the existence of laws of this kind, though facilitating a solution to the problem of induction, creates its own problem. The problem it creates is simply that, given the kind of necessity they involve, it is hard to see how we can make sense of such laws—how the relevant notion of a law can be considered coherent.

It is in relation to this new problem that, in the final phase of the discussion, I construct my argument for the existence of God. For I argue that, given the problem, we can only achieve a satisfactory account of the situation if we accept that there is a God of the relevant (broadly Judaeo-Christian) type, and that it is he who is the creator of the natural world and the source of its laws. With the argument for theism in place, I bring the discussion to a close by looking again at the issue of induction, and showing how my earlier proposal needs to be reworked, in a certain key respect, in response to the theistic outcome.

With the course of the discussion outlined, let us now turn to the initial topic: the problem of induction. And we need to start by getting clear about what the problem is. Although he does not use the term 'induction', the classic statement of the problem was provided by David Hume, in sections IV and V of his *An Enquiry Concerning Human Understanding*. And if you have not already done so, I would encourage you to read his powerful account.

II

Here is a coin, which I am holding in my hand. I could release it from my grasp. My firm expectation is that, if I did, the coin would fall—fall straight down till it reached some solid surface to give it support. I am quite confident that this would be the outcome—or would be unless there were some special change in the circumstances presently obtaining, like a sudden strong gust of wind or the force of an explosion. But why should I be so confident? The expected downward movement of the coin is only one of infinitely many directions in which the coin could move. And then, in addition, there are such possibilities as the coin staying suspended in mid-air, or its breaking into a hundred fragments which move in different directions, or its disappearing altogether. If it were a matter of assigning equal chances to all the logically possible outcomes, the likelihood of the downward movement would be infinitesimally small.

Well, the basic reason why I expect the coin to fall is because that is the outcome which is in line with how, in my experience, objects like this are known to have behaved in the past. Coins, and other similar objects, have, when thus released, always fallen—fallen straight down—or at least they have done so unless there was some special reason (like the gust of wind or the explosion) to explain why they did not. But then the question becomes: why should this kind of past regularity be a good reason for expecting future cases to follow suit? It obviously does not hold as a matter of *logic* that if things have happened in a certain way in the past, then they will go on happening in that way in the future. From the premises that all unsupported coins fall, and that this, if released, will be an unsupported coin, I can indeed validly deduce that this, if released, will fall. But from the premises that all unsupported coins have *up until now* fallen, and that this, if released, will be an unsupported coin, I obviously *cannot* validly deduce that this, if released, will fall. But if my inference from the past regularity to the future instance is not *deductively* valid, what is its rationale? Can it be justified at all?

It might be thought that what lies behind it, and justifies it, is the principle that nature is uniform—that the fundamental ways in which things behave in different parts and phases of the universe are constant. But such a principle can only help to justify the inference if I know the principle to be correct, or at least have some good reason to believe it. And what could such a reason be? The principle is not one which can be known a priori: it is not a self-evident truth, or something deducible from self-evident truths. It is conceivable that different parts or phases of the universe work in quite different ways; and we cannot then, on purely a priori grounds, rule out the possibility of some radical change in how things like coins will behave in future. So my only reason for accepting the principle of uniformity seems to be that it has held well enough hitherto. But, of course, if this is my only reason for accepting the principle, then I am relying on the same kind of inference to justify accepting the principle as I was employing in the first place to justify my expectation regarding the coin—an inference from a knowledge of how things have been in the past to a conclusion that they will go on in the same way in the future. So, in effect, appealing to the principle of uniformity to justify my original inference would just beg the question. If that kind of inference needed justification in the original case, it would equally need it in the case of the principle too. In short, I seem to have made no progress in finding a rationale for my expectation about the coin. I remain confident that if released, it will fall. But I cannot seem to find any grounds or justification for this confidence.

Now this is an illustration of the problem of induction. Inductive inference, as I shall here understand it, is a form of *extrapolative* inference.[1] We know that a certain regularity has held among the observed (examined) cases; and, by induction, we infer that this regularity will extend to some not as yet observed (not as yet examined) case or class of cases. So we know that, in our experience so far, coins, and such like, when released in such and such circumstances, have always fallen, and we conclude that this coin, if now released in these circumstances, will fall. Or again, we know that, in our experience so far, ravens have always been black, and we conclude that all ravens in a certain (as yet unexamined) wood are black. Or again, we know that, in our experience so far, water has always expanded when frozen, and we conclude that water, always and everywhere, expands when frozen. Quite generally, in the most straightforward cases, the form of the inference is from the knowledge that all the examined F-things have been G to the conclusion that a certain unexamined F-thing is G, or that a certain group of unexamined F-things are G, or that all F-things are G. Notice how the conclusion can vary in extrapolative scope: it may be merely the conclusion that *a particular* unexamined case will turn out a certain way ('*this* coin, if released *now*, will fall'), or it may be, more strongly, the conclusion that *a certain range* of unexamined cases will turn out that way ('all the ravens *in yonder wood* are black'), or it may be, still more strongly, the conclusion that *all* unexamined cases will turn out that way ('water, *always and everywhere*, expands when frozen'). The form of the inference is subject to other kinds of variation too. Thus sometimes the knowledge which forms the basis of the inference is not that *all* the examined cases are of a certain type, but only that *most* are, or that a *certain proportion* are. And, correspondingly, the conclusion inductively inferred is sometimes merely that a certain unexamined case will *probably* be of the relevant type, or that the relevant type will occur among the unexamined cases with a certain *relative frequency*. But, for the time being at least, it will be best to put these further variations on one side and focus on the more straightforward types of inference we first identified—where we move from a knowledge of how things have *universally* been with respect to the examined cases to a conclusion about how they will

---

[1] Some philosophers use the term 'induction' in a broader sense, to cover certain other non-deductive forms of inference too. In my usage, induction is always extrapolative.

categorically be with respect to the unexamined case, or with respect to *each* of the relevant unexamined cases.

I have said that, in inductive inference, we move from the knowledge that a regularity has held among the examined cases to the conclusion that it will continue to hold for some unexamined case or group of cases. I should add that, when I speak here of a *regularity*, I mean one that involves a genuine qualitative similarity over the domain of the cases it covers, rather than a similarity which is created by the employment of a special predicate. I am responding here, of course, to Nelson Goodman's famous essay 'The New Riddle of Induction'.[2] Thus suppose (slightly changing Goodman's own example) we introduce a colour predicate 'gred', defined as true of any object at a time t if and only if *either* t is earlier than noon tomorrow and at t the object is green *or* t is not earlier than noon tomorrow and at t the object is red. All the emeralds so far examined have been found to be, at the times of their examination, green, and so also qualify at those times as gred. But if someone were to infer from this that emeralds are gred at *all* times at which they exist, including times that are later than noon tomorrow, that would not be a case of inferring the continuation of a regularity in the relevant sense. For the relevant similarity between gred objects before and after noon tomorrow is just a linguistic artefact— created by the use of the predicate, and not by the fact that something genuinely qualitative stays the same. It might indeed turn out that emeralds retain their gredness after the critical time. But if it does, that will not be because emeralds stay the same colour, but because they change in colour from green to red, and such a change will mark the termination of a regularity, not a continuation. For this reason, an inference from the past gredness of emeralds to their future gredness does not count as inductive for my purposes. I realize that some philosophers, Goodman included, would be sceptical about my distinction between a *genuine* similarity and one that is a *linguistic artefact*; and indeed Goodman's whole argument seems to rest on the implicit assumption that such a distinction is not available. But, to my mind, the distinction is perfectly clear, and, in the context of these lectures, I am simply going to take it for granted.[3]

---

[2] In his *Fact, Fiction, and Forecast*, 4th edn. (Cambridge, Mass.: Harvard University Press, 1983), ch. 3.

[3] I have discussed the issue in a little more detail in my *Ayer* (London: Routledge & Kegan Paul, 1985) Pt. III, sect. 4.

We constantly rely on induction in our everyday forming of expectations about the future, and indeed about the unexamined aspects of the present and the past; and, on the face of it, we also rely on it in the quest for well-founded scientific theories, though, as we shall shortly see, one eminent philosopher of science has famously disputed this. In the case of our everyday thinking, the reliance on induction is not always, indeed not typically, a matter of employing this mode of inference *explicitly*—explicitly citing the regularity that has held in the examined cases and explicitly drawing from this an extrapolative conclusion about the character of the unexamined case or cases. Usually, the forming of the expectation occurs automatically—without the backing of reflective thought. Thus we see a coin released and, without any intervening process of reasoning, find ourselves expecting it to fall. Or we are told that a raven has taken up residence in a certain tree, and, without consciously appealing to past evidence, assume that it is black. But even where it is automatic, we are still responding in an inductive way to evidence drawn from past experience. It is our knowledge of how objects like coins have regularly behaved in the past that prompts us to expect similar behaviour in the coin that has just been released, and our knowledge that hitherto observed ravens have always been black that prompts us to expect the particular raven we have been told about to be black. And these are instances of inductive reasoning, even if their inferential structure is not consciously articulated.

We constantly rely on induction both in our everyday forming of expectations and (on the face of it) in our scientific theorizing. But, as we saw in the example of the coin, once we call this mode of reasoning into question, it is not easy to see how it can be rationally justified. It is this combination of factors—our reliance on induction on the one hand and the lack of an obvious justification on the other—which creates the *problem* of induction.

III

Philosophers have responded to this problem in many different ways. But before we consider these responses, we need to make sure that we have a proper understanding of its nature. There is one mistake in particular which it is very easy to make and which leads those who make it to underestimate the problem's severity. It is a mistake, in fact, which tends to affect the interpretation of sceptical problems in general, but it is only the case of induction that will here concern us.

The sceptic about induction is calling in question the legitimacy of the extrapolative mode of inference—the mode of inference whereby we reach conclusions about certain unexamined cases by extrapolating from how things are known to have been with respect to the examined cases. Now it is easy to suppose, particularly when one is first introduced to the topic, that what is at issue here is whether we have, on the basis of this kind of inference, the right to be *sure*—to be *certain*—about the outcome in these unexamined cases. Thus it might be thought that what the sceptic is pointing out and underlining is that there is a *logical gap* between the knowledge we have about the examined cases and the conclusions which we ordinarily reach about the unexamined cases, and that, just because of this gap, we cannot be sure that these conclusions are correct. However strong the evidence from an inductive standpoint, we have to allow for the possibility that the unexamined cases may turn out differently from the examined, and so we ought, to that extent, to keep an open mind about the outcome. We should settle for merely claiming that there are *grounds for believing* that the unexamined cases will turn out the same way as the examined, and, with increasing inductive evidence, increasingly strong grounds for belief. What is in principle beyond our reach, it might be thought the sceptic is claiming, is rationally based *certainty*.

If this were all that the sceptic was claiming, his challenge would not be so worrying. It is true that, in the course of everyday life, we often find ourselves with complete certainty about how things will turn out in the unexamined cases. We do not, for example, have any doubt at all about the direction in which an unsupported coin will move, so long as there are no special factors which make the circumstances unusual. We just take it for granted that objects like this fall downwards until they reach something to support them. But, at least from the standpoint of philosophical reflection, we could surely settle for the result that we do not have the right to be absolutely sure. After all, there is no denying that, even after a long run, regularities do sometimes fail: we had thought that something was how things were universally, but have been forced to admit, on discovering a counterinstance, that that is not so. It does not have to be something as dramatic as a miracle. It can just be a matter of discovering that nature is more varied than we had thought. Take the classic example. Up to a certain date we—we *Europeans*—thought that all swans were white, but then, with the discovery of Australia, we discovered that they are sometimes black. Admittedly, where a regularity which has held in a particular region, or over a certain period, is found to fail for some other region or period, we expect there to be other regularities which cover the relevant cases, and which reveal nature as ultimately uniform. So if English swans are white and Australian swans are black, we expect there to be some genetic difference between the two types of swans which correlates with, and explains, the colour difference. Even so, the suggestion that we should, on reflection, at least entertain the possibility of the universe's turning out to be not wholly uniform—of its exhibiting different fundamental ways of working in different regions or over different periods—does not seem crazy, or to reflect any eccentrically sceptical approach. It just seems like the rationally cautious, intellectually honest response to the undeniable fact that the unexamined cases are indeed *unexamined*, and that the final, criterial, test has to be to wait and see how things turn out.

But what needs to be stressed, here, is that the sceptic about induction is not just pressing the need for this rationally cautious and honest response. He is not just insisting that, at the level of reflective thought, we should avoid absolute certainty about outcomes of which we have no direct knowledge. What he is claiming, much more strongly, is that, with respect to these outcomes, there is no rational basis for any kind of expectation at all. So, in the case of the coin, it is not just that, if the sceptic is right, I do not have the right to be *certain* that, if released, the coin will fall. It is that, if he is right, I do not have any rational grounds for even *expecting* it to fall—for thinking that falling is what is *likely* to happen. I do not have rational grounds for thinking any outcome more likely than any other. In short, the sceptic is insisting that, with respect to the unexamined cases, our situation is one of total, unqualified ignorance—that the knowledge we have of how things have been so far, however rich, and however much regularity they reveal, offers absolutely no rational guidance. This, of course, is to represent the sceptic not just as rejecting induction, but as rejecting *any method* by which one might use the examined cases as a basis for predicting the unexamined. But that indeed is his position. The reason for focusing on the inductive method is simply that it is the method that we ordinarily employ, and so it is with respect to *that* method that the sceptic's position poses a challenge.

Whether this challenge can be met remains to be seen. What I hope is now clear is the full extent of what is at stake. What is also surely clear is that, however we may respond to the challenge philosophically, there is no chance at all of our being able to absorb the sceptical position into our ordinary thinking. Remaining totally agnostic about all not-as-yet examined cases is not, in our everyday lives, a psychologically possible option.

IV

Given what is at stake, it is hardly surprising that the majority of philosophers who have focused attention on the problem of induction have tried to show how the sceptic's argument can be resisted. There are, however, some notable exceptions. The most notable is Hume himself, the originator of the problem. He recognized that the sceptical conclusion was not one to which we could adjust our ordinary modes of thought. But he was content to leave the situation in that state: the sceptic winning the philosophical argument at the level of our reflective thinking, but not affecting our disposition to extrapolative reasoning in the affairs of everyday life. In fact, Hume went further in the direction of doublethink. For having advanced the sceptical case with such force and single-mindedness, he then continued his philosophical investigations as if there was no problem. So, for example, when, in the *Enquiry*, he goes on to consider the issues of free will and determinism, and after that the issue of miracles, he simply takes it for granted that nature is uniform, and that we have good reason to accept, and indeed accept with confidence, the obtaining of certain universal regularities on the basis of the limited regularities that have shown up in the cases so far examined. There is an especial irony here in his dealing with the issue of miracles. For he makes a point of the utter irrationality of giving credence to reports of miracles precisely on the grounds that, where our ordinary experience of how the world works suggests that such events do not happen (events like walking on water and turning water into wine), reason obliges us to accept the universal regularity and dismiss the alleged counterinstance.

A more recent philosopher who has famously sided with the sceptic is Karl Popper.[4] Popper's main interest in the issue is to do with the methodology of science; and the apparent bleakness of his rejection of induction is tempered by his insistence that, contrary to what is commonly taken for granted, science does not need inductive reasoning in order to make the theoretical progress we expect of it. Science, according to Popper, does not need a method of establishing the *truth* or *likely truth* of its theories: it can confine itself to a method of *falsification*. Thus, presented with the range of data for which a theory is sought, science can advance some theory as a provisional hypothesis—a hypothesis which at least covers and perhaps explains the data in question, and which is to be provisionally entertained

---

[4] Thus see his *The Logic of Scientific Discovery* (London: Hutchinson, 1959), Pt. I, *Conjectures and Refutations* (London: Routledge & Kegan Paul, 1963), ch. 1, and *Objective Knowledge* (Oxford: Oxford University Press, 1972), ch. 1.

without the claim that it is true or even worthy of acceptance. Science can then subject the theory to a range of further tests, to see whether what it predicts in this or that further, and as yet unexamined, situation is correct. If the predictions are correct, we retain the theory, still as a provisional hypothesis, but with as it were the enhanced credit of having shown itself able to survive those tests. (Popper speaks of this as *corroboration*, rather than *confirmation*.) If, on the other hand, one of the predictions fails, then we know that the theory is mistaken and can reject it accordingly. And, having rejected it, we must then construct some new theory to put in its place—a theory which covers both the original data and the new data resulting from the tests—and this new theory will then become the new current provisional hypothesis, itself to be subjected to further tests. This, as Popper sees it, is how scientific progress is made—using a procedure designed for the falsification of theories, rather than one which aims at their verification.

As an account of scientific method, at least in physics and chemistry, this sounds quite plausible. But where I think Popper goes wrong is in supposing that the procedure would work in a satisfactory way without the backing of induction.[5] The point where, it seems to me, induction is needed is in deciding what kind of theory to choose as a replacement for one which has been shown, by the failure of one of its predictions, to be mistaken. Thus suppose we are provisionally entertaining the theory that whenever an A-type particle meets a B-type particle, they produce a C-type particle. This has held good in all the situations so far investigated. We then put the theory to the test in a further situation, which we may think is not significantly different from the others, and the predicted result does not occur. We check very carefully on what has happened, and cannot avoid the conclusion that, on this occasion, there was a genuine meeting of a genuine A-type particle and a genuine B-type particle, with no resulting C-type particle. So we are forced to acknowledge that the original theory is mistaken. But where do we go from there? Well, Popper would say, as any *scientist* would say, that we should try to find some relevant difference between the situation where the prediction failed and all the others where it succeeded, and then come up with a unitary theory which covers both types of result—a theory which represents the world as behaving in a uniform way after all. But an alternative response would just be to accept

---

[5] My argument here develops a point which (as far as I know) was first made by A. J. Ayer. Thus see his *The Problem of Knowledge*, (London: Penguin Books, 1956), 73–4.

that the world is not wholly regular, and that, on this particular occasion, for no interesting reason, there was a different result. In other words, we might just replace the original theory by one which claims that whenever an A-type particle meets a B-type particle, they produce a C-type particle *except on that occasion*. Now, of course, if we were to put forward such a theory as our new provisional hypothesis, it would immediately invite a retesting of it in the same kind of conditions (the conditions in which the original theory failed), and no doubt when that retest was done, the same negative result would emerge, forcing us to reject the new theory too. But, in the face of any such refutation, we could always respond in the same conservative way, by retaining the original theory, and simply expanding the class of specified exceptions. Now, from a scientific standpoint, such a procedure would be seen as just perverse—something designed to lock us into an unending series of refutations, without making any theoretical progress. But notice that the assumption underlying this scientific verdict is that nature is *uniform*, and that once the original hypothesis has been found to fail on one occasion, we should expect it to fail again when exactly the same type of situation recurs. And if we could not rely on this assumption of uniformity, then, as far as I can see, there is no way, except by arbitrary stipulation, in which the perverse procedure could be ruled out. But our only grounds for accepting that nature is uniform are that it has been found to be uniform over the cases so far examined; and these grounds will only entitle us to expect uniformity over the unexamined cases if we can rely on the rationality of induction. So if science is to have a principled way of excluding the envisaged procedure—which I assume that Popper himself would think crucial—it has to rely, at this point, on the rationality of induction, contrary to what Popper supposes.

V

Hume and Popper are two major thinkers who have sided with the sceptic. But, as I said, the main tendency among philosophers who have focused on this issue has been to try to show how the sceptic can be resisted. And this will be the goal of my own investigation too. Of course, opposing the sceptic does not involve claiming that *all* forms of inductive inference are rational. One does not need to be a sceptic to recognize that there are a number of ways in which inductive inferences can be rationally defective in their own terms. For example, the examined cases may be insufficiently numerous; or there may be other things we know which strongly evidentially point in a contrary direction; or the relevant unexamined case or cases may be in conditions that are sharply different from those of the examined cases. All the defender of induction is committed to claiming is that inductive inferences are rational when they satisfy the appropriate conditions. In effect, he is committed to claiming that, *other things being equal*, the holding of a regularity over the examined cases provides evidential support for the conclusion that it will continue to hold for the unexamined cases, and that, *when the relevant conditions are satisfied*, this support is sufficiently strong to justify a belief or expectation that things will turn out that way. The sceptic, of course, is insisting that there are no circumstances in which such beliefs or expectations are justified or have any degree of rational support.

There are many different ways in which philosophers have tried to defeat the sceptic, and we shall need to explore a number of these in detail in due course. But, among the various proposals, there are three in particular which are, to my mind, non-starters. What I want to do next, to prepare the way for the main discussion, is to identify these three proposals, and explain why I think that they should be dismissed.

The first proposal is that we should offer a justification of induction by appeal to its past success. The argument is that induction, appropriately employed, has served us well as a method of prediction in the past, and, on this basis, we are entitled to expect it to serve us well in future. In other words, we can justify a reliance on induction by employing an inductive inference with respect to the predominant success of its own past applications. This, it seems to me—as indeed it seems to the vast majority of philosophers—is clearly question-begging and of no help at all in defeating the sceptic. It is true that the reasoning involved is not, as is sometimes alleged, *circular*: using induction to argue for its own reliability does not involve assuming such reliability, explicitly or implicitly, as a premise, or as the basis of a premise. And some philosophers have concluded that, without such circularity, the reasoning is not vulnerable to objection at all.[6] But I cannot see how we can get round the point that if there is a sceptical problem about extrapolating from the past regularities in the workings of

---

[6] Thus see R. B. Braithwaite, *Scientific Explanation* (Cambridge: Cambridge University Press, 1953), 264–92, reprinted in Richard Swinburne (ed.), *The Justification of Induction* (Oxford: Oxford University Press, 1974), 102–26, and Max Black, *Problems of Analysis* (London: Routledge & Kegan Paul, 1954), ch. 11, and 'Self-Supporting Inductive Arguments', *Journal of Philosophy* 55 (1958), 718–25, reprinted in Swinburne, *Justification of Induction*, 127–34.

the world to their future continuance, there is equally a sceptical problem about extrapolating from the past success of the extrapolative method to its future continuance. Indeed, it is surely clear that it is only in so far as we could independently solve the first problem, and thereby have grounds for expecting the continuation of the regularities, that we could have grounds for expecting the future success of the extrapolative method.

The second proposal, which was first made by Hans Reichenbach, is that we should try to justify induction *pragmatically*.[7] The argument can be developed in a number of subtly different ways, but its basic approach is reminiscent of Pascal's wager. Beyond the cases we have examined, we are, it is conceded, ignorant as to whether the universe works in a uniform way or not. But if it does, or if its workings are at least *predominantly* uniform, then induction, it is claimed, promises to be a generally successful method of inference. And if it does not, then no method of inference from examined to unexamined cases has any prospect of success. So we have much to gain and nothing to lose by employing induction. Even in its own terms, I think that this argument is fallacious; for I think that we can envisage specific forms of non-uniform universe for which a specific non-inductive method of inference would be advantageous. But even if the argument were correct, there is an obvious reason why we should set it aside in the present context. For it is not offering any challenge to the sceptic's conclusion. It is purporting to give us a practical reason for using induction. But it is not offering us any grounds for believing that induction will continue to be successful, nor grounds for believing, in any particular instance, that a regularity which has held for the examined cases will continue to hold for some unexamined case or group of cases. For that reason, it is simply irrelevant to the theoretical issue that here concerns us.

The third proposal, which became popular in the heyday of linguistic analysis, is that we should take it to be true *by definition* that, when they satisfy the appropriate conditions, inductive inferences are rational.[8] The argument here is that what we *mean* by saying, of an inference from the examined to the unexamined, that it is 'rational', is precisely that it is

---

[7] Thus see Hans Reichenbach, *Experience and Prediction* (Chicago: University of Chicago Press, 1938), ch. 5. For a further development of the approach, see also Wesley C. Salmon, 'Inductive Inference', in B. Baumrin (ed.), *Philosophy of Science: The Delaware Seminar* (New York: Interscience Publishers, 1963), 353–70. An extract from this is reprinted in Swinburne, *Justification of Induction*, 85–97.

[8] For classic expositions of this proposal, see Paul Edwards, 'Russell's Doubts about Induction', *Mind* 68 (1949), 141–63, reprinted in Swinburne, *Justification of Induction*, 26–47, and P. F. Strawson, *Introduction to Logical Theory*, ch. 9, sect. II.

sanctioned by our ordinary inductive criteria—by our standard ways of deciding what is an acceptable form of inference from an inductive standpoint. And if this is so, then, in challenging the rationality of inferences which are thus sanctioned, the sceptic is showing that he has failed to grasp the meaning of the term 'rational'—the content of the concept of rationality—as it applies in this area. He has failed to notice that, once it is known that the evidence provides adequate support for the conclusion by the standards which are internal to our inductive practice—standards which concern such factors as the number of cases examined, the range of types of circumstance from which they are drawn, the proportion of such cases that have the relevant feature, and the strength of the conclusion inferred—there is no further issue of rationality that can be coherently raised. But the objection to this argument is that the concept of rationality, as it applies in this or indeed in any other area, is in fact a *normative* one. To speak of an inference as *rational* is to imply that it is *worthy of endorsement*, that it *ought to be accepted*. And even if it is true that inferences of the relevant sort are rational in this normative sense, there is clearly no way in which this could be established by merely unpacking what is implicit in the meaning of the term 'rational', or in the content of the concept of rationality. Nor, of course, could the argument be salvaged by introducing a new concept of rationality that was free of any normative element and guaranteed to apply to inferences of the relevant sort. For it is precisely the normative issue that the sceptic is addressing. His claim is not that inductive inferences cannot pass the test of acceptability by reference to our ordinary inductive criteria, but that these criteria themselves have no objective warrant, and that, because they have no objective warrant, the inferences they license are not ultimately worthy of acceptance.[9]

VI

I have identified three proposals for answering the sceptic which, as I see it, are non-starters and should be dismissed at the outset. With these out of the way, we are almost ready to begin the main part of our investigation. But there is one final preliminary point that needs to be made. For before we focus in detail on any further proposal as to how the sceptic might be

---

[9] For a fuller discussion of these issues, see Simon Blackburn, *Reason and Prediction* (Cambridge: Cambridge University Press, 1973), chs. 1–2.

resisted, we need to take note of a crucial distinction between two very different forms which such resistance could take.

The sceptic is claiming that inductive inferences are irrational. And the basis of this claim is simply that he can see no way of *establishing* their rationality. In effect, he is putting the onus of proof on those who would endorse induction to make good their case. He is issuing a challenge to the inductivist to provide a rational justification of induction, and insisting that it is irrational to form expectations in the inductive way until a justification has been supplied. The most straightforward way of resisting the sceptic would be to take up this challenge and try to meet it—try to provide a justification for induction, try to show that inductive reasoning, when it is of the appropriate type, has a rational basis. The three anti-sceptical proposals I considered and rejected above were all attempts—albeit unsuccessful attempts—to meet the challenge in this way; and, of course, there are other attempts at justification which we have yet to consider.

But there is also a quite different approach which the defender of induction might take. Instead of taking up the sceptic's challenge and trying to meet it, he might claim that the challenge should never have been made. Thus he might claim that induction is something whose rationality should just be taken for granted—something that should be recognized as a basic form of sound reasoning, not standing in need of justification. There is no way of trying to validate our methods of *deductive* reasoning which does not, by employing those same methods, in effect presuppose their validity. But this is not thought to create a sceptical problem. On the contrary, we are happy to regard our modes of deductive reasoning as rationally acceptable in their own right, without needing anything else to justify them. In the same way, it might be insisted that inductive reasoning, when properly constituted, is something rationally acceptable in its own right— something which we are entitled to endorse without having to establish its soundness on some independent basis. This, if I interpret him aright, is the position adopted by A. J. Ayer.[10] We must be careful not to confuse this position with the view, already dismissed, that it is true *by definition* that inductive inferences of the relevant sort are rational. The claim that induction is a basic form of sound reasoning, or that it is something rationally acceptable in its own right, is being put forward as an irreducibly normative judgement, not as signalling the way in which such expressions as 'sound reasoning' and 'rational acceptability' are to be defined.

---

[10] See especially his *Problem of Knowledge*, ch. 2, sect. viii.

From a dialectical standpoint, this way of resisting the sceptic would not be as effective as a successful pursuit of the first. For unless induction is *shown* to be rational, the sceptic can simply dig his heels in and insist that he cannot discern the rationality that is being claimed. The only sure way of silencing the sceptic is to acknowledge the legitimacy of his challenge and show how it can be met. Nonetheless, I suspect that, of all the possible responses to the sceptic, this second approach is the one that commands the greatest current support. One reason for this is simply that, after so much expenditure of effort, apparently to no avail, most philosophers have now despaired of finding any adequate justification for induction; and, being unwilling to accept the sceptic's conclusion, they find themselves with no other means of opposing it. But there is also something else that can make the approach seem congenial. Whatever its *philosophical* status, induction is certainly a *psychologically* fundamental form of reasoning at the level of our ordinary thinking. We do not, in our ordinary thinking, recognize any need to justify our readiness to extrapolate from hitherto exemplified regularities to their future continuance. Rather, this readiness presents itself to us as an aspect of normal human rationality—as simply the rational way of being responsive to the available evidence. It is not surprising, then, that when they come to reflect on the status of this reasoning, many philosophers feel drawn towards endorsing this commonsense perspective.

My own view, as will emerge, is that induction is *not* something whose rationality should be taken for granted and that it *does* stand in need of justification. Over the next two lectures I shall be explaining why I think that this is so and how I think a justification can be provided.

LECTURE 2
Some Attempted Solutions

I

In the first lecture, I provided an account of the problem of induction. Induction, as I here understand it, is that form of empirical inference based on extrapolation. We find a certain kind of regularity in the domain of the examined cases, and infer the continuation of this regularity with respect to some unexamined case or group of cases. So, knowing that all ravens so far examined have been black, we might infer from this that a particular unexamined raven is black. Or knowing that all bodies so far examined have behaved gravitationally, we might infer from this that bodies, everywhere and at all times, behave gravitationally. These kinds of extrapolative inference are ones that we constantly use, or implicitly rely on, in our everyday practical lives, and, for the most part, with conspicuous success. The problem arises at the level of philosophical reflection, when we try to discover what, if anything, makes them rational. As I stressed, the problem is not that it is hard to see what could give us the right to be *sure* that such inferences will succeed, or will do so when they satisfy certain conditions: acknowledging that we are not entitled to *certainty* about the unexamined cases is not, on reflection, disturbing. What is at issue is whether there is a rational basis for *prediction at all*. Having hitherto only encountered black ravens, are we rationally entitled even to *expect* the next raven we encounter to be black? Having hitherto found that unsupported bodies fall, am I rationally entitled to think it at least very *likely* that, if I release this coin now, it will fall? Intuitively, it seems that there must be such entitlement. The problem is to find what provides it. According to the sceptic, inductive reasoning is wholly devoid of a rational basis, and the holding of a regularity in our experience hitherto never provides any grounds at all for expecting it to hold in our future experience.

18 · *Some Attempted Solutions*

I have already considered three proposals for answering the sceptic, which I have dismissed as non-starters. The first was that we should try to provide a rational basis for induction by appeal to its past success. This was seen as clearly question-begging, since we would only be entitled to think of its past success as affording grounds for expecting its future success if we already knew that induction was rational. The second proposal was that we should try to justify induction pragmatically, on the grounds that if nature is predominantly uniform, induction promises to be a generally successful method of inference, and if nature is not predominantly uniform, then no method of inference from examined to unexamined cases has any prospect of success. My main reason for rejecting this approach was that it is simply not relevant to the sceptical problem that concerns us. For, even if it gives us a practical reason for using induction, it does not give us any grounds for believing that induction will continue to be successful, or for forming an inductive expectation in any particular case. The third proposal was that we should take it to be true by definition that, when they satisfy the appropriate conditions, inductive inferences are rational, since what it *means* to speak of an inference from the examined to the unexamined as rational is precisely that it passes the test of acceptability imposed by our ordinary inductive criteria. The objection to this was that the concept of rationality is in fact a normative one: to characterize an inference as rational is to imply that it is *worthy of endorsement*, that it *ought to be accepted*. And there is clearly no way in which it could be true merely by definition that inferences which are sanctioned by our ordinary inductive criteria are rational in this normative sense.

With these three proposals rejected at the outset, let us now consider what other ways of answering the sceptic may be available.

II

One way in which philosophers have commonly tried to establish the credentials of inductive reasoning is by appeal to some a priori theory of probability. The general idea of such appeals is that there are certain abstract truths of probability which we can know a priori (without recourse to empirical evidence) and which are philosophically uncontroversial; and we can then provide a justification of inductive reasoning, or at least some degree of justification, by showing how these abstract truths apply to the concrete factors in the inductive situation. Because the relevant truths are philosophically uncontroversial, they are ones that even the sceptic about induction would be obliged to accept.

There are a number of ways of trying to provide a justification of induction along these lines, and it seems to me that they all fail. The failure can come about in three ways. There are cases where what the attempt establishes is not even relevant to the issue of induction. There are cases where, despite its aprioristic intentions, the attempt turns out to depend, implicitly, on certain empirical assumptions, and ones that are not warranted while the rationality of induction is under suspicion. And, among those latter cases, there are ones where, even when the empirical assumptions are granted, the extrapolative inferences which get legitimized are of a highly restricted kind, and do not cover the main uses of induction either in science or in everyday life. I shall not have time to discuss all the different attempts which have been made or which we can envisage. Nor, dialectically, do I need to; for the case I shall eventually offer in favour of my own solution to the problem of induction will, I hope, be convincing in its own terms. But I think it will be instructive to focus on two attempts in particular, which are of interest in their own right, and which will serve to illustrate the different ways in which the inadequacy of this whole approach can manifest itself.

Before I consider these two proposals, there are some points of clarification that need to be made.

To begin with, we need to recognize, at the outset, that there are two quite different kinds of probability that will be relevant to our discussion, and they must not be confused. One kind is what is sometimes known as *epistemic* probability. It is the probability of the truth of a certain proposition relative to certain evidence. In other words, it is the degree of confidence that we would be rationally entitled to have in the truth of a certain proposition on the basis of certain evidence—the basis of the acceptance of certain propositions represented as already known. So a detective investigating a murder might discover Jones's fingerprints on the murder weapon, and conclude that, on the basis of this finding and the rest of what he knows, he is entitled to a high degree of confidence that Jones is the guilty party. And this is equivalent to saying that, as the detective sees things, the guilt of this person is epistemically very probable relative to the relevant evidence. It should be stressed that, in order for there to be a fact of epistemic probability, it is not necessary that the relevant evidence be *actual*. A proposition can have a certain probability of truth relative to information *hypothetically* possessed, and the propositions which form the content of this hypothetical information do not even have to be true.

The other kind of probability is what we might term *natural*, and it is to do, not with evidential support or rational belief, but with the presence of bias and chance in the workings of the world. It is exemplified by cases in which, in the framework of the laws of nature, the properties of a certain situation give it a propensity (of a certain strength) to give rise to a certain type of outcome, or in which the properties of a certain object give it a propensity (of a certain strength) to behave in a certain way in certain conditions. For example, if someone's immune system is severely damaged, this will make him highly prone to infection in normal types of environment, and, in that sense, will make the occurrence of infection highly likely unless prophylactic arrangements are put in place; and this likelihood will be an instance of *natural* probability, distinct from any fact about what, on certain evidence, it would be rational to believe. Or again, if someone were to construct a coin in such a way as to give it a causal bias in favour of coming up heads when tossed, this bias would make it very likely for the heads outcome to predominate when the coin is tossed a sufficiently large number of times; and this too would be an instance of natural, rather than epistemic, probability. Although the natural and epistemic kinds of probability are quite different, they are, in one obvious respect, closely linked. For the knowledge of a natural probability automatically constitutes evidence relative to which there is an associated epistemic probability. Thus if we know that the damage to someone's immune system has left him with a natural propensity to infection, we thereby have grounds for expecting that, without protective measures in place, infection will occur; and if we know that the construction of a coin is such as to give it a strong natural bias in favour of heads, this entitles us to be confident that the heads outcome will correspondingly predominate if we toss the coin a hundred times.

When probability is represented mathematically, its degrees of strength are measured by the real numbers from 0 to 1. In the epistemic case, we get a probability of 1 when there is a rational warrant for being certain of the truth of the relevant proposition, and a probability of 0 when there is a rational warrant for being certain of its falsity. In the natural case, we get a probability of 1 when the occurrence of the relevant type of event or state of affairs is rendered inevitable, and a probability of 0 when it is rendered impossible. The significance of the values that lie between 1 and 0 follows accordingly. So, for example, epistemically, 1/2 marks the point where the degree of warranted confidence in the truth of a proposition is equal to the degree of warranted confidence in its falsity; and, naturally, it marks the point where the chance of the occurrence of the relevant type of event or state of affairs is equal to the chance of its non-occurrence. In many instances, the use of real numbers to measure the degree of the relevant probability is clearly an idealization: in reality, the degrees do not have that numerical exactness. But, even in those cases, the fiction of supposing that there is an exact numerical measure is useful in setting out the logical relations between different probability claims. For example, irrespective of whether or not they have exact numerical values, we want to say that, relative to any evidence, the truth of a proposition is probable to whatever degree the truth of its negation fails to be probable, and this is conveniently expressed by saying that the sum of the two probabilities is equal to 1. We should also note that, where a natural probability falls between 0 and 1, this need not mean that, in this area, the workings of nature are ultimately non-deterministic. The fact that damage to someone's immune system makes him *prone* to infection, without making infection *inevitable*, does not mean that the actual course of events in the person's subsequent medical history is not, at each point, fully determined by the totality of factors that are causally relevant. And the fact that a coin is constructed so as to give it equal chances of heads and tails for an arbitrary toss does not mean that there is a failure of determinism with respect to the outcome of any particular toss. Cases where nature *does* seem to work in an ultimately non-deterministic way will become relevant to our discussion in due course.

Of the two kinds of probability, it is the epistemic variety that has an immediate connection with the topic of induction and the issue of its justification. Induction, after all, is a method of inference from evidence to conclusion, and, in each case of its employment, the inference is rational if and only if the evidence warrants a sufficient degree of confidence in the truth of the conclusion. So the issue of whether induction can be justified is precisely the issue of whether a certain class of claims of epistemic probability can be shown to be true. It is hardly surprising, then, that the two attempts at a justification that I am about to consider are extensively concerned with matters of epistemic probability. Even so, matters of natural probability will also importantly feature.

Let me, then, turn to the discussion of these two proposals. As I indicated, they are illustrative of a general approach to the problem of induction—an approach which tries to justify inductive reasoning by appeal to certain truths of probability that are knowable a priori and philosophically uncontroversial. In considering them now, I shall, in broad outline, follow the

22 · Some Attempted Solutions

account I previously gave in my book on the philosophy of A. J. Ayer,[1] and, in the case of the first attempt, the core of my argument is directly drawn from Ayer's own discussion in *Probability and Evidence*.[2] I shall, of course, try to make sure that, whenever I speak of probability, it is always clear which of the two kinds I have in mind.

III

The first attempt appeals to a principle of probability which standardly features as an axiom in formal systems of probability, and which indeed qualifies as something knowable a priori and philosophically uncontroversial. It can occur in more than one form. In the form that here concerns us, the principle is concerned with epistemic probability, and states that, for any propositions P and Q, and body of evidence E, the probability of the truth of the conjunction of P and Q, relative to E, equals the probability of the truth of P relative to E multiplied by the probability of the truth of Q relative to the conjunction of P and E. Or put more succinctly:

$$\text{Prob}([P \& Q] \text{ on } E) = \text{Prob}(P \text{ on } E) \times \text{Prob}(Q \text{ on } [P \& E])$$

In other words, the degree of confidence we are entitled to have in the truth of the conjunction of propositions P and Q on the basis of evidence E equals the degree of confidence we are entitled to have in the truth of P on the basis of E multiplied by the degree of confidence we are entitled to have in the truth of Q on the basis of the conjunction of P and E. Let us refer to it as the *multiplication* principle. To illustrate how the principle works, let us take a case where we can give the relevant probabilities precise numerical values. Thus suppose we know that someone has been dealt two playing cards from a standard pack, by a method that was not biased in favour of any particular card or subset of cards, and we want to work out the probability of both cards being spades relative to this information. We know that there are 13 spades in the pack of 52. So, relative to our information, the probability that the first card dealt was a spade is 13/52, that is, 1/4; and, relative to the conjunction of that information and the supposition that the first card was a spade, the probability that

---

[1] Ayer, Pt. III, sect. 3.
[2] A. J. Ayer, *Probability and Evidence* (London: Macmillan, 1972), 30–3.

the second card was a spade is 12/51, that is, 4/17. The multiplication principle then allows us to conclude, correctly, that the probability of both cards being spades, relative to our original information, is $1/4 \times 4/17$, that is, 1/17.

Now it might seem that, even on its own, this uncontroversial principle provides some degree of justification for induction. To follow the reasoning, let us focus on a concrete case.[3] Suppose that all ravens so far examined have been black, and let Rupert be some as yet unexamined raven. And let G be the generalization that all ravens are black, S the singular proposition that Rupert is black, and E our present information. This information includes the knowledge that Rupert is an as yet unexamined raven, and that all the ravens so far examined have been black, but leaves open the colour of Rupert and all the other unexamined ravens. And finally, let us assume that there are only finitely many ravens. If there is any problem about the legitimacy of this assumption, we can always restrict the relevant domain of ravens in a way that guarantees finiteness, without undermining the point of the example (for instance, we could limit the domain to ravens existing between 10,000 B.C. and A.D. 10,000). With the finiteness assumption in place, we can take the probability of G on E to be greater than 0.

Now, by two applications of the multiplication principle, we have:

(1)   Prob ([G & S] on E = Prob (G on E) × Prob (S on [G & E])
(2)   Prob ([S & G] on E = Prob (S on E) × Prob (G on [S & E])

Since the expressions on the left side of these equations are synonymous, we get (by equating the right halves):[4]

(3)   Prob (G on E) × Prob (S on [G & E])
      = Prob (S on E) × Prob (G on [S & E])

which (given that Prob (G on E), and hence Prob (G on [S & E]), is greater than 0) can be reformulated as:

(4) $\dfrac{\text{Prob (G on E)}}{\text{Prob (G on [S \& E])}} = \dfrac{\text{Prob (S on E)}}{\text{Prob (S on [G \& E])}}$

---

[3] The core of the reasoning that I here illustrate comes from Jean Nicod, *Foundations of Geometry and Induction* (London: Routledge & Kegan Paul, 1930), 266–8.
[4] What follows is, of course, just a variant, in a specific form, of Bayes's theorem.

24 · *Some Attempted Solutions*

Now focus on the right half of this equation. Since E includes the information that Rupert is a raven, G and E jointly entail S. So (looking at what is underneath the line) we can assert:

(5) Prob (S on [G & E]) = 1

But we know that E leaves open Rupert's colour, and so leaves open the truth value of S. So (looking at what is above the line) we must accept:

(6) Prob (S on E) < 1

So, on the right side of the equation, we have the number 1 below the line and a number less than 1 above the line, and so we have a smaller number over a larger number. It follows that, in order to preserve the equation, we need a similar relationship on the left. In other words, we know that

(7) Prob (G on E) < Prob (G on [S & E])

But what this shows is that, if we were now to discover that Rupert is black, allowing us to add this new item of knowledge to our existing information, the probability of the truth of the generalization, relative to our total information, would increase. The discovery that Rupert was black would entitle us to a greater degree of confidence that all ravens were black.

This is just one case. But obviously an analogous argument can be constructed for any case of the same general kind. So we are forced to conclude, quite generally, that, with analogous assumptions in place, the probability of the truth of a generalization, relative to current information, increases with each new instance in which it is found to hold, given no counterinstance. And, at first sight, this seems to provide at least a partial justification of induction. It seems to show that, in standard circumstances, the greater the number of positive instances of a regularity that we have found, without finding a counterinstance, the stronger our grounds for expecting the regularity to extend to the whole domain, and so the stronger our grounds for expecting it to hold for the unexamined cases. And this, in turn, seems to take us a significant step nearer to the conclusion that, when a regularity has held good over a sufficient number of cases, and when all the other relevant conditions are satisfied, there are sufficient grounds for an extrapolative inference.

All this, however, is just an illusion. There is nothing wrong, in the example, with the reasoning that leads to (7). And this indeed does show, quite generally, that, with the relevant assumptions in place, the likelihood of a generalization's being true, relative to current evidence, increases with each new favourable instance, given no counterinstance. But this result has absolutely nothing to do with induction. It merely reflects the trivial fact that, with each new favourable instance, there are fewer cases left in which the generalization could fail. This can be brought out by focusing on a case where we *know* that induction can be of no help. Thus suppose we know that an unbiased coin has, by an unbiased method, been tossed ten times, but we do not yet know the outcomes. Relative to this information, we can set the epistemic probability of all the outcomes being heads at $1/2^{10}$; for the probability of heads for any particular toss is $1/2$, and all the outcomes are independent. Now suppose we subsequently learn that the outcome of the first toss was heads. The multiplication principle tells us, as we have seen, that if we add this datum to our previous information, the probability, on the new total information, of all the outcomes being heads increases. And, of course, we can see why this is so. For there are now only nine outcomes left where the generalization could fail. So, relative to our new current information, the probability becomes $1/2^9$, which is indeed the value assigned by the principle. And with the further revelation that the outcome of the second toss was heads, the probability would go up to $1/2^8$. But none of this has got anything to do with induction. For each such increase in the probability of the truth of the generalization—the probability of all the outcomes being heads—does not make it any easier to predict any of the as yet unrevealed outcomes. It tells us that there are fewer outcomes left where a counterinstance could be forthcoming; but, for each outcome left, the probability of its being heads stays at $1/2$—the value fixed by our knowledge that the coin and the method of tossing are unbiased. So what the multiplication principle tells us is correct, but it does not afford any basis for extrapolation. And this holds true of any case in which the principle is applied in the way envisaged.

IV

The second attempt to justify induction by appeal to some a priori theory of probability focuses on certain principles of sampling.[5] A precise account of these principles, and the mathematical truths that underlie

---

[5] Among others, David Stove has offered a justification of induction along these lines in his *The Rationality of Induction* (Oxford: Oxford University Press, 1986).

them, would be technically complex and I think counterproductive in the present context. But the basic points, which will suffice for our purposes, can be put quite simply.

Suppose we know that there are exactly 1,000 marbles in a bag, each either red or green, but we do not know in what proportions. And let us assume that, in this initial situation, all hypotheses about the proportions of the two colours are equally plausible—equally epistemically probable relative to our current information. We then draw out 100 marbles at random, *knowing* the draw to be random, of which 90 turn out to be red and 10 to be green. We have as yet no direct knowledge about the colours of the remaining 900 marbles: our evidence leaves open the possibility that they are all red, the possibility that they are all green, and all the possibilities in between. But it seems that, purely a priori grounds, we can be reasonably confident that the ratio of red to green marbles in the total population does not greatly differ from the ratio of 9 to 1 found in the sample. This confidence would rest on five points. First, what is meant by saying that the draw was random is that the balls were selected by a method that gave an equal chance—an equal degree of natural probability—of selection to each possible sample of the relevant size, and so was not biased in favour of either colour. Second, the closer the ratio in the population comes to that in the sample, the greater is the proportion of possible samples of that size—100-marble subsets of the original 1,000—that have that sample's ratio. Third, given that the sample was selected at random, by a method that gave an equal chance of selection to each 100-marble subset, the greater the proportion of such subsets with the 9 to 1 ratio, the greater the prior natural probability of the sample drawn turning out to have that ratio. Fourth, given that the different hypotheses about the ratio in the population were equally plausible initially, and that the 9 to 1 ratio in the sample is the only new piece of relevant evidence, a hypothesis H1 becomes more plausible than a hypothesis H2 in the light of this evidence (comes to acquire a higher epistemic probability) to the extent that the prior natural probability of the sample having that ratio would be greater under the truth of H1 than under the truth of H2. And fifth, the size of the sample is sufficient to ensure that even quite small differences in the ratio in the population would create quite sharp differences in the relevant prior probabilities; and, by point four, these differences will feed through to the relative plausibilities of the corresponding hypotheses in the light of the sample ratio that has actually occurred. (Quite generally, of course, the larger the sample, the greater these differences.) In short, and putting everything together, we can be reasonably confident that the ratio in the 1,000-marble population does not greatly differ from the 9 to 1 ratio of the sample, because, if it did, there would have been much less chance (a much smaller natural probability) of our randomly drawing a sample with that ratio, and because, in default of any other information that bears on the issue, it is reasonable to think that the ratio that has emerged is one that was relatively likely to emerge, given the circumstances of the draw, rather than one that was relatively unlikely. We have reached this conclusion in the framework of certain specific assumptions about the numerical factors involved—the total number of marbles, the number of relevant colours, the size of the sample, and the distribution of the colours in the sample. But, of course, we could vary these assumptions in a wide range of ways without altering the general character of the result.

Now the set-up of drawing marbles from a bag is an artificial one: it is not often that we find ourselves needing to make predictions about the unexamined cases in that sort of way. But it might seem that the reasoning involved in it could be applied quite generally to situations where we are wanting to gauge the distribution of some property among the members of a larger class on the basis of a sample for which the distribution is known; and this might lead us to think that we have here the makings of a general justification of induction. For why should we not represent *any* inductive situation in these terms? Thus the argument might run: 'Hitherto, ravens examined have turned out to be black. So we can be reasonably confident that the total population of ravens is, or is predominantly, black. For if it contained more than a tiny fraction of non-black members, there would have been much less chance (a much smaller natural probability) of our now finding ourselves in a situation in which no non-black raven has been detected.' Or again it might run: '90 per cent of the people we have so far come across have been right-handed. So we can be reasonably confident that a roughly similar proportion of people quite generally are right-handed. For if this proportion differed considerably, there would have been much less chance (a much smaller natural probability) of our finding the 90 per cent frequency among the cases examined.' Admittedly, in applying the reasoning to these kinds of case, we would have to ensure that the relevant population, like that of the marbles, was finite. For if it were infinite, it would make no sense to speak of the *proportion* of its members that had the relevant feature. But this presents no problem. If there is a danger that the population we have initially chosen is infinite, we can easily select a finite portion of it that covers the area of our predictive concern.

Now there can be no denying that, unlike the earlier case, this appeal to the principles of sampling is relevant to the issue of extrapolation: it is purporting to justify an inference from what we have found to hold in the sample to what we can reasonably expect about the total population; and the claim about what we can reasonably expect about the population has direct implications for what we can reasonably expect about its unexamined portion. In this respect, the attempt to provide a justification for induction is on track. But, as we shall now see, there are other reasons why it fails.

The first point to notice is that, even if the argument were successful for the case of the marbles, and other cases of that sort, it could not, contrary to what was suggested, be applied to cases of inductive reasoning in general. In the case of the marbles, we made the assumption that the sample was drawn *at random*, and we have taken this to mean that the method of selection gave equal chances of selection to all possible relevantly sized samples. This assumption was crucial. Without it, we would not be entitled to assume that the smaller the proportion of possible samples with the 9 to 1 ratio, the less naturally likely that ratio was to show up in the sample drawn; and so there would be no grounds for expecting the ratios in the sample drawn and in the total population to be reasonably close. But the assumption of randomness cannot standardly be made in ordinary cases of induction. For, in such cases, the unexamined cases whose character we are trying to gauge are almost always ones that did not have the same chance of being selected. Indeed, in the most typical type of case, they had no chance of being selected at all, since they lay, relative to the time of the inference, in the future. But it is only to the extent that the unexamined items were available and liable to be selected that we can see the findings about the actual sample as having any evidential bearing on their character—at least when we are merely relying on the a priori principles of sampling. And, in the extreme, but typical, case in which the relevant items were not available at all, then, as far as these principles go, the findings about the sample are entirely irrelevant.

To illustrate the point, consider the two hypotheses: H1, that all ravens are black; and H2, that all the ravens up to the present time have been black, but, from now on, they will all be white. All the ravens we have so far examined have been black. But how can we use this fact to show that, relative to our evidence, H1 is more plausible—has a higher epistemic probability—than H2? There is no denying that if the future ravens are all white, then the colour distribution in our current sample is, relative to the whole range of similar-sized subsets in the total population, much less typical than it would be if these future ravens were all black. But this does not help if, as is clearly the case, the future ravens have had no chance of being examined, and so have had no chance of occurring in our sample. The analogy would be this: after randomly drawing the sample of marbles from the bag, the bag is emptied and refilled with new marbles, and we are asked to estimate the distribution of colours in this new population from the sample drawn from the old. Obviously, we have no reason to extrapolate unless we have some independent reason for thinking that the new population is likely to be similar to the old. Principles of sampling as such are impotent to decide the matter, since the new marbles have not been subjected to any sampling test. In the same way, we can make no extrapolative inference about the future colour of ravens from their colour hitherto, unless we have an independent reason for assuming that ravens have, or are likely to have, the same colour at different times; and it is just this kind of assumption—a raven-specific version of the assumption of the uniformity of nature—that the sceptic is calling in question.

This still leaves the possibility of claiming that the a priori principles of sampling *do* afford a justification for extrapolative inference in cases, like that of the marbles, where we normally suppose that the randomness of the selection of the sample can be (at least approximately) ensured. And while this would not provide, or come anywhere near to providing, the full-blooded defence of induction that we would like, it would at least be a step in the right direction. However, even in cases like that of the marbles, the sceptic will not be prepared to yield any ground. For we can only make sure that the drawing of the sample is random in the relevant sense—that the method gives equal chances of selection to all possible samples of the relevant size—by relying on certain empirical assumptions about how the world works, and these assumptions will not be ones on which, from the standpoint of the sceptic, we are entitled to rely. Thus, in the case of the marbles, we may thoroughly shake the bag in advance, draw out the marbles without looking inside, and take whatever other measures we can to facilitate an unbiased selection. But none of this affords us any grounds for believing that the selection is unbiased unless we already know, or have grounds for believing, certain propositions about how things behave in this kind of situation—for example, that shaking a bag of marbles has a jumbling influence on its contents, rather than one of (say) making marbles of a certain colour rise to the top, and that marbles in a bag do not adjust their positions, in response to the entry of one's hand, in a way that makes the extraction of one colour more likely. These are, by ordinary standards, very plausible propositions; indeed, we ordinarily take them for granted. But they are not ones that we know a priori. Our grounds for accepting them, and applying them to the particular case at hand, stem from our knowledge of how things have regularly behaved hitherto. And so the sceptic will say that it is only if we are entitled to rely on induction that we can have reason to think that the drawing of the sample is random in the relevant sense.

V

I have looked at two attempts to find a rational basis for inductive inference by appeal to certain truths of probability theory—truths that are knowable a priori and philosophically uncontroversial. Neither attempt was successful. The first was not relevant to the issue of induction at all. The second had at best a marginal relevance, and it additionally rested on empirical assumptions that begged the question. I think that all such attempts fail in one of the ways which these two cases illustrate, and from now on I shall assume that this whole approach has to be abandoned.[6]

Where do we go from here? I have already rejected as non-starters the three ways of trying to justify induction mentioned earlier—the inductive, the pragmatic, and the definitional ways. If, in addition, we accept that we cannot justify induction by an appeal to the truths of probability theory—at least to truths that are knowable a priori and philosophically uncontroversial—we may well come to the conclusion that induction cannot be justified at all. And this, in turn, could lead us to side, as philosophers, with the sceptic, who claims that induction is simply irrational. (I say *as philosophers* because, as already noted, we would not be able to adjust our *ordinary* ways of thinking to reflect the sceptical position.) On this last point, however, there is, as I pointed out in the first lecture, an alternative approach available. For, while conceding that there is no way of *justifying* induction—of showing that it is rational on some independent basis—we could insist that it does not stand in need of justification. We could insist that, like deduction, it is a basic form of sound reasoning, whose rationality should just be taken for granted. I shall speak of this as the *simple view*, and it is on this view that I now

---

[6] For further discussion and criticism of the approach, including a consideration of the theories of Carnap and Harrod, see Ayer, *Probability and Evidence*, 33–53 and 91–110.

want to focus. As I said in the earlier context, my guess is that the simple view represents the most popular approach to induction among current philosophers, partly because of a widespread pessimism about the feasibility of resisting the sceptic in any other way, and partly because the view harmonizes with how induction presents itself at the level of our ordinary thinking.

Given the difficulty of finding an independent justification of induction, I can certainly see the attraction of the simple view. Even so, I think that the view can be shown to be mistaken. For I think that there are types of case where accepting the simple view would commit us to endorsing inferences that are clearly irrational. I shall focus on a particular example, and here, as earlier, my discussion will follow, in broad outline, the discussion in my book on the philosophy of A. J. Ayer.[7]

Suppose we have what we know to be an unbiased coin: one which is evenly weighted and has no other property—categorical or dispositional—which makes it more likely to come down on one side rather than the other when tossed. In addition, we have what we know to be an unbiased coin-tossing machine: one which is scrupulously designed to vary in a random way the force with which it tosses the coin from one occasion to the next. And, finally, let us assume that we know that there is no special factor in the conditions in which we are going to use the machine which imposes an influence in favour of one type of outcome. Suppose we then get our machine to toss the coin a hundred times, and, to our surprise, the coin comes up heads on each occasion. Can we use this run of heads as a basis for predicting the outcome of the next toss? It is easy to see how someone might think that we can. Indeed, this could come about in two contrasting ways. Thus, on the one hand, we can envisage someone who, focusing on his knowledge that there is no bias in favour of either type of outcome, and believing that this requires that, if the series of tosses were to continue long enough, there would be an approximately equal distribution of heads and tails, thinks that, to help even things out, tails is the more likely outcome. On the other hand, we can envisage someone who, focusing on the long run of heads, and believing in the uniformity of nature over time, expects the run to continue to the next trial. But, on reflection, we can see that both these responses would be irrational. If there is any reason for expecting, in the long run, an approximately equal distribution of heads and tails, it is not that the tosses are subject to a special egalitarian

---

[7] Ayer, Pt. III, sect. 4.

bias—a bias which would allow the past ratio of heads to tails to have an effect on future outcomes—but that they are not subject to a bias at all. And this automatically excludes any rational prediction about any particular toss, however uneven the distribution in the preceding series. Likewise, given the knowledge that there is no bias, we cannot interpret the consistency of the previous outcomes as anything more than a coincidence. And if it is purely coincidental, we have no reason to expect it to continue to the next trial. Thus, however you look at it, the only rational response to the outcome of the next toss is to acknowledge our complete ignorance—to admit that the outcome is wholly unpredictable, and that the previous run of heads is evidentially irrelevant.

Now what is interesting about this case is that one of the two responses that we have rejected as irrational seems to be the response that would count as rational *by inductive standards*. Someone who predicts heads for the next toss on the basis of the previous run seems to be doing just what induction tells him he should do, namely projecting a past regularity on to the future. So the example poses an immediate challenge for the defender of the simple view. How can he see induction as a basic form of sound reasoning if the prediction which it here seems to license is not rational? There would be an analogous question, of course, for *anyone* who accepts the rationality of induction. But it is only the issue for the simple view that presently concerns us.

The general strategy which a defender of the simple view would have to pursue, to try to deal with the challenge, is not hard to discern. As I stressed in Lecture 1, accepting the rationality of induction does not involve accepting the rationality of *every form* of inductive inference. For it is not in dispute that there are a number of ways in which, even from an inductive standpoint, such inferences can be rationally defective. All that accepting the rationality of induction involves is accepting that, *other things being equal*, the holding of a regularity over the examined cases provides evidential support for the conclusion that it will continue to hold for the unexamined cases, and that, *when the appropriate conditions are satisfied*, this support is sufficient to justify an expectation that things will turn out that way. So what the defender of the simple view has to show, to meet the relevant challenge, is that, in the particular case in question, other things are *not* relevantly equal or the appropriate conditions are *not* satisfied, and that, in consequence, an inductive inference is not warranted. He has to stand by his claim that induction is a basic form of sound reasoning, which does not stand in need of justification, but show that there are special reasons why it cannot be legitimately employed in the present instance.

So what are the possibilities here? Well, as far as I can see, there are just two things that the defender of the simple view could say, and neither of them is effective.

The first thing he could say is that, while the past run of heads, in itself, evidentially points to a heads outcome for the next toss, this support does not suffice to justify an expectation of that outcome when we take account of *all* the empirical evidence that inductively bears on the issue. After all, we already know, from other observations, that when unbiased coins have been tossed in unbiased ways, the tendency has been for the numbers of heads and tails outcomes, for a given coin, to be approximately equal. So the defender of the simple view might say that the reason why it would be illegitimate to predict a continuation of the run in the case of this particular coin is just that the evidence drawn from it gets swamped by the evidence drawn from coins in general. Induction is rational, but a prediction of heads is not something which, taking account of *all* the available evidence, induction supports.

But this response misses the central point. For, irrespective of our evidence about other coins, the assumptions we have made about *this* coin ensure that any prediction about the outcome of the next toss is unwarranted. If it were merely a matter of the insufficiency of our inductive evidence when set against our evidence about coins in general, we could remedy this by supposing a larger number of previous trials over which the run of heads had been maintained. We could suppose that the coin had been tossed a thousand, or ten thousand, or even a million times, and had come up heads on each occasion. As the length of the run of heads increased, so the inductive significance of the evidence drawn from other coins would diminish; and, at some point, we would be bound to get sufficient evidence of the uniform behaviour of *this* coin to outweigh, from an inductive standpoint, any other consideration. But the fact is that if, as we are assuming, we know that there is no bias in the situation, then we know that any run of heads, however protracted, is purely coincidental, and must be discounted as a basis for prediction.

This immediately suggests the second way in which the defender of the simple view might try to meet the challenge. For he might say that, while induction is a basic form of sound reasoning, we obviously should not apply it to a case where we start with an assumption which implicitly denies the appropriateness of its application. By putting in place the assumption of no bias—the assumption that we know that there is nothing in the situation which creates a bias in favour of one type of outcome over the other—we ensure that we know that the run is a mere coincidence, and so of no evidential value in estimating the distribution of heads and tails over the trials that remain. And if we know that the run is of no evidential value in that respect, we know that induction cannot be rationally applied. So the defender of the simple view might simply say that while we are entitled to expect the continuation of a hitherto exemplified regularity when the appropriate conditions are satisfied, one of the conditions which has to be satisfied is that the holding of the regularity over the examined cases is not known to be just coincidental.

The problem with this response is that, while the requirement proposed is clearly needed, it is hard to see what its rationale would be *from the standpoint of the simple view*. To say that the past holding of a regularity is a *coincidence* is to say that there is nothing which accounts for it—no reason why it occurred. But the fact that there is nothing which accounts for a regularity does not entail that it will not continue, and so does not entail that it cannot be successfully used as the basis for an extrapolative inference. So if knowledge of coincidence makes the step of extrapolation unwarranted, we need to be told why. The answer on offer—and I am not disputing its correctness—is that where it is known to be just coincidental that things have been regular, the fact of the regularity is, for the purposes of prediction, of no evidential value. But how would this lack of evidential value become apparent to a defender of the simple view? If he takes induction to be a basic form of sound reasoning, how could he come to see the coincidental character of the regularity as preventing its constituting evidence in inductive terms? Once it is accepted that the rationality of induction is something fundamental, and does not need to be established on an independent basis, there seems to be nothing in the nature of inductive reasoning to which considerations of coincidence are relevant.

The true character of the situation becomes clear when we consider how we would respond to the coin-tossing example if the assumption of no bias were dropped. Thus, in this new version of the example, we do not know, in advance of the trials, that there is no bias in the situation— nothing in the character of the coin or the machine or the surrounding conditions which imposes an influence in favour of one type of outcome. We may believe that there is no such bias, but the belief is one which we are permitted to revise in the light of our empirical findings. As before, the coin is tossed a hundred times and comes up heads on each occasion. And, as before, the question is: can we rationally predict the outcome of the next toss? Well, the dropping of the assumption of no bias does seem to facilitate a step of extrapolation: it does seem to legitimize the inference from the past regularity to its future continuance. But what is interesting is the way in which it does this. Our reasoning would not be: 'Now that we have dropped the assumption, we have removed the only obstacle to what is, other things being equal, an inherently rational mode of inference—a direct inference from how things have been to how they will be.' Rather, we would try to justify the extrapolation by an argument which explicitly involved the postulation of a bias. We would argue that the previous run provides convincing evidence of the presence of a strong, and perhaps overriding, bias in favour of heads. And having inferred the bias from the run, we would then appeal to the bias to justify the prediction of heads for the next toss. Thus we would regard the step of extrapolation as rational, not because it exemplifies a basic form of sound reasoning, but because we can justify it on the basis of two other steps of inference of a quite different kind—an inference from the previous run to the presence of a bias, and an inference from the bias to the outcome of the next toss. And the reason why this step of extrapolation would be blocked by the assumption of no bias—an assumption which would force us to see the run as merely coincidental—is simply that it depends on an inference to a conclusion which the assumption explicitly denies.

We can now see that the example of the coin is interesting in more than one way. It was originally offered as a case which posed a challenge to the simple view, and, if I am right, this challenge has now turned into a decisive objection. With the assumption of no bias in place, we are not entitled to predict the continuation of the run of heads to the next toss, and, as far as I can see, someone who takes induction to be a basic form of sound reasoning cannot explain why this is so. But there is now a further point, and one which may prove to be of crucial importance. For, once we drop the assumption of no bias, we try to justify the extrapolative step by dividing it into two further steps of inference, neither of which is itself extrapolative. The first of these steps, that from the previous run to the presence of a bias, is, presumably, an inference to the best explanation; the thought, presumably, is that a run of that length cannot be credibly attributed to chance, and that the most plausible explanation for it is that there is some constant factor in the situation—something in the character of the coin or the machine or the surrounding conditions—which exerts a special causal influence, and perhaps a determining influence, in favour of the heads outcome. The second step, from the postulation of a bias to the prediction about the next toss is, in its core, deductive: if we accept the presence of the bias in favour of heads, we are logically committed to concluding that, given no relevant change in the character of the situation, a heads outcome is rendered inevitable or likely. The potential importance of this lies in the possibility that we have, in this method of reasoning, the key to a solution of the whole sceptical problem. For might it not be that, in all cases where extrapolation is rational, we can justify the extrapolative step in a broadly similar way—by dividing it into explanatory and deductive steps of inference, which are not as such extrapolative, and thus not vulnerable to the sceptic's attack? It is this suggestion that I shall take up and develop in the next lecture.

LECTURE 3
The Nomological-Explanatory Solution

I

I have considered various unsuccessful attempts to solve the problem of induction. It is now time to present what I believe to be, in its core, the correct solution. As I indicated in Lecture 1, this solution involves recognizing the existence of *laws of nature*, and it is this involvement that will eventually bring us into the area of theological interest. I need to begin by explaining what, in this context, I mean by a 'law of nature', or 'natural law'.

The term 'law', as it occurs in the context of a discussion of the natural world, can be used in three distinct, though related, senses. In the first place, it can be used to refer to those claims by which, at various times, scientists have tried to characterize the fundamental ways of working of the natural world. For example, we may speak of *Newton's first law of motion*, and mean by this his thesis that bodies continue in a state of rest or uniform motion unless acted on by some force; and, similarly, we may speak of *Newton's law of gravity*, and mean by this his thesis that, for any pair of bodies, existing at any time, there is, at that time, a force of attraction between them with the value that his equation specifies. Taken in this sense, laws are not part of nature, but part of our theorizing about it. They are human artefacts, products of the scientific enterprise.[1] Secondly, the term 'law' can be used to refer, not to these scientific claims, but to the natural regularities—the

---

[1] They can also, of course, be false. This is why it is possible for Nancy Cartwright to argue (in her *How the Laws of Physics Lie* (Oxford: Oxford University Press, 1983)) that, despite their explanatory value, the fundamental laws of physics are false.

uniform ways of working—which the claims are attempts to record. Thus let us, for the sake of argument, assume that Newton's account of gravity is correct. Then, in this second sense, the law of gravity will be not the Newtonian thesis, but the natural regularity which it records—the uniform manner in which the relevant force of attraction is distributed over pairs of bodies at times. In this sense, laws are quite independent of the human mind and the human scientific enterprise. They are part of the natural world, and are what they are irrespective of how our theories represent them. Thirdly, the term 'law' can, as in the second case, be used to denote aspects of the natural world, but aspects that consist not in the regularities which characterize the world, but in the forms of natural necessity which (in a certain sense) control it—the natural necessities which ensure that the world is regular in the relevant ways. So, in this sense, to recognize a law of gravity would not be merely to recognize that there is a uniform manner in which bodies attract one another, but to recognize a principle of necessity underlying this uniformity—to recognize that it is naturally necessary for bodies to attract one another in that manner, and to behave in the ways in which, according to the total character of the conditions in which they find themselves, this attraction demands. Some philosophers would insist that we cannot make sense of necessity of this natural kind. This will become a crucial issue in due course, but, for the moment, it is something that I am going to put on one side.

Now it is in the third of these senses that I am using the term 'law' in these lectures. Thus when I say that the solution which I am going to propose to the problem of induction involves recognizing the existence of laws of nature, what I mean by such laws are not scientific theories about the regularities in nature, nor even the regularities themselves, but the forms of necessity which ensure that these regularities obtain. Note that, if there are laws in this sense, the necessity they involve has wide scope in relation to the regularities they ensure. To recognize a law of gravity is to recognize that it is naturally necessary for bodies to behave, or to attract one another, gravitationally. But what is here meant by saying that it is naturally necessary for bodies to behave gravitationally is not that, for any body x, and any time t at which x exists, it is naturally necessary for x to behave gravitationally at t, but that it is naturally necessary that, for any body x, and any time t at which x exists, x behaves gravitationally at t. Quite generally, a law, in the relevant sense, is not a regularity concerning instances of natural necessity, but the natural necessity of a certain type of regularity.

There is one other thing that we should note at the outset. The term 'law' is a noun, signifying a certain kind of entity. But the status of laws as entities is, in a sense, only superficial—the product of grammar, rather than a reflection of how things fundamentally are. For to speak of the existence of a certain type of law is, in effect, to speak of the obtaining of a certain type of fact—the fact *of its being a law that* (of its being naturally necessary that) things are regular in a certain way. Of course, from a grammatical standpoint, facts themselves are a kind of entity. But it is not as entities that facts fundamentally feature in the world. The fundamental way of recording the obtaining of the fact that things are thus and so is by simply stating that things are thus and so, without making any reference to the fact as such. And, likewise, the fundamental way of recording the existence or obtaining of a law is not by referring to a law entity, but by stating that it is a law that (that it is naturally necessary that) things are regular in such and such a way.

II

It might seem, at first, that the very idea of seeking a solution to the problem of induction which involves the recognition of laws of nature in the relevant sense is absurd. It is not difficult, of course, to see how, if we were *entitled* to recognize the existence of such laws, and *entitled* to take their content to be of a certain kind, then we could make well-founded predictions about the outcomes of the unexamined cases. If, say, I were now entitled to believe in a law of gravity, which ensured the gravitational behaviour of all bodies across space and time, then I would be entitled to believe that if I were to release the coin I am holding, it would fall—or, at least, would do so unless there were some special change in the circumstances obtaining. But what might seem, at first sight, absurd is the idea that we could be entitled to believe in the relevant laws without recourse to induction itself. For what possible grounds could we have for supposing that it is a law of nature that things are regular in a certain way except by finding that this regularity has held good in our experience of the world hitherto, and then concluding, by a step of extrapolation, that things have to be regular in this way quite generally? Indeed, it seems that, to reach this conclusion, we would have not only to rely on induction, but to use it to sustain a larger step of extrapolation than in the examples we have so far envisaged. Up until now, the strongest inductive conclusion we have envisaged takes the form of claiming that the relevant regularity, observed to hold in the examined cases, holds universally *in the actual world*. For example, the argument might run: 'All ravens so far examined have been black. So all ravens (anywhere, at any time) are black.' Or again: 'All bodies so far examined have behaved gravitationally. So all bodies (anywhere, at any time) behave gravitationally.' The conclusions reached are universal, but only apply to the domain of *actual* cases. But what we are now envisaging is a conclusion concerning how it is *necessary* for things to be, and this extends the regularity to cover not only the unexamined cases that actually exist, but a range of counterfactual situations too. So, if we recognize a law of gravity—a law which is a form of natural necessity—we are committed to saying not only that all bodies, in the actual situations which occur, behave gravitationally, but that *had* I released this coin a moment ago, it *would have* fallen, and that if the sun *had* twice its current mass, this *would* affect the orbits of the planets in such and such ways. It seems, then, that if the recognition of laws of nature is going to feature at all in our discussion of induction, it will feature in a way that exacerbates the problem rather than contributes to its solution. For it seems to mean that we shall need to look to induction to do a greater amount of work.

This, in effect, is the point that A. J. Ayer is making, in his *Central Questions of Philosophy*, when he considers and instantly dismisses the suggestion that claims of natural necessity might help with the sceptical problem:

> If on the basis of the fact that all the A's hitherto observed have been B's, we are seeking for an assurance that the next A we come upon will be a B, the knowledge, if we could have it, that all A's are B's would be quite enough; to strengthen the premise by saying that they not only are but must be B's adds nothing to the validity of the inference. The only way in which this move could be helpful would be if it were somehow easier to discover that all A's must be B's than that they merely were so; and perhaps this is what its advocates believe. But how can they possibly be right?... It is no good claiming that empirical hypotheses of this... sort are known to be true by intuition.... But then, if it is a matter of evidence, it must be easier to discover, or at least find some good reason for believing, that such and such an association of properties always does obtain, than that it must obtain; for it requires less for the evidence to establish.[2]

At first sight, this seems very plausible.

---

[2] A. J. Ayer, *The Central Questions of Philosophy* (London: Penguin Books, 1974), 149–50.

It *seems* very plausible, but, in fact, there is a crucial possibility which it overlooks. To appreciate this possibility, we need to start by taking note of something which is very familiar in modern discussions of the methodology of science, but whose potential significance for the problem of induction has largely gone unnoticed. The familiar point is that there is a form of empirical inference, which is much employed in science, and which we normally assume to be rational, but which is not *inductive* in the relevant sense.

Induction, in the sense in which I am using the term in these lectures, is *extrapolative*. We make an inductive inference when, from our knowledge that a certain regularity has held among the examined cases, we infer that it will continue to hold for some unexamined case or group of cases. But not all supposedly rational empirical inferences are of this kind. Consider, for example, the way in which chemists have supposedly established that water is H_2O. No doubt there was, in their procedure, a step of extrapolative induction, namely from the chemical composition of the water samples examined to the composition of water in general. But this was not the only step of inference involved. For the composition of the samples was not directly observed: it was detected by inference from how the samples responded to certain tests. The rationale for such an inference was the explanatory power of the conclusion it yielded. The conclusion was accepted because it explained the experimental findings—or at least it did so in the framework of a more comprehensive chemical theory which was itself accepted largely on explanatory grounds. Thus the conclusion was reached, not by *extrapolation*, but by *an inference to the best explanation*. And this, of course, is not an isolated case: the same explanatory mode of inference is what science employs quite generally, whenever it is attempting to reach conclusions about types of entities and properties that are beyond the reach of direct scrutiny. Without this mode of inference, the sciences of chemistry and particle physics would simply not exist.[3]

---

[3] Some radically empiricist philosophers of science reject the rationality of inference to the best explanation and are correspondingly sceptical about the possibility of establishing, or finding good grounds for believing, claims about unobservables. Thus see, in particular, Pierre Duhem, *The Aim and Structure of Physical Theory* (New York: Atheneum, 1962), and, more recently, Bas van Fraassen, *The Scientific Image* (Oxford: Oxford University Press, 1980) and *Laws and Symmetry* (Oxford: Oxford University Press, 1989). I do not find the arguments of these philosophers persuasive, but this is not something that I have space to deal with here. My hope is that the ways in which I make use of this mode of inference in what follows will seem acceptable on their merits.

Now the issue which we are presently considering is whether there might be some way in which the recognition of laws of nature (of the relevantly necessitational kind) could feature in a solution to the problem of induction. And it seemed, at first sight, that the answer must be negative. For it seemed that any entitlement to recognize the existence of a law would itself depend on the employment of an inductive inference. And, indeed, an inductive inference to the postulation of a *law* would presumably be even harder to justify than one to the postulation of a *universal regularity*, since it would involve a stronger conclusion. As Ayer put it: 'If it is matter of evidence, it must be easier to discover, or at least find good reason for believing, that such and such an association of properties always does obtain, than that it must obtain; for it requires less for the evidence to establish.' But what this overlooks is the possibility that we might be able to establish, or find grounds for accepting, the stronger conclusion—the conclusion which postulates a law of nature—by an *inference to the best explanation*. For, although it stands at a greater logical distance from the evidence, it might be precisely because the stronger conclusion is stronger that it has the explanatory power required to make it worthy of acceptance. And so it might be precisely because we are justified in accepting, on explanatory grounds, that a certain regularity holds as a matter of *natural law* that we are justified in accepting, as a logical consequence, that it holds as a matter of *fact*. It is this possibility that I want now to develop.

III

We already have a clue as to how we might develop it from the coin-tossing example discussed in the previous lecture. An apparently normal coin is tossed a hundred times and, to our surprise, comes up heads on each occasion. The question posed was: what, if anything, should we predict about the next toss? In the original version of the example, it was assumed that we knew that the coin and the method of tossing were unbiased, and, quite generally, that there was no special factor in the situation which causally favoured one type of outcome over the other. And we saw that, on this assumption, there were no rational grounds for making any prediction at all. In particular, there were no rational grounds for expecting the previous run of heads to continue, since the knowledge that there had been nothing to bias the coin in favour of a heads outcome obliged us to regard the run as a mere coincidence, and so as evidentially irrelevant. This result was then seen to conflict with the view that induction is a basic form of sound reasoning, whose rationality should just be taken for granted. But we also considered a revised version of the example, in which the assumption of no bias was dropped. The same question was posed, but in a framework in which it had not been stipulated in advance that there was nothing in the situation to impose a bias in favour of one type of outcome. The answer which then commended itself was quite different from the one that we endorsed on the original version. Thus we found it natural to suppose that we could legitimately see the run of heads as indicating the presence of strong and perhaps overriding bias in favour of heads—a bias sustained by some factor in the character of the coin or the machine or the surrounding conditions—and that we could then appeal to the presence of this bias as grounds for expecting a further occurrence of heads on the next toss. In other words, it seemed reasonable to expect the run to continue, not because extrapolative expectations are inherently rational, but because the previous regularity could be reasonably construed as a manifestation of a special source of influence—the bias—which makes the heads outcome, on any arbitrary occasion, inevitable or extremely likely.

Now it is this second version of the example which is of importance in the present context. And what makes it important is the nature of the reasoning which underlies our natural response. We see the run of heads as evidence of a bias. But why? Well, presumably our reasoning would run as follows. The fact that the coin has come up heads a hundred times in succession calls for explanation. It is true that this run *could be* just a coincidence: it is *possible* that, on each occasion, the factors which causally explain why the coin landed in the way it did are no different, in general character, from the factors operating in the case of any normal coin, tossed in normal circumstances, and that it was just a fluke that the sets of factors operating on all the different occasions happened to lead to the same type of outcome. But while this is *possible*, it is hardly *plausible*. It is vastly more plausible to suppose that the run of heads has some explanation; and, of course, the implausibility of supposing that the run is a coincidence, and the corresponding plausibility of taking it to have an explanation, can be further increased by increasing the length of the series over which the run is assumed to hold. There must surely be some point—at a thousand tosses, at ten thousand, at a hundred thousand, or whatever—at which the hypothesis of coincidence becomes literally incredible and the pressure to believe in the existence of an explanation becomes irresistible. But, granted that the run calls for explanation, by far the most plausible explanatory hypothesis would be that either the coin or the machine or the surrounding conditions are so constituted as to impose a constant bias on the outcome—a bias which compels or strongly disposes the coin to come up heads whenever it is tossed. So we are justified in taking the run as evidence of a bias by means of an inference to the best explanation— an inference which is not, in itself, a step of extrapolative induction—and we can then appeal to the presence of the bias to justify our expectation that the run will continue.

Now the suggestion I want to make is that we can see this line of reasoning as a model for how we can be justified in postulating laws of nature, and how we can then use this to justify the predictions which we want to make in the context of induction. For I want to argue that we can be justified in postulating laws as a way of explaining the regularities which have held good in our past experience, and can then appeal to the presence of these laws to justify the belief that the regularities will, or will on certain conditions, continue to hold for the unexamined cases. Just as we are entitled to believe that the run of heads, if sufficiently protracted, is not just a coincidence, but manifests an inherent bias in the coin-tossing situation towards a particular type of outcome, so we are entitled to believe, quite generally, that the regularities we encounter in nature, as we have so far sampled it, are not just coincidental, but manifestations of nature's inherent bias in favour of certain kinds of outcome—a bias which is imposed by its *laws*. And just as our entitlement to postulate a bias in the coin-tossing situation justifies our prediction of heads for the next toss, so our entitlement to postulate this law-imposed bias in nature justifies our prediction that nature will continue to exhibit the relevant forms of regularity in future. In effect, of course, the reasoning involved in the case of the coin is not just a *model* for what I am now proposing, but a special *instance* of it. For, in explaining the run of heads as a manifestation of a bias, we are presumably implicitly acknowledging the existence and explanatory role of laws. For presumably we shall want to say that what creates the bias is the presence of some factor which, *in the framework of the laws of nature*, is empowered to determine or influence the outcome in the relevant way.

Although the case of the coin can be thought of as an instance of the general line of reasoning I have in mind, it is a very complex one. It will be better to begin by focusing on something simpler, and I think the case of gravity will be the best one for our purposes. Even this case can become complicated when it is handled in terms of the General Theory of Relativity, where, in contrast with the traditional Newtonian account, gravitational behaviour is represented as reflecting not a special force of attraction, but the ways in which bodies affect and are affected by the geometry of space-time. But although it would be possible to present the case in these terms, and although this may be what the fine detail of the scientific evidence ultimately requires, it will be vastly easier, and I think more illuminating, if we continue to think of the situation in the traditional way. And this is what I shall do, not only in the present context, but throughout the rest of the discussion. As far as I can see, there is nothing of philosophical significance that could get distorted by this procedure.

Let us assume, then, that hitherto, as far as our experience reveals, bodies have always behaved gravitationally; and let us take this to mean that they have always behaved in ways that conform to the theory of gravity advanced by Newton—the theory that represents the force of gravitational attraction between any two bodies at any time as directly proportional to the product of their masses and inversely proportional to the square of their distance. On this basis, let us suppose, we are confident that bodies will continue to behave gravitationally in future. The question is: can we find rational grounds for this confidence? I suggest that we can in the following way. The past consistency of gravitational behaviour calls for explanation. For given the infinite variety of ways in which bodies might have behaved non-gravitationally, and the innumerable occasions on which some form of non-gravitational behaviour might have occurred and been detected, it would be astonishing if this consistency were merely coincidental—something that has occurred for no reason. But if the past consistency calls for explanation, what should that explanation be? The most plausible account is surely that gravitational behaviour is the product of natural necessity: bodies have always behaved gravitationally in our experience hitherto because it is a law of nature that bodies behave in this way, or are subject to the relevant forces of attraction which such behaviour reflects. But if we are justified in postulating this law to explain the past consistency, we are justified, to the same degree, in expecting gravitational behaviour in future. For if it is naturally *necessary* that bodies behave gravitationally, it follows, as a matter of logic, that they *always do*.[4] So our confidence that bodies will continue to behave gravitationally is well-founded—or, at least, can become so when it is defended in this way.

---

[4] As we shall see in Lecture 5, there is a slight complication about this claim. For it might be thought that we can make sense of the possibility of laws being contravened. But this is something that is best ignored in the present context.

The past regularity does indeed, by means of an inference to the best explanation, afford rational grounds for expecting its future continuation.

This is just one case, and an especially straightforward one. But if the reasoning involved is sound, it seems to offer the prospect of a solution to the whole problem of induction. For it seems that, in any case where we find some extensive regularity in nature within the compass of our experience so far, and where everything would be appropriate, from an inductive standpoint, for a step of extrapolative inference, we could hope to fall back on a similar kind of reasoning to justify such an inference. The reasoning need not have precisely the same form in each case. In the gravitational example, the regularity was explained by postulating a law which directly covered the form of behaviour in question: the past consistency of gravitational behaviour was explained by postulating a law of gravity, which makes it naturally necessary for bodies to behave in that way. In such a case, the nomological postulate forms the *total* explanation of the regularity in question. But there are other cases where the total explanation would need to conjoin the postulation of a certain law or laws with the recognition of certain standing conditions—conditions which would be thought of as combining with the laws to ensure the obtaining of the regularity that we have empirically detected. For example, in the case of the regularity of the elliptical orbits of the planets, the most plausible explanation, in the light of all that we know, or independently have reason to accept on explanatory grounds, is not that there is a law of elliptical planetary motion, or specific laws for the different planets, but that there are certain more fundamental laws of motion and gravity which combine with certain stable conditions of the solar system to account for the regularities we observe. And this kind of explanation—in terms of a combination of laws and standing conditions—would obviously be the appropriate one in a wide range of other cases, including, of course, the example of the coin. It should be noted that where the explanation does take this form, the move from the acceptance of the explanatory hypothesis to the prediction about the unexamined cases is not so clear-cut. In the gravitational example, it is a matter of a straight deduction from the postulation of the law to the conclusion that the unexamined cases conform to it: it is naturally *necessary* for bodies to behave gravitationally, and so tomorrow they *will*. But where the explanation appeals to the presence of standing conditions, the prediction will only be forthcoming on the assumption that the conditions continue to obtain: the planets can be predicted to continue to pursue their elliptical orbits *provided that* nothing occurs to disturb the conditions which, in combination with the laws, are responsible for sustaining these orbits; the coin can be predicted to retain its tendency to come up heads *provided that* nothing occurs to alter the factor which, in the framework of the laws, creates the bias. So whereas the prediction is *absolute* in the case where the regularity is explained by the nomological postulate alone, it is only a *conditional* prediction in the case where standing conditions are accorded an explanatory role—though, of course, this still leaves room for an appeal to additional evidence to support the assumption (again ultimately by means of explanatory inference) that the standing conditions will continue to be in place.

We should also note that, in many cases where there is a conspicuous regularity in how things have been hitherto, and where the regularity seems too extensive to be deemed coincidental, we are not, in our current state of knowledge, in a position to be able to select and rationally defend a *specific* explanation. Sometimes, in such cases, we are in a position to offer a *schematic* explanation, leaving the details to be worked out by future scientific research. I guess this would be our current position with respect to the regularity of the blackness of ravens—a regularity which will presumably stem from some aspect of the common genetic makeup of ravens, but where the precise nature of that aspect and the way in which it influences the pigment of the feathers are yet to be discovered. Sometimes, we can hardly do any more, by way of explanation, than insist that there is *some* set of laws and standing conditions which are responsible for the observed regularity, without committing ourselves, even generically, to the nature of the factors involved. Obviously, the less specific our explanatory hypothesis, the less clear-cut its application to the unexamined cases. We can still justify a conditional prediction: the regularity will continue to hold for the unexamined cases so long as the standing conditions involved continue to stand. But the less we know about the nature of these conditions, the harder it will be to find reasons for assuming that they *will* continue to stand.

Drawing the various strands together, and leaving room for certain later refinements, I can set out the basic elements of the position I want to defend as follows:

1. There is a significant range of cases where the knowledge of a hitherto exemplified regularity (a regularity which has held among the examined cases) provides rational grounds for an extrapolative inference (for expecting the continuation of the regularity with respect to some unexamined case or group of cases).

48 · The Nomological-Explanatory Solution

2. In any case where there are such grounds, they can be made explicit by breaking the inference down into two further steps of inference, neither of which is, as such, extrapolative.
3. The first of these steps is an inference to the best explanation. What the explanation is advanced to explain is the occurrence of the hitherto exemplified regularity whose extrapolation is at issue. And this regularity calls for explanation because it is too extensive to be deemed coincidental—deemed to be something that has occurred for no reason.
4. This explanation is a nomological one: it involves the postulation of some law or set of laws of nature, sometimes precisely specified, sometimes not. In certain cases, the postulation of these laws will form the whole explanation of the relevant regularity. This is so, for example, in the gravitational case, where the postulated law of gravity suffices, on its own, to ensure the universal observance of gravitational behaviour. In other cases, the explanation will additionally involve the recognition of certain standing conditions, sometimes precisely specified, sometimes not. So, in the case of the planets, what is taken to ensure their regular pursuit of certain elliptical orbits is the combination of the laws of nature and certain constant aspects of how the solar system is constituted.
5. The other step of inference is a deduction from the explanation—a deduction that the regularity (thus explained) will continue to hold for the unexamined case or cases, or will do so subject to the continued obtaining of the relevant standing conditions. Which of these latter options applies depends on the nature of the explanation. If the explanation just consists in the postulation of a law, or set of laws, ensuring that things are regular in the relevant way, then the deduced prediction will be unconditional. Thus, if the past regularity of gravitational behaviour is explained by postulating a law of gravity—a law which makes it naturally necessary for bodies to behave gravitationally—then the explanation logically entails that the unexamined bodies behave gravitationally too. On the other hand, if the explanation combines the postulation of laws with an appeal to certain standing conditions, then all that can be deduced is that the regularity will continue to hold for the unexamined cases if the relevant conditions continue to obtain.

Following the terminology of my earlier writings, I shall speak of this account of the matter as the *nomological-explanatory solution* (NES)—*solution*, because I am offering it as a way of solving the problem of induction, *nomological-explanatory*, because of the central role that it accords to nomological (law-postulating) forms of explanation.[5]

As I have already stressed, I am taking laws of nature to be not mere factual regularities, but forms of natural necessity. Given the role they have to play in the context of NES, we can see why this is crucial. For if laws were just factual regularities, holding universally over space and time, they would not serve the purposes of explanation in the relevant sense, and I would have done nothing to show that their postulation could be justified by an inference of a non-extrapolative kind. Thus suppose we construed the law of gravity as merely the fact that bodies always behave gravitationally. There is, I suppose, a sense in which the postulation of this universal regularity might be taken to explain the past consistency of gravitational behaviour—the sense in which we explain a fact when we subsume it under something more general. But it cannot be this sort of explanation that is involved in NES. For unless there were some further step of inference to underpin it, an inference to this sort of explanation would have to be an ordinary step of extrapolative induction, and hence vulnerable to the sceptic's attack. The reason why we can hope to do better with laws of a genuinely necessitational kind is that, if I am right, their postulation can be justified by reasoning of a quite different sort. Thus we are justified in postulating a law of gravity, as a form of natural necessity, because it eliminates what would otherwise be an astonishing coincidence: it enables us to avoid the seemingly incredible conclusion that the past consistency of gravitational behaviour, over such a vast range of bodies, occasions, and circumstances, has occurred for no reason. Merely subsuming this past consistency under a universal regularity would do nothing to diminish the coincidence; indeed, it would just extend it to cover a wider domain.

This brings us back to the key point mentioned earlier. The conclusion that a regularity is naturally necessary is stronger than the conclusion that it just obtains; and, at first sight, this seems to mean that it will be harder to justify. But it is precisely because it is stronger that there is the possibility of justifying its acceptance on explanatory, and hence non-extrapolative, grounds, and thereby justifying an acceptance of the weaker conclusion it entails. It is this point that NES exploits.

---

[5] Thus see my 'Induction, Explanation, and Natural Necessity', *Proceedings of the Aristotelian Society* 83 (1982–3), 87–101, and *Ayer*, Pt. III, sect. 5.

IV

I have set out, in the five-clause account above, the basic elements of my proposed solution to the problem of induction. But, before going any further, there is one respect in which I want to modify this account, in a way that restricts the scope of the solution to a certain range of cases.

As I have formulated it, NES is claiming that, in any case where there are rational grounds for an extrapolative inference of the relevant sort, these grounds can be made explicit by breaking the inference down into two further steps of inference, of which the first is an inference to the best nomological explanation. But, in our ordinary inductive practice, we often make extrapolative inferences about matters which it is not easy to think of as law-governed in the relevant sense. What I have in mind here are cases in which the extrapolation concerns aspects of human psychology, and, in particular, ones involving the exercise of reason and choice. To take a simple example, suppose that John proposes marriage to Mary, and she declines. Next week, he proposes again, and she again declines. He goes on, week after week, pressing his suit, and she remains adamantly unwilling. There comes a time when we become pretty confident about how Mary will respond on the next occasion when the proposal is made; and it is hard to think that there would be no grounds for such confidence when we try to set things out in the most rational way. At the same time, it is not easy to think that the consistency of Mary's behaviour is to be ultimately explained in terms of the operation of natural laws. The consistency can only be accounted for in terms of Mary's psychology, and the factors which would feature in any such psychological explanation—factors of belief and desire, and the process of rational deliberation and choice—are not ones which can be plausibly thought of as operating in a law-controlled, mechanistic way. And, in consequence, justifying an extrapolative inference by means of NES seems to be excluded in principle.

Now it would be possible for the advocate of NES to retain its claims in their present form and simply dig his heels in over this kind of case. Thus he could insist that NES provides the only method of giving extrapolative inferences a rational foundation, and that if cases like that of Mary are resistant to nomological treatment, then we are simply not warranted in making such inferences with respect to them. I do not myself find this response plausible. It seems to me that, even when we exclude the possibility of a nomological approach to such cases, we can still, in broad outline, plausibly envisage how extrapolative inferences could be justified.

The Nomological-Explanatory Solution · 51

Indeed—though this is not something that I can hope to pursue in these lectures—I think we can plausibly envisage a method of justification which is akin to the method involved in NES, with the subject's rationality taking the place of laws, and with his beliefs and desires taking the place of the standing conditions. My own (dialectically more cautious) response will simply be to put this whole matter on one side and restrict the scope of the claims of NES to areas where this kind of problem does not arise. So, instead of taking NES to be claiming that, in *any* case where there are rational grounds for making an extrapolative inference, these grounds can be made explicit in the specified way, I shall, from now on, take it to be offering this claim only for cases in which the hitherto exemplified regularities whose extrapolation is at issue are not to do with human decision-making or any other aspects of human psychology that might be thought to create special problems for a nomological approach. Indeed, in practice, I shall think of NES as exclusively concerned with the status of extrapolative inferences about the workings of the *physical world*.

With this restriction in place, I am offering NES as a solution to the problem of induction—a solution that provides a rational justification of inductive reasoning in the face of the sceptic's attack. But there is something else that I now need to underline. For, as well as recognizing the restriction on the range of cases to which it applies, it is important that we do not misunderstand the *sense* in which NES is seeking to provide a justification of inductive reasoning.

NES is claiming—with the appropriate restriction in scope—that, in so far as there are rational grounds for moving from the knowledge that a regularity has held in our experience hitherto to the conclusion that it will continue to hold for the unexamined cases, these grounds can be made explicit by breaking this move down into two steps of inference of the specified kind. What it is *not* claiming is that this two-stage process of reasoning is something that we typically employ in our everyday inductive practice. Obviously, such a claim would be unsustainable. As Hume recognized, our everyday inductive practice reflects a natural disposition of the mind to form expectations in an extrapolative way, and, for the most part, we exercise this disposition without feeling any need to give the inferences a further rational foundation. Indeed, as I stressed in Lecture 1, the disposition typically operates in an *automatic* way, without giving rise to a conscious process of reasoning at all. The sense, then, in which NES is offering a justification of induction is not that it is purporting to reveal the rationality of inductive reasoning in the form in which it ordinarily occurs, but that it is purporting to provide a sound method of reasoning which is equipped to cover the same inferential ground, or at least to do so in those cases where the ground can be rationally covered at all. We should not see this as a deficiency in the NES position—as a respect in which it is failing to deliver all that it should. For NES is responding to the problem of induction in precisely the form in which the sceptic poses it. The sceptic is not merely claiming that extrapolative inferences lack rational warrant as they occur in the context of our everyday lives. He is claiming that such inferences lack rational warrant altogether. He is claiming that, however we reflect on the situation, we cannot discern any way in which the knowledge of hitherto exemplified regularities provides rational grounds for forming expectations about the outcomes in unexamined cases. NES is purporting to reveal such a way.

V

I have tried to introduce NES, and spell out its rationale, in a way that makes it prima facie plausible. And, by restricting its scope to inferences concerning the physical realm, I have protected it from one possible form of challenge. But there remain a number of crucial objections that can be brought against it, and these will have to be considered and met before I can think of claiming that the case for NES is irresistible. These objections are ones that I am going to look at in the next two lectures. Among them is the objection which will set the agenda for the next main phase of our discussion, when I focus on the problem created by the notion of natural necessity.

The objections I shall be looking at are ones that challenge NES at its most fundamental points. But I want to conclude the present discussion by raising an issue which, while not threatening the basic thrust of the solution I am proposing, does present it with a complication.

So far, we have been exclusively concerned with cases in which the hitherto exemplified regularities have been universal in form—each regularity consisting in the fact that *all* the cases examined have turned out in a certain way—and the issue of extrapolation has turned on our entitlement to infer that this will continue to be the uniform outcome for the relevant class of unexamined cases. But it often happens that the hitherto exemplified regularities whose extrapolation is at issue are of a statistical rather than a universal kind; and, in such cases, the issue of extrapolation will turn on our entitlement to infer not that a certain type of outcome will be *uniform* over the relevant class of unexamined cases, but that it will continue to occur with the *same relative frequency*. For example, we might notice that whenever we have sown seeds of a certain type in certain conditions, approximately three-quarters of them have germinated; and the question of extrapolation will then be whether we are entitled to infer that this same frequency of germination will continue in the case of future sowings. Now, in general, the application of NES to these kinds of case does not require us to suppose that the laws that ultimately account for the regularities are of a special kind—a kind which distinctively reflects the statistical character of what they explain. So, in the case of the seeds, there is nothing which discourages us from supposing that the laws that lie behind the observed regularity are of the standard, deterministic, sort—assigning constant types of outcome to constant types of condition—and that the reason why the seeds do not respond in a uniform way is to do with some variation in their internal character or in the factors that affect them after they are sown. Quite generally, even where the detected regularities are only statistical, there is normally nothing to suggest that the underlying regularities are anything other than universal (universal regularities about the instantiation of categorical physical properties), and that the laws which account for them are anything other than deterministic.

There is one area, however, where the occurrence of statistical regularities seems to have a more far-reaching significance, and where the application of NES is correspondingly less straightforward. For when we investigate the workings of the world at the level of particle physics, we encounter regularities that are not only statistical, but that also empirically present themselves as *basic*—as regularities with no more fundamental regularities underlying them. And if these regularities really are basic, then the laws that we shall need to postulate, if we are to explain them nomologically, will indeed have to be of a special, statistically oriented, kind. Now the fact that a statistical regularity is basic, and can only be nomologically explained by postulating a law of a special kind, does not necessarily require any radical change of approach. For example, if we found that, as a basic regularity, particles of a certain type, in certain conditions, always moved in one of four determinate directions, and that these four determinate types of outcome tended to be more or less equally distributed over randomly chosen samples of sufficient size, we could straightforwardly explain the regularity simply by postulating a law that requires particles of that type, in those conditions, to behave in one of those four ways. Explaining the *evenness* of the distribution of the four types of outcome would not require us to postulate any additional—evenness-encouraging—constraint. For the evenness would be adequately accounted for by the absence of anything to bias things in favour of one type of outcome more than another. But many of the statistical regularities that we encounter in particle physics cannot be explained in that simple way, by merely appealing to a disjunctive law, and leaving everything else to chance; and it is here, it seems, that we are going to need a radically new approach. To take a familiar example, there are certain seemingly basic statistical regularities that characterize the rate at which the atoms (more precisely, the atomic nuclei) of radioactive substances decay over time. Specifically, we find that, for a given substance and a given length of time, there is a certain number between 0 and 1 such that, whenever we take a sufficiently large sample of atoms of that substance at a certain time and then check on the proportion of them that decay over a period of that length, the resulting fraction almost always approximates to that number. Now we cannot explain these regularities by merely postulating laws that prescribe disjunctions of outcomes. Nor, again, can we explain them by postulating laws that make it naturally necessary for samples of the relevantly sufficient size to exhibit frequencies of decay of the relevant sort; for not all samples of such a size do exhibit such frequencies. Rather, once we accept that the regularities are basic, it seems that the only way we can nomologically account for them is by postulating *probabilistic* laws—laws that, instead of assigning certain types of outcome (or ranges of types of outcome) to certain types of situation, assign certain degrees of natural probability of certain types of outcome to certain types of situation. Specifically, it seems that we would need to suppose that, for each radioactive substance, there is a certain function f from lengths of period to probability degrees, such that, for any period length d, it is a law of nature that, for any atom of that substance, existing at any time, the probability of its decaying within a period of length d from that time is f(d). In other words, it seems that, in order to explain the stable *frequencies* of decay with respect to *samples* of atoms, we would need to postulate laws that impose the corresponding *probabilities* of decay on *individual* atoms. Despite their probabilistic character, such laws would still be forms of natural *necessity*; and, though the detected regularities they would be postulated to explain are statistical, the regularities they would render naturally necessary would be universal. It is just that these universal regularities are not ones concerning the types of outcome that occur in certain types of condition, but ones concerning the *probabilities* of certain types of outcome occurring in certain types of condition.

Now if we are allowed to appeal to probabilistic laws of this sort, the statistical regularities that we encounter in the behaviour of particles present no special problem for the approach to induction that I am advocating. We simply have to make allowance for the fact that, where the explanatory hypotheses are thus probabilistic, the conclusions drawn about the unexamined cases (whether individual cases or samples of cases) will have to be probabilistic too. But it is just over the legitimacy of recognizing probabilistic laws that there might seem to be a problem. For it might be wondered whether we can really make sense of the sort of probabilities involved. In general, recognizing natural probabilities does not require us to think of them as fundamental ingredients of reality. Thus, in recognizing that, for a normally constructed coin, there is an approximately 1/2 probability of a heads outcome for an arbitrary toss, we do not have to suppose that there are any factors fundamentally involved in coin tossing apart from the intrinsic character of the coin, the conditions in which it is tossed, the method of tossing, and laws of an ordinary, deterministic, kind. But in cases where the laws that govern the relevant phenomena are taken to be probabilistic, the probabilities they assign to things do have to be thought of as fundamental. Thus if we take it to be a law of nature that any atom of radium has, at any time, a certain probability of decaying within a certain period, then, given any such atom, existing at a certain time, we not only have to think of it as possessing this probability of decay, but we also have to think of its possession of this probability as something fundamental about it, and as something with a fundamental influence on its future. It is this that creates the source of worry. There is no difficulty in understanding how natural probabilities can obtain in a *non*-fundamental form, as the *product* of laws and physical conditions. But it might well be wondered whether we can make sense of such probabilities as metaphysically freestanding, whereby a certain type of event has a certain likelihood of occurring without there being anything more fundamental that makes that the case. Nor is it any good countering that, in the case envisaged, the probabilities would obtain as a result of the obtaining of the laws, and so would not be free-standing after all. The relevant point is that, if the laws are probabilistic, the probabilities that result from them would have to have an ontological life of their own. They would not be items that the laws and conditions *logically create*, but items whose obtaining the laws *control*. And it is in that sense that they would be metaphysically free-standing.

The Nomological-Explanatory Solution

You can see now how, given the solution I am proposing to the problem of induction, the phenomena of particle physics present me with a complication. I want to say that, like other forms of extensive regularity, the statistical regularities that characterize such phenomena call for explanation, and, on the approach I have been advocating, any such explanation would have to be nomological. But it seems that many of these regularities could only be explained by appeal to probabilistic laws, and the legitimacy of such an appeal is in question. Of course, I could always try to bypass the potential problem by insisting that, if it turns out that we cannot make sense of probabilistic laws, we should conclude that the regularities in question are not basic after all. For the fact that there is no empirical evidence of the presence of underlying regularities does not prove that they do not exist: there could be physical factors at work in the relevant situation that we have not yet managed to detect, and perhaps are not even capable of detecting. But, for obvious reasons, I would feel uncomfortable if this were my only way of dealing with the situation. It would be preferable by far if there were a way of handling things within the framework of what the empirical evidence seems to indicate.

This is as far as I want to take the discussion at this stage. On the crucial question of whether we can make sense of probabilistic laws, I have offered no verdict; and until a verdict is reached, we do not know whether there is a specific problem here which my approach faces. But, for the time being, I want to leave this whole topic on one side and focus on matters of more central concern. I shall return to it in the final lecture, when my account of the nature of laws is in place, and when I shall be in a position to look at things in a significantly new perspective.

LECTURE 4

Two Objections to NES

I

Induction is that form of reasoning whereby, from our knowledge that a certain regularity has held good among the cases examined, we infer that it will continue to hold for some unexamined case or group of cases. The sceptic claims that such extrapolative inferences have no rational warrant. The claim is not merely that we are not rationally entitled to make such inferences with *certainty*, but that the evidence of the hitherto exemplified regularity provides no rational grounds for even forming *expectations* about the unexamined cases. We may know that all ravens so far examined have been black; but this gives us no rational grounds for expecting ravens to be black tomorrow. We may know that, whenever they have been relevantly monitored, bodies have always behaved gravitationally; but this provides no rational grounds for thinking that such gravitational behaviour will continue.

In the previous lecture, I set out, in outline, the way in which I think that the sceptic's claim can be successfully resisted. The position for which I argued can be summarized like this:

1. There is a significant range of cases where the knowledge of a hitherto exemplified regularity provides rational grounds for an extrapolative inference.
2. In any such case—or, at least, any case which is exclusively concerned with the workings of the *physical world*—the grounds can be made explicit by breaking the inference down into two further steps of inference, neither of which is, as such, extrapolative.
3. The first of these two steps is an inference to the best (the most plausible) explanation. What the explanation is advanced to explain

is the occurrence of the hitherto exemplified regularity whose extrapolation is at issue. And this regularity calls for explanation because it is too extensive to be deemed coincidental—deemed to be something that has occurred for no reason.
4. This explanation involves the postulation of some law or set of laws of nature, sometimes precisely specified, sometimes not. In the simplest cases, the postulation of these laws will form the whole explanation of the relevant regularity. In other cases, the explanation will additionally involve the recognition of certain standing conditions—sometimes precisely specified, sometimes not. Which of these forms of explanation is appropriate depends on other things we independently know or have reason to believe about the world.
5. The second step of inference is a deduction from the explanation—a deduction that the regularity (thus explained) will continue to hold for the unexamined case or cases, or will do so subject to the continued obtaining of the relevant standing conditions.

I labelled this the *nomological-explanatory solution* (NES).

In the simplest cases, as I have said, the explanatory hypotheses envisaged by NES just consist in the postulation of some law or set of laws, without the additional recognition of standing conditions. I illustrated this type of case by focusing on the example of gravity. The sceptic claims that we have no grounds for supposing that the past regularity of gravitational behaviour will continue (or that the regularity over the examined cases will also hold for the unexamined). The answer offered by NES is that the past (hitherto exemplified) regularity calls for explanation, that the most plausible way of explaining it is by postulating a law of gravity, rendering gravitational behaviour naturally necessary, and that once we accept this explanation, we can move deductively to the extrapolative conclusion. We can move deductively to this conclusion because it is a matter of logic that if it is necessary that bodies behave gravitationally, then they always do.

Thus set out and illustrated, NES is, I think, looking plausible. But, as I acknowledged, there are certain objections which can be brought against it, and which I need to answer before I can think of claiming that its correctness is established. There are, as I see it, three objections which need to be addressed, relating to different aspects of the proposed solution. I shall look at two of these in the present lecture. The third will need more extensive treatment; indeed, it will set the agenda for the whole of our subsequent discussion.

II

NES depends on the assumption that if a hitherto exemplified regularity is sufficiently extensive, it calls for explanation, and does so simply in virtue of the phenomenon of regularity it exhibits. It is by relying on this assumption that it is able to present its case for postulating laws of nature (as, or as part of, what accounts for the regularities), and it is by the postulation of such laws that it is able to offer a justification for the relevant forms of extrapolative inference.

To say that a regularity *calls for* explanation is to say that it is rational to believe that it has an explanation (to believe that there is a *reason* why things have been regular in that way), and that it is rational to believe this independently of our knowledge of what the explanation is or is likely to be. The fact that something calls for explanation in this sense does not, of course, entail that it has one. Nor does the fact that something calls for explanation *prior* to an investigation into what its explanation might be entail that it will continue to call for explanation *subsequent* to that investigation. For the investigation might reveal, contrary to expectation, that the thing in question does not have an explanation after all, or none that we could plausibly recognize. This last point is of no worry, at this stage, to the defender of NES. In claiming that hitherto exemplified regularities call for explanation, he is working in a framework where nothing has yet been discovered which casts doubt on the availability of credible explanations. And indeed his very next move is to offer an account of how, by appeal to laws, credible explanations can be found.

You may have noticed that I am using the term 'explanation' in two senses. Thus when I speak of something as *calling for* explanation, I mean by 'explanation' an *explanatory account*—an account which it is up to us to construct and which purports to specify the reason why the thing exists or obtains. But when I speak of something as *having* an explanation, I mean by 'explanation' whatever it is that a correct explanatory account would specify—whatever it is that, independently of our theorizing, constitutes the reason why the thing in question exists or obtains. This twofold usage of the term, and of its cognates, is perfectly standard; and, since it is also very convenient, I shall continue to mix the two uses in what follows. I think it will always be obvious, on each occasion of use, which sense I intend.

NES depends on the assumption that, when sufficiently extensive, hitherto exemplified regularities call for explanation, and do so simply in virtue of the phenomenon of regularity they exhibit. Let us refer to this assumption as the *call-for-explanation* claim, or, for short, CFE. It is NES's dependence on CFE that gives rise to the first objection. For many philosophers would say that, even when they are relevantly extensive, regularities do not call for explanation in this way.

We need to start by getting clear about what is at issue here. Philosophers who reject CFE do not want to deny that hitherto exemplified regularities can often be scientifically explained in terms of more fundamental regularities. For example, they would be happy to accept that the hitherto exemplified regularity of coins falling, when released in circumstances like these, can be explained in terms of the more fundamental regularity of bodies behaving, or attracting one another, gravitationally. Nor do they want to deny that, even when we do not know *how* a certain regularity is to be explained in terms of more fundamental regularities, other things we know about the circumstances of the regularity and the general workings of the world may make it rational to believe that it *has* an explanation of that sort. But what these philosophers insist is that, wherever there are grounds for thinking that a hitherto exemplified regularity has an explanation, these grounds depend on our possession of empirical evidence, additional to our knowledge of the obtaining of the regularity itself. In other words, what they deny is that hitherto exemplified regularities ever call for explanation *simply in virtue of the regularity they exhibit*. And it is this that brings them into conflict with CFE. For what CFE claims is that, quite independently of any additional empirical evidence, the phenomenon of regularity *as such*, when sufficiently extensive, calls for explanation. This is crucial to the purposes of NES. For unless extensive regularity *as such* calls for explanation, then, when we get down to the level of those regularities that are, qua regularities, explanatorily fundamental, there would be no grounds for thinking that there is anything which accounts for them, and so no grounds for postulating laws to play the explanatory role that NES envisages.

CFE, then, claims that hitherto exemplified regularities of sufficient extent call for explanation, and do so simply in virtue of the phenomenon of regularity they exhibit, while those who reject CFE insist that, where there are grounds for thinking that a regularity has an explanation, it is always because of our possession of additional empirical evidence. Let us refer to this latter position as the *empiricist view*; and, as something which stands in opposition to NES, let us speak of it as the *empiricist objection*. Clearly, this would be the position of all radically empiricist philosophers in the tradition of Hume and Ayer.

Considered in the abstract, the empiricist view has a certain prima facie plausibility. There is no *conceptual* problem about the notion of an extensive regularity which obtains for no reason: there is no hint here of any kind of unintelligibility or incoherence. And, granted that there is no conceptual problem with this notion, it might seem, in the abstract, that, in any particular case, there could be nothing other than our empirical knowledge of the circumstances surrounding this case, and of the general workings of the world, that could bear on the question of whether we should expect the regularity to have an explanation. However, I think that when we concretely focus on actual or hypothetical cases of extensive regularity, and raise the issue of explanation in the right way, we can see that this is not so, and that the implications of CFE are correct. Or, at least, I think that this is something we shall be able to see, provided we approach things with an open mind, and do not allow our intuitions to be dominated by a prior commitment to a radically empiricist outlook.

III

I have already tried to make clear the basic rationale for CFE when I focused on the case of gravity in the context of my original exposition of NES, and I shall begin by setting out the relevant reasoning again, though in a little more detail.

The case turns on the following three facts, or what we are assuming to be facts. First, given any body existing at a certain time, there is an infinite (indeed, a non-denumerably infinite) range of logically possible forms of behaviour open to that body at that time, only one of which would be, in the prevailing conditions, gravitational. We can illustrate this, as in the first lecture, by thinking of the situation that would obtain if I were to release this coin, and noting that, of the infinite range of directions in which it might move, only the straight-downwards movement would, in the circumstances, meet the requirements of gravity. Secondly, there has been a vast number of occasions when bodies have been observed, or scientifically monitored, in ways that would have revealed the occurrence of non-gravitational behaviour, had such behaviour occurred and been sufficiently distinctive in its non-gravitational character. For example, there have been countless occasions when we have observed an object resting on a supporting surface, and when we would have noticed if, without any new force acting on it, it had started to rise. Thirdly, on none of these occasions has non-gravitational behaviour been detected. This, I suppose, might be thought to be an exaggeration. Certainly, there have been reported sightings of non-gravitational behaviour—for example, reports of levitation. But, even if some of these reports are true, they can be safely ignored in the present context: they are sufficiently rare as to make no significant difference to the extent of the hitherto exemplified regularity, and do not affect the issue of explanation that concerns us—the issue of whether the regularity, qua regularity, calls for explanation.

Now consider the hypothesis (H) that this consistency in the gravitational behaviour of bodies over the cases examined has occurred *for no reason*—that nothing has been responsible for ensuring or to any degree encouraging it, that it is no more than a pure coincidence that all the different instances of bodies behaving at a time have turned out to conform to this common pattern. There is no denying that H is a coherent hypothesis; nor, as far as I can see, is there anything else which conclusively establishes its falsity. Nonetheless, the situation postulated by H would surely be a very strange one—a situation whose obtaining, if we knew of it, would warrant huge surprise. For it would surely be objectively hugely surprising that, with so much opportunity for non-gravitational behaviour to occur and manifest itself, and with nothing to prevent or discourage it, such behaviour has never shown up. It would be surprising in the same kind of way as it would be surprising if, knowing that there was nothing to impose a bias in favour of heads, we tossed a coin a large number of times and it came up heads on each occasion. Moreover, what would make it surprising is not to do with any additional empirical evidence. The thought is not, for example, that we have found empirically that, where there is nothing to ensure or promote regularity, irregularity tends to prevail. The thought is simply that, irrespective of what happens in practice, there is something very odd *in the abstract* about a situation in which events keep on conforming to a common pattern by chance—without anything to prevent or discourage deviance.

But if the situation postulated by H is one whose obtaining would be objectively hugely surprising, then the rational expectation must be that this situation does not obtain, and that there is something which accounts for the past consistency of gravitational behaviour. Or, at least, this must be the rational expectation provided that we have no independent reason for thinking that no plausible explanation is available; and, as things presently stand, this proviso is satisfied. So the implications of CFE hold good in this case: there is indeed a call to explain the gravitational regularity, and one which stems simply from the phenomenon of regularity it exhibits. Moreover, if the implications of CFE hold good in this case, they will obviously hold good in other cases of a similar kind. Thus, wherever a hitherto exemplified regularity is sufficiently extensive, there is the same kind of warrant for surprise on the supposition that there is nothing which accounts for it, and the same kind of consequential reason to think that this supposition is false.

This, then, as I see it, is the basic rationale for CFE, and the core of the way to rebut the empiricist objection. And it might seem, at first, that I could afford to leave matters like that. But, in fact, there is one crucial respect in which the argument needs to be further elaborated if the case for CFE is to be fully clear.

I have represented the situation postulated by H as a very strange one, whose obtaining (if we knew of it) would warrant huge surprise. For, as I put it, 'it would surely be objectively hugely surprising that, with so much opportunity for non-gravitational behaviour to occur and manifest itself, and with nothing to prevent or discourage it, such behaviour has never shown up'. And, intuitively, that sounds right. But, on closer scrutiny, it might be wondered what the basis of this surprise is supposed to be. Let us start by considering the issue in the context of coin tossing, where the relevant factors are easier to handle. Suppose we have two coins, A and B. We toss each one in turn a hundred times, knowing that, in each case, there is no kind of bias at work—nothing that would ensure or encourage the emergence of any particular type of sequence of outcomes, or the emergence of a sequence drawn from any particular group of such types. Coin A comes up heads on each occasion, while, with coin B, the outcomes are fifty heads and fifty tails, arranged in no conspicuous order or pattern. Applying my reasoning to this case, I want to say that the emergence of the occurrence of A's run of heads is objectively surprising, because it is surprising that, with nothing to require or encourage the constant heads outcome, the tails alternative never occurred. And again, intuitively, that sounds right. But suppose I were to apply the same reasoning to the case of B. Suppose I claimed that the occurrence of B's particular sequence of outcomes, whatever it was, is also objectively surprising, because it is surprising that, with nothing to require or encourage the emergence of this type of sequence, it still happened that, in the case of each toss, the outcome conformed to it. Such a claim would be clearly absurd: in so far as there is no conspicuous order or pattern in the sequence type in question, there is no warrant for surprise that this type should happen to get realized when things are left to chance. But if the reasoning would be fallacious in the case of B, what justifies it in the case of A? How do the two cases relevantly differ? It is here that my argument stands in need of further elaboration. I want to say that there is something objectively surprising about a situation in which an extensive regularity emerges without there being anything that accounts for it. But I need to be able to explain why more surprise attaches to the reasonless emergence of a *regularity* than to the reasonless emergence of *any* type of complex of events. And it is precisely this issue that arises, in a conveniently manageable form, in the example of A and B.

One thing is clear. I cannot say that what relevantly distinguishes the cases of A and B is that, prior to any knowledge of the outcomes, the epistemic probability of the occurrence of the A-sequence was lower than that of the occurrence of the B-sequence. Let K be the knowledge that the two coins have been tossed a hundred times and that, in each case, there was no bias in favour of the emergence of any particular type of sequence of outcomes, or group of such types. And let us call the two types of sequence that respectively occur in the cases of A and B, T1 and T2. Then it is true that, relative to K, the epistemic probability of A's sequence of outcomes being of type T1 is very low. Thus, for each toss, we can set the probability of a heads outcome at $1/2$, since, with the knowledge of the lack of any bias, the warranted degree of expectation for heads and tails would be equal; and so the probability of all the outcomes turning out to be heads can be set at $1/2^{100}$, which is exceedingly small. But it is also true that, relative to K, the epistemic probability of B's sequence of outcomes being of type T2 is exceedingly small. For since the probabilities of heads and tails for a given toss are the same—each being $1/2$—the probability of occurrence for *any* type of hundred-item sequence is $1/2^{100}$. So if there is warrant for retrospective surprise at the sequence of outcomes that occurs in the case of A (which is indeed what I would claim), but not at the sequence that occurs in the case of B (which is uncontroversial), this cannot be because of some difference in the prior epistemic probabilities of the occurrence of the two types of sequence. It cannot be because, in advance of a knowledge of the outcomes, there are stronger grounds for expecting the non-occurrence of a T1-sequence than for expecting the non-occurrence of a T2-sequence.

Presumably, if there is a warrant for surprise in the case of A, but not in the case of B, this must turn not so much on the *determinate* character of the outcomes that occur in the two cases, as on the fact that the A-sequence is conspicuously orderly and the B-sequence is not. But the problem is still over identifying just what it is that makes that difference relevant. It is tempting, at first, to appeal, once again, to a simple point of prior probability. However we decide to distinguish what is conspicuously orderly from what is not (and, at the margin, the distinction will obviously be arbitrary), the set of conspicuously orderly types of sequence will form only a tiny minority of the totality of types; and, for each coin, this means that, relative to K, the epistemic probability of the emergence of a sequence that is conspicuously orderly is very low, and the epistemic probability of the emergence of a sequence that is not conspicuously orderly is correspondingly very high. But is it still not clear how that is to provide a basis for the difference in respect of surprise. Let α be the set of conspicuously orderly types of sequence (however, exactly, this set is to be demarcated), and let β be some equinumerous set of non-orderly types to which T2 belongs. Since α and β are equinumerous, we have to accept that, relative to K, their epistemic probabilities of exemplification are equal. So, if we are entitled to be surprised at the occurrence of the T1-sequence in the case of A, on the grounds that T1 belongs to the set of conspicuously orderly types α, which has a very low probability of exemplification, why are we not entitled to be equally surprised at the occurrence of the T2-sequence in the case of B, on the grounds that T2 belongs to β, which has an equally low probability of exemplification? We seem to have made no progress.

But now notice something interesting. It is true that the mere fact that T2 belongs to β and that β has a very low prior probability of exemplification does not entitle us to be surprised when a T2-sequence occurs in the case of B. But suppose that, quite independently of the outcomes that occur in the case of B, there is something that marks β out as having some special significance in comparison with other equinumerous sets of types. To take one example, suppose that, in advance of tossing the coins, we wrote down a list of certain possible sequences of outcomes, representing heads by 'h' and tails by 't', and that β is the set of types that feature in this list. Then, in those special circumstances, the subsequent occurrence of the T2-sequence in the case of B does indeed warrant surprise. For, although there is nothing about the character of this sequence in itself that warrants surprise, what is objectively surprising is that, just by chance—by mere coincidence—the sequence happens to instantiate one of the members of that set of sequence types that is independently marked out for us by the earlier construction of the list. Of course, the warrant for surprise still depends, in part, on the fact that the set of types that is thus marked

66 · Two Objections to NES

out is a relatively small subset of the totality of types, and so has a relatively low prior probability of exemplification. If the list we drew up in advance covered, say, half the possibilities, then obviously there would be no reason to be surprised that, just by chance, one of these possibilities happened to be realized when we tossed the coin. But the particular point of interest is that, while the low probability of the exemplification of β is not, on its own, sufficient to make the occurrence of a β-sequence retrospectively surprising, it does suffice for such surprise when it combines with the fact that β is already, and quite independently, marked out as a subset of special significance. In other words, the strong prior grounds that exist, in the abstract, for expecting the non-occurrence of a β-sequence (simply because β is a relatively small subset of the totality) come to yield subsequent grounds for surprise at the actual occurrence of such a sequence because there is something independent of that occurrence that, as it were, puts β in the frame.

This point, I think, helps us to understand the relevant difference between the cases of A and B in the context of the original example, where there is nothing that puts β in the frame. In both cases, as we have noted, there is the same exceedingly low epistemic probability of the occurrence of the relevant type of sequence of outcomes relative to K; and just as the set of conspicuously orderly types, α, to which T1 belongs, is a relatively small subset of the totality of types, with a consequentially low probability of exemplification relative to K, so likewise β, to which T2 belongs, is an equally small subset of the totality of types, with an equally low probability of exemplification relative to K. But whereas there is nothing to mark β out as a subset of special significance—nothing, that is, apart from the fact that it is one of the subsets that contains the sequence type that occurred in the case of B—there is indeed something that marks out α as a subset of special significance, and does so quite independently of its containing the sequence type that occurred in the case of A. What marks it out is not some other *concrete* item, such as a previously constructed list of its members; or, at least, if there is such an item, that is not what is relevant in the present context. What is relevant is the fact that α is marked out *in the abstract* as of special significance, simply by its being the set of types that are conspicuously orderly. It is this fact that explains why there is a warrant for retrospective surprise when the run of heads occurs. For what creates the warrant for surprise is the fact that the sequence of outcomes that occurs happens, by mere chance, to be of a type that belongs to that select group of types that is thus independently marked out. Thus, just as we would be entitled to be surprised, indeed astonished, in a case where, just by chance—by mere coincidence—a sequence of outcomes with no conspicuous order happens to match one of a small list of possible sequences that has been independently drawn up in advance, so, in the case presently envisaged, we are entitled to be surprised, and again astonished, that, just by chance—by mere coincidence—the sequence of outcomes happens to instantiate a type that features in that small group of types that are set apart from the others by their orderly character. Once again, of course, we need to bear in mind that considerations of prior probability are relevant too. The fact that a subset of types is independently marked out by something does not create grounds for surprise in a situation of its chance exemplification if the prior epistemic probability of such exemplification is already reasonably high. (Thus just as α is independently marked out by the *orderly* character of its members, so the complementary subset of types that are not members of α is independently marked out by the *non-orderly* character of its members. But this does not yield any warranted surprise when, as in the case of B, a member of this subset happens, by chance, to occur.) What creates the grounds for surprise, in the case of A, is the combination of the fact that, by chance, the sequence that occurs is of a type that belongs to a subset of types that is independently marked out by the character of its members, and the fact that, by being so small in comparison with what remains, this subset has only a very low epistemic probability of exemplification relative to K.

Now it is in these same terms that we must understand why, in the case of an extensive regularity in nature, the situation would be objectively surprising if the regularity had occurred for no reason—with nothing to require or encourage things to be regular in that way. Let us continue to focus on the case of gravity. The grounds for surprise, if we suppose that things have been gravitationally regular for no reason, is created by the combination of two factors, relating to different aspects of the phenomenon of regularity involved. The first factor covers the point of prior epistemic probability. Thus, on any natural way of dividing up the behavioural possibilities, it will turn out that, in the abstract space of relevant types of relevantly sized behavioural complexes, regularity-exemplifying types are a comparative rarity; and so, on the supposition that outcomes are left to chance (or at least are not subject to any form of regularity-promoting influence), there is a correspondingly low rational expectation—low prior epistemic probability—of such a type being realized in a given case. The second factor is that, quite independently of what occurs in this or in any other particular case, regularity-exemplifying types are marked out, by their regularity-exemplifying character, as of special significance. They form a group of types that are set apart from other types by their distinctive character. Neither factor, on its own, would suffice to create grounds for surprise. There is no warrant for surprise in a situation where something unlikely happens, if there is nothing that relevantly distinguishes that outcome from the alternatives that might have occurred. Nor is there any warrant for surprise in a situation where what happens is marked out as in some way special, if the occurrence of something that is thus special was in any case likely. It is to the two factors in combination that we need to appeal. What is so surprising about the situation envisaged—the situation in which things have been gravitationally regular for no reason—is that there is a certain select group of types, such that (i) these types collectively make up only a tiny portion of the range of possibilities, so that there is only a very low prior epistemic probability of things conforming to one of these types when outcomes are left to chance, (ii) these types are independently marked out as of special significance by being forms of regularity, and (iii) just by coincidence—coincidence on a grand scale—the way in which bodies have behaved, over the vast number of occasions in which things have been monitored, happens to match one of these special types. The warrant for this surprise is something that we can recognize a priori: it does not involve an appeal to empirical evidence of how the world works. And, granted that it is recognizable in the case of gravity, it must be recognizable in any other case of a similar kind, where we focus on an extensive regularity that has held in our experience so far, and suppose that there is nothing that has required or encouraged things to be regular in the relevant way.

This, then, as I see it, is what provides the ultimate basis for CFE. Where an extensive regularity has held in our experience so far, there is a call to explain it, simply on account of the phenomenon of regularity it exhibits. What creates this call is that the situation that would obtain if there were no explanation (nothing that had required or encouraged things to be regular in that way) would be objectively hugely surprising. And the source of this surprise would be the strangeness of the fact that, just by coincidence, and on a such a large scale, the way in which things had turned out happened to match one of a narrowly circumscribed group of complex behavioural possibilities that were independently marked out as of special significance by being forms of regularity. For reasons mentioned earlier, there is a sense in which this endorsement of CFE is only provisional.

For although it would be very surprising if the extensive regularities we have encountered have no explanation, it is conceivable that further investigation will reveal that there is no plausible mode of explanation available and that the surprising outcome has to be accepted. But, as I have stressed, we have no reason to think that the call for explanation will be silenced in this way. And, indeed, with the option of accounting for the regularities by the postulation of laws, it seems that a plausible form of explanation has already been identified.

IV

Let us assume, then, that, when sufficiently extensive, hitherto exemplified regularities call for explanation, and do so simply in virtue of the phenomenon of regularity they exhibit. And let us also provisionally assume, in line with NES, that the most plausible way of accounting for them is by supposing that they are consequences of laws, or of combinations of laws and standing conditions. Even so, it might be thought that, in envisaging the kinds of explanation that it does, NES is begging the question against the sceptic—that, in effect, these explanations have been chosen to sustain the legitimacy of extrapolative inference, rather than because they can be justified in their own terms. To see how this new objection arises, let us once again focus on the familiar case of gravity. As before, I shall ignore reported sightings of non-gravitational behaviour and assume that the gravitational regularity has held without exception in our experience so far. The sceptical issue is then over whether we are entitled to expect this regularity to continue to hold in the future and over the unexamined cases quite generally.[1]

We are assuming that the hitherto holding of the regularity calls for explanation, and that the explanation has to be wholly or partly in terms of laws. And let us further assume, as was earlier envisaged, that the appropriate form of the explanation is of the simplest type, where we just postulate a law of gravity, without an additional appeal to standing conditions. Following the procedure envisaged by NES, we are then supposed to be able to move to the extrapolative conclusion by deduction from the nomological postulate. Thus we are supposed to be able to reason that,

---

[1] The present discussion of the objection follows closely my earlier discussions in 'Induction, Explanation, and Natural Necessity' and in my *Ayer*, Pt. III, sect. 5.

because it is naturally necessary that bodies behave gravitationally, it logically follows that they always do, and hence that they do, in particular, in the cases not yet examined. But it only takes a moment's reflection to see that this procedure depends on a crucial further assumption, and it is here that the opportunity for objection arises. For we can only reach the conclusion that bodies *always* behave gravitationally if we assume the relevant law to be *universal in scope*—a law which imposes the same gravitational necessity on *all* bodies, in *all* places, at *all* times. And it is not clear what entitles us to make this assumption. For if the sole basis for postulating the law is the need to provide an explanation of the regularity over the cases examined, why should we not select a law which, while covering these cases, is restricted in its scope to some particular set of bodies or some particular portion of the space-time continuum? To take the most obvious example, where our extrapolative concern is with how things will turn out in the future, consider the following three nomological hypotheses, with T as the present moment:

A. It is a law that bodies always behave gravitationally.
B. It is a law that, at all times before T, bodies behave gravitationally.
C. It is a law that, at all times before T, bodies behave gravitationally; and there is no stronger gravitational law (no law relevant to the period from T onwards).

To justify the conclusion that bodies will continue to behave gravitationally, we have to justify an acceptance of A in preference to C. But how can this be done by an explanatory inference, granted that both A and C, by entailing B, account for the gravitational regularity so far? The objector will say that the only way in which we could try to justify an acceptance of A would be by falling back on extrapolative induction, arguing that if gravitational behaviour has been naturally necessary hitherto, it is likely to be naturally necessary in future. And, if this is so, we have not yet solved the sceptical problem. Nor, indeed, will we have made progress towards a solution. For if we have to resort to induction at this point, we might just as well apply it directly to the hitherto exemplified regularity without bringing in nomological explanation at all. We might just as well say that because bodies have always behaved gravitationally hitherto, we can reasonably expect such behaviour in future. Obviously, there are analogous ways of developing the objection, in which the alternatives to A involve a restriction to a certain set of bodies or to a certain region of space (defined by reference to some body or bodies). But I shall continue to focus on the case of the time-restricted law already before us.

Does this new objection to NES succeed? Well, in the example on which we are focusing, it is certainly true that B, and hence both A and C, offer explanations of the past regularity. But this alone is not enough to sustain the objection. For what NES envisages is that we can find grounds for accepting the right kind of nomological hypothesis—one that will legitimize the projection of the regularity on to future cases—by an inference to the *best* explanation; in effect, by an inference to an explanation which is both plausible and decisively more plausible than any alternative explanation. So what the objector needs to show is that, as explanations, C is not, or is not decisively, inferior to A; or put another way, he has to show that B is not inferior, or decisively inferior, to A as a *terminus* of nomological explanation. And, on this point, I think that the defender of NES can stand his ground. For it seems to me that a law whose scope is restricted to some particular period is more mysterious, inherently more puzzling, than one which is temporally universal. Thus if someone were seriously to propose C as the correct account, our response would be to ask *why* the relevant law should be time-discriminatory in that way. Why should a certain moment have this unique significance in the structure of the universe, that bodies are gravitationally constrained in the period up to it, but not thereafter? Barring the postulation of a malicious demon, these questions are unanswerable: any answer we could receive would only serve to show that the nomological situation was not as suggested—that the change in the constraints on gravitational behaviour was to be ultimately explained in terms of time-impartial laws and a difference, relevant to the operation of these laws, in the conditions which obtain in the two periods. Because these why-questions seem pertinent and yet are *ex hypothesi* unanswerable, we are left feeling that, as hypothesized, nature would be inherently puzzling, and would preclude an explanation of our empirical data which was both correct and, from the standpoint of our rational concerns, fully satisfactory. And it is for this reason that, presented with the datum of the past gravitational consistency, and the alternative explanatory hypotheses A and C, we are justified in regarding A as decisively superior. It is decisively superior because, unlike C, it dispels one mystery without creating another: it dispels the mystery of unexplained regularity without creating the mystery of capricious necessity. In the same way, we would be justified in taking A to be decisively superior to other hypotheses with restrictions of a similar kind to C, both to hypotheses that restrict the gravitational law to some (different) particular period of time, and to hypotheses that restrict the law to some particular set of bodies or some particular region of space.

The objector might reply that I am here guilty of double standards. I have argued that, in the case of behaviour, we ought to be surprised by the occurrence of *unexplained regularity*, and I am now claiming that, in the case of necessity, we ought to be surprised by the occurrence of *caprice*. But why should our expectations for behaviour and necessity be so strikingly different? If there is no problem in expecting irregular behaviour when there are no laws (or anything else) to forbid it, why should there be a problem in building a measure of irregularity into the laws themselves? Or if it is reasonable to expect the laws to be uniform over bodies, space, and time (given no evidence against this), why should it not be reasonable to expect uniformities of behaviour without the backing of laws (or anything else)? It seems that I am relying on opposite standards of rationality in the two cases.

Well, in a sense, I am. But this is just because the cases are quite different. What makes them so is that, unlike the concept of behaviour, the concept of a law of nature has some notion of generality built into it. Thus try to imagine a law that is restricted in scope to a single object at a single time, so that it prescribes how that object is to behave at that time, but does not do so by prescribing anything more general. It is surely clear that a law of such total singularity cannot be coherently envisaged. We cannot make sense of the claim that it is nomologically required that a particular object behave in a certain way at a particular time except as a claim which is implicitly more general, concerning what is required of objects of a certain type in situations of a certain kind. This is not to say that we cannot conceive of there being laws whose scope is *to some degree* restricted by a singular reference. We can, I think, conceive of there being the law postulated by C, whose scope is restricted to a certain period. But this is only because the restriction leaves room for enough generality of scope for the notion of law to gain purchase. In itself, a singular restriction is something which runs counter to the grain of nomological explanation. This is why, if there is a need for nomological explanation at all, we serve its purposes better by postulating laws without such restrictions, so long as we can do so compatibly with our data. And, in particular, this is why, given the consistency of gravitational behaviour in our experience so far, we rightly regard A as a more satisfactory explanation than C, or any other explanation of a similarly restricted kind. None of these considerations, which apply to our concept of a law, carry over to our concept of behaviour. There is no implicit generality in our concept of an object's behaving in a certain way at a certain time—none, at least, except in so far as the possession of certain behavioural dispositions may be implicit in our concept of the type of object in question. And, indeed, it is precisely when instances of behaviour keep on conforming to a common pattern that there is a call to explain the situation.

Now, at this point, a determined objector might try to press his case in a different way. He may concede the point I have been arguing for—that the inclusion of arbitrary restrictions in the scope of the laws we postulate would leave us with a further source of puzzlement, and so detract from the plausibility of the explanations offered. And, accordingly, he may concede that, in the particular case on which we have been focusing, there is a clear-cut reason for preferring A to C. But he might also insist that the substance of his objection can be put in a way that does not depend on the possibility of appealing to nomological hypotheses of the relevantly restricted kind. Let me explain.

The kind of restrictions that we have been considering are ones that involve picking out a particular period, region, or set of bodies, and restricting what would otherwise be a universally applicable law to what takes place within that period or region, or with respect to those bodies. Crucially, the restriction here is a purely *singular* one: it is not achieved by finding some general property or complex of properties which distinguishes what is selected from other items in the relevant category (other periods, regions, or sets of bodies), and which is then held to be nomologically relevant to the resulting forms of behaviour. Rather, the restriction is achieved by simply *referring* to the relevant item (or to some item which is appropriately related to it) and making its *identity* (or the identity of the related item) what is nomologically relevant. But it would be possible to achieve a nomological restriction in a different kind of way. For having mentally selected the period, region, or set of bodies to which we want to restrict the relevance of the law, we could then find some purely general predicate which distinguishes it from other items of the relevant category, and use this predicate, rather than a designator, in the formulation of the law. So, in the case on which we are focusing, we could introduce nomological hypotheses like B and C, but achieve the restriction to the past—the pre-T period—by the use of a predicate which, while it applies to all past times, and as far as we know to no other times, does not involve, explicitly or implicitly, any singular reference to the present moment, or to any other particular. There are a number of ways of doing this. To take just one example, let us stipulate n to be the exact number of years ago of the Big Bang, and V to be the determinate type of this event. We can then introduce a predicate 'F' defined as true of all and only times that are less than n years later than some earlier V-event. Put more precisely, 'F' is defined as true of time t if and only if, for some event y, y is earlier than t and y is of type V and the distance in years between t and y is less than n. We can then replace B and C by respectively:

D. It is a law that at all F times bodies behave gravitationally.
E. It is a law that at all F times bodies behave gravitationally; and there is no stronger gravitational law.

Although we know that 'F' is true of all past times subsequent to the Big Bang, we have no reason to think that it is true of any future time. So accepting D, or E, would provide no basis for expecting gravitational behaviour in the future. At the same time, the law involved is not essentially restricted in scope by the form of its content: the times on which the necessity of gravitational behaviour is imposed are identified by their instantiation of a purely general property, rather than by means of a singular reference. So these new nomological hypotheses would enable the objector to reformulate his point in a way that avoided, at least ostensibly, the problem of nomological caprice. He could insist that, although they do not license any expectations about the future, D, and hence E, adequately explain the gravitational regularity so far. And he could insist that, unlike what was envisaged earlier, the relevant law, being formally universal in scope, is not time-discriminatory. It does not assign a special significance to the present moment; it simply assigns a special significance to a general property which, as far as we know, only applies to times that are earlier than this moment.

This, then, is how a determined objector might try to reinstate his point in response to the criticism of his original approach. But I mention the possibility more for the sake of completeness than because it represents a serious option. For such a response would clearly be just a contrived manœuvre, designed to evade the letter of the original criticism, rather than something which deals with the criticism in its substance. Let us continue to focus on the particular example. The crucial point is that the relevant property which is introduced into the gravitational law, and which has the effect of contingently restricting its application to the period up to the present, is selected not because there is anything to suggest that it is of nomological relevance to how bodies behave, but purely because it is expected to have the relevant restrictive effect without involving an explicit reference to the period in question. And so entertaining E as a serious rival to A has no rationale other than a determination to block the entitlement to extrapolation. The situation here would be analogous to that in which someone who purports to accept the principle of universalizability in ethics, but wants nonetheless to adopt a moral position which is advantageous to himself, insists that his basic moral principle is that everything should be done to further the interests of anyone whose fingerprints are thus and so—where he displays a photograph of his own prints as the specification of the type in question. The upshot is that, while E is an available explanatory option, its plausibility does not come anywhere near that of A. Given the way that F-ness has been selected, it would be astonishing and deeply puzzling if it turned out that, by chance, this property did have the nomological relevance E assigns to it—every bit as astonishing and puzzling as it would be if the present moment had the significance assigned to it by C. Analogous remarks would apply to other hypotheses reached by a similar procedure, where the restriction to the relevant period, region, or group of bodies is effected by the use of a predicate which, while avoiding singular references, is specially selected to achieve that restrictive purpose.

It seems to me, then, that, whether the relevant restrictions are achieved by singular references or by the use of specially devised predicates, the second line of objection to NES fails, and that the defender of the solution has the resources to justify his preference for explanations which, by postulating laws that impose uniform constraints across bodies, space, and time, are suited to the purposes of extrapolation.

V

I have now looked at two lines of objection to NES. The first stemmed from what I called the empiricist view, which rejects the claim that extensive regularity as such calls for explanation. The second turned on the claim that, even if extensive regularities need to be explained, we cannot, without begging the question, justify the choice of nomological explanations that license extrapolation. I hope that both these objections have now been adequately answered.[2]

---

[2] I should mention that, in the case of the second objection, the answer I have offered is relative to the perspective in which the issue has so far presented itself. Our understanding of this issue will eventually change, in the light of the account of laws that we come to accept, and, at that point (in Lecture 10), my handling of the issue will be adjusted accordingly.

There remains, however, one further objection, and I think the most crucial. NES is claiming that, when sufficiently extensive, hitherto exemplified regularities call for explanation, and it is assuming that the appropriate way to explain them is by postulating laws of nature—laws which either on their own, or in conjunction with certain standing conditions, ensure that things are regular in the relevant ways. But it might be said that the very notion of a law of nature, in the sense I intend, is incoherent. There is, indeed, no problem with the notion of a law of nature as a fundamental *regularity* in the workings of the natural world; nor any problem with the notion of a law as a *claim of science* which attempts to record such a regularity. And, as we saw, the term 'law' can be used in both these ways. But what I am taking the term to mean, and what it has to mean for the purposes of NES, is a form of *natural necessity*—something in virtue of which things *have* to happen in a regular way. And it is *this* notion of a law of nature that might be thought incoherent.

This is the issue that I shall turn to in the next lecture. And, in doing so, I am, at last, beginning to move our discussion into the area of theological interest. For it will be in relation to the problem over the coherence of the notion of a law that I shall construct my argument for the existence of God.

LECTURE 5
The Problem of Laws

I

In the third lecture, I proposed a certain solution to the problem of induction—a solution which I called the *nomological-explanatory solution* (NES). The solution claims that, in so far as it is rationally defensible, extrapolative inference with respect to the physical realm can be justified by being recast as the product of two other steps of inference, neither of which is, as such, extrapolative. The first of these steps is an inference to the best explanation—the best (the most plausible) explanation of the hitherto exemplified regularity whose extrapolation is at issue. This explanation always involves the postulation of some law or set of laws of nature, and, in certain cases, also involves an appeal to the presence of certain standing conditions. The second step of inference is a deduction from the explanation thus inferred. When the explanation just consists in the postulation of a law or set of laws, what is deduced is that the regularity (thus explained) will continue to hold for the relevant unexamined case or cases. Where the explanation also involves an appeal to certain standing conditions, what is deduced is that the regularity will continue to hold for the unexamined cases provided that these conditions continue to obtain.

In the last lecture, I considered and rejected two objections to NES. The first was that the regularities which have held in our experience hitherto do not stand in need of explanation, with the consequence that the envisaged justification of the relevant extrapolative inferences cannot get started. Against this, I tried to show just how implausible it is to suppose, in the case of an extensively exemplified regularity, that things have been regular for no reason—that it is just a coincidence that the various objects and events involved have conformed to a common pattern. The second objection was that the nomological explanations envisaged by NES have been specially chosen to sustain the relevant step of extrapolation, and that this choice begs the question against the sceptic. In response to this I tried to show that the kind of explanations envisaged can be defended as the best (the most plausible) ones on independent grounds—grounds which are to do with avoiding gratuitous sources of puzzlement and surprise, not to do with rigging things in favour of a justification of induction.

But there is still one further way in which NES can be challenged. NES claims that past regularities call for explanation and that the appropriate way to explain them is by postulating laws of nature, as forms of natural necessity. But it might be said that the very notion of a law of nature, in the intended sense, is incoherent—that we simply cannot make sense of there being forms of natural necessity of the kind required. It is to this crucial challenge that I now turn. As I mentioned, this challenge will set the agenda for the rest of our discussion, and it will be in relation to it that I shall construct my argument for the existence of God.

II

It will be some time before I am ready to present that argument. But I want to make it clear, at the outset, that what I have in mind is quite different from two other ways of arguing for theism, which also focus on issues concerning the laws of nature.

The first of these can be thought of as a law-specific version of the cosmological argument. As we have seen, the regularities in nature, when sufficiently extensive, call for explanation, and, on the face of it, the way to explain them is by appeal to the existence of laws. But equally, it might be said, we need to appeal to something further to explain why there are *laws*. For how has it come about that things are constrained to behave in certain regular ways unless there is something which has imposed, or continuously imposes, these forms of constraint—something which is causally responsible for (as it were) laying out the nomological tramlines? But if we are looking for a causal explanation of the laws, we shall presumably have to look for a source of causal agency outside the natural realm; for, within that realm, there is surely no source of agency that operates independently of the laws themselves. And if we are looking for a source of agency outside the natural realm, the conclusion that the laws are imposed by God, if not quite mandatory, is at least very plausible.

If this first argument can be thought of as a law-specific version of the *cosmological argument*, the second can be thought of as a law-specific version of the *argument from design*. Like the first, it turns on the claim that the laws of nature call for explanation, but the focus of attention is not on the question of why there are laws at all, but on the question of why the laws that obtain have the specific content they do. The reasoning runs as follows. The universe, or at least our planet within it, contains a rich variety of forms of life, some of them, and human beings *par excellence*, of enormous sophistication. Such forms of life could not have come about without the world being constituted and organized in a range of specific ways, and these forms of constitution and organization depend, at a number of points, on the detailed content of the laws of nature. The fineness of detail involved here is very great. Even a slight variation in the content of the laws would have had a catastrophic effect, preventing not only the emergence of the forms of life that actually exist, but also the emergence of any life forms of comparable complexity; indeed, in most cases, any variation would have prevented the emergence of life altogether. But it is hard to believe that it is just by good fortune that the content of the laws is, in this finely tuned way, just what is required for the emergence of significant life. Rather, we should conclude that the laws have been put in place by God, and that he has chosen their content with the precise purpose of permitting the existence of the forms of life that he wants there to be.

Both these lines of argument have, I think, some plausibility. But the reason I have drawn attention to them is not because I want to endorse them, or even attempt to assess their merits. I mention them because I want to stress the contrast between the issues they involve and the issue that I want to focus on in my own discussion. In both these arguments, it is taken for granted that we can make sense of what a law of nature is, prior to the claim that the existence or content of the laws calls for divine explanation. It is supposed that we can understand, without reference to God, what it is for there to be laws of nature, and can then draw on that understanding to see that there is a pertinent why-question which only theism can answer. But the argument for theism that I want to develop is precisely concerned with the issue of whether we can make sense of laws of nature at all. It is an argument which turns on the claim that there is a prima facie problem over the intelligibility of the notion of a law, and that, in the end, we can only satisfactorily deal with this problem in a theistic way.

80 · The Problem of Laws

III

Questions about whether we can make sense of a certain kind of thing—whether the notion of a certain kind of thing is intelligible—are a familiar feature of philosophical debate. But there are two quite different ways in which philosophers can approach such issues. One way involves starting out with a preconceived philosophical theory about what kinds of thing we can make sense of—what kinds of intelligible concept are possible—and then applying this theory to the particular case at issue to see whether the case meets the requirements which the theory specifies. The classic example of this is the empiricist criterion of intelligibility espoused by David Hume.[1] Hume held that, in order for a concept to be intelligible—indeed, in order for it to be a *genuine* concept at all—it has to draw its whole content from the materials supplied by sensory and introspective experience (in his terminology, *ideas* have to be either copies of previous *impressions* or analysable into simpler ideas which are copies of impressions). And he then invoked this criterion in an attempt to show that some of the things that we normally suppose ourselves to be able to understand, we cannot really understand, because the content of our supposed understanding is not wholly drawn from the materials of experience in the required way. By this means, he tried to show that we cannot form intelligible notions of, for example, substance, the self, and, in so far as it is held to involve a relation of objective 'necessary connexion', causation.[2]

The other way of approaching an issue about whether we can make sense of a certain kind of thing—whether the notion of such a thing is intelligible—is quite different. For it just consists in considering the issue on its merits, without any preconceived view of the requirements of intelligibility beyond the ordinary and philosophically uncontroversial

---

[1] See his *A Treatise of Human Nature*, ed. L. Selby-Bigge, 2nd edn. revised P. Nidditch (Oxford: Oxford University Press, 1978), Bk. 1, Pt. 1, sect. 1, and *An Enquiry Concerning Human Understanding*, ed. L. Selby-Bigge, 3rd edn. revised P. Nidditch (Oxford: Oxford University Press, 1975), sect. 2.

[2] 'Necessary connexion' was the expression which Hume used to signify that element in the cause-effect relation that is additional to temporal precedence and spatial and temporal contiguity. I should mention, in passing, that, in recent years, a number of philosophers have challenged the traditional view that Hume denied that we can form an intelligible notion of objective necessary connexion. Thus see, in particular, G. Strawson, *The Secret Connexion* (Oxford: Oxford University Press, 1989). For a good critique of this modern challenge see S. Blackburn, 'Hume, and Thick Connexions', *Philosophy and Phenomenological Research* 50 (suppl. vol., 1990), 237–50.

principles of reason itself. So if a philosopher were to focus on such notions as substance, the self, and causation in this ideologically neutral spirit, he would not, as Hume, start by invoking some philosophically inspired criterion of what is intelligible or genuinely conceivable. Rather, he would just try to spell out, in a philosophically perspicuous way, what these notions amount to, and only convict them of unintelligibility if something comes to light which makes this plain—plain from that ideologically neutral viewpoint. So, in the case, say, of the notion of substance, he would not be prepared to say that we cannot make sense of this notion simply on the grounds that we cannot form a conception of substance in purely experiential terms. Rather, he would try to get clear about what is involved in the notion, and only reject it as unintelligible if some conceptual problem is revealed that anyone of sufficient intelligence and conceptual sophistication can recognize, whatever his philosophical leanings.

Now of these two approaches, it is the first that has been involved in the main traditional attack on the notion of a law of nature. For the main attack has come from philosophers who, like Hume, have a radically empiricist view of what counts as intelligible, and who think that the notion of a law of nature, as a form of natural necessity, does not meet the relevant requirements. This radically empiricist attack can itself be developed in different ways, according to the kind of criterion of intelligibility which is adopted. On the one hand, there is, as we have seen, the Humean criterion, which is applied to *concepts* (in Hume's terminology, *ideas*) and which requires intelligible concepts to draw their content from the materials supplied by experience. The notion of a law of nature is then thought to be something that cannot be traced back to the materials of experience in this way. On the other hand, there is a more modern form of empiricism, which is primarily concerned with the intelligibility of *propositions*, and which restricts such intelligibility to cases where the proposition is potentially amenable to a certain kind of empirical verification. (Philosophers who hold this verificationist view often differ about the kind of verification required.) And, from this standpoint, the problem with the notion of a law is that propositions which assert or imply the obtaining of laws are not amenable to verification in the relevant way.

These empiricist rejections of the notion of a law, whether they pursue a Humean or a verificationist line of attack, are, in my view, misconceived; for I simply cannot see any rational justification for the empiricist theories that underlie them. No one wants to deny the enormous contribution which experience makes to the development of our conceptual scheme.

But it seems to me to be no more than an unwarranted dogma to insist that *all* our concepts draw *all* their content from the materials supplied by experience, or that propositions are *bound* to be unintelligible unless they are potentially open to empirical verification of the relevant sort. These are matters which I have dealt with in some detail elsewhere, and I shall not pursue them any further here.[3] The prima facie problem which *I* discern in the notion of a law, and which will eventually lead to my argument for theism, arises in the context of the second methodological approach, in which we look at the issue of intelligibility on its merits. Thus it seems to me that, without commitment to a particular philosophical theory of what intelligibility requires, we only have to focus on the way in which we have so far characterized laws, and pose the right questions, to perceive a clear-cut difficulty in making sense of what laws would be. It is to the task of bringing out this difficulty that I now turn.

IV

A law of nature, as we are conceiving of it, is an instance of a certain kind of necessity. Thus its being a law that bodies behave gravitationally is the same as its being, in a certain way, necessary that bodies behave gravitationally. Let us refer to the necessity involved as *nomic* necessity. I have spoken of such necessity as a form of 'natural' necessity. In part, the point of the label 'natural' is to indicate the realm of reality to which the necessity applies: a nomic necessity is, whatever else, a necessity with respect to the occurrence and arrangement of *natural* phenomena, a way in which events or states of affairs in the *natural* realm are constrained. But the label is also intended to signal the fact that the necessity in question is of a distinctive kind, and, in particular, different in character from *logical* necessity. The need to distinguish these two forms of necessity becomes apparent as soon as we consider a case of logical necessity which is itself concerned with the natural realm. Thus take the logical necessity of bodies being extended. The sort *body* and the property *extension* are universals pertaining to the natural realm. But obviously we do not want to say that the necessity of bodies being extended is an instance of nomic necessity—the necessity involved in laws. It is necessary that bodies are extended and necessary that bodies behave gravitationally, but the kinds of necessity involved are different.

---

[3] In Part I of my *Ayer*.

One obvious way in which such necessities differ is that there is a clear contrast between the ways in which they are discerned—between the kinds of ground that we have for accepting that they obtain. In the case of nomic necessity, our grounds are always empirical. Thus, in the case of gravity, we detect the relevant regularity in how bodies have behaved hitherto, and take this, via an explanatory inference, to be evidence of the presence of a natural law. And, quite generally, the only way we can come to have grounds for recognizing the presence of a natural law is by finding that we need to postulate such a law in order to explain our empirical data. But, in the case of logical necessity, at least logical necessity *in its standard form*, our basic method of establishing that such necessities obtain is a priori—a method of pure rational thought, without recourse to empirical evidence. So, in the example we considered, we know merely by unpacking what is implicit in our concept of a body that such a thing cannot exist without having voluminous extension. Such extension is a defining feature of body, and it would simply make no sense to suppose that something could qualify as a body but lack that attribute. Of course, we could always make it a defining feature of a certain type of thing that it should obey a certain type of law; for example, we could introduce the concept of *Newtonian matter* to signify matter which obeys a Newton-type law of gravity. But this would not mean that we could establish the existence of such a law a priori—by unpacking what is implicit in our concept of the type of thing in question. All it would mean is that until we had empirical evidence that such a law obtained, we would have no reason to think that this type of thing was instantiated.

But there is also, it seems to me, another way in which logical and nomic necessity differ, and it is on this point that I mainly want to focus. When we say that it is necessary that bodies are extended, or, what is equivalent, that it is impossible for there to be a body which is not extended, we mean this without proviso or qualification. The possibility of an unextended body is excluded *absolutely*. And this is true of all cases of what we think of as *logical* necessity. But, in the case of *nomic* necessity, the claim of necessity does not, as I see it, have this unqualified and absolute character. In recognizing a law of gravity, we are recognizing that, in some sense, it is *necessary* that bodies, or bodies of the relevant sorts in the relevant kind of space, behave (or attract one another) gravitationally. But the relevant sense is not one that excludes altogether the possibility of things being otherwise—the possibility of situations in which bodies, or bodies of the relevant sorts, in the relevant kind of space, fail to behave (or attract one another) gravitationally. In contrast with logical necessity, the necessity of gravitational behaviour is not, as we may put it, a form of *strict* necessity. And this is so for nomic necessity quite generally.

One way in which it could be thought that nomic necessity is non-strict is by supposing that it is possible for laws of nature to be contravened—possible for there to be cases in which a law obtains, but something occurs which is contrary to what it requires. This may sound strange. For how can something be a genuine law if it leaves room for its own contravention? But the point is that, although it makes no sense to suppose that a law of nature could be contravened when the natural realm is left to its own devices—when there is nothing other than its own conditions and laws to influence what takes place within it—it might still be thought that there could be some *supernatural* source of agency with the power to interfere in the workings of nature and override the constraints of law on particular occasions. At the same time, such a view would clearly be controversial. Many philosophers would insist that the notion of the contravention of a law is simply incoherent—that something would not count as a genuine law (a genuine form of natural necessity) if it had counterinstances. And, indeed, in my own characterization and defence of NES, I have so far worked on the assumption that contravention is logically excluded, and that from the claim that it is a law of nature that things behave in a certain way, we can logically deduce that they always do. For the time being, I am going to put this whole issue on one side. I shall return to it in the final lecture, after my account of the nature of laws is in place.

But, quite apart from any possibility of laws being contravened, there is a much more obvious way in which, as I see it, we are obliged to think of nomic necessity as non-strict. In explaining this point, it will be convenient to employ the terminology of 'possible worlds'. What is meant by a 'possible world' is simply a total way in which things (past, present, and future) might have been. In employing this terminology, I am not suggesting that we should take the existence of such worlds seriously. There are, indeed, philosophers who do this—David Lewis is the most obvious example.[4] But, as far as I am concerned, referring to possible worlds is just a convenient device for speaking about possibilities in a precise and systematic way. It does not, as they say, carry ontological commitment.

Let us say that a possible world W is *compositionally relevant* to a law L if and only if the types of ontological and qualitative ingredient which

---

[4] See, for example, Lewis's *Counterfactuals* (Oxford: Basil Blackwell, 1973), 84–91.

feature in W include all that is needed for the formation of states of affairs that would be counterinstances to L, that is, states of affairs that do not accord with how L, in the actual world, requires things to be. So, in the case of the law of gravity, a world containing the sorts of space and matter which the law concerns would be compositionally relevant to it in this sense, since such a world would be furnished with all the types of ingredients needed for states of affairs in which bodies of the relevant sorts behaved non-gravitationally; while a world whose only substances were mental, or an abstract world whose only basic ingredients were numbers and numerical properties, would not be compositionally relevant to it. (Note that where the ingredients of a world suffice for the formation of *counterinstances* to a certain law, they also suffice for the formation of *positive exemplifications* of it, and vice versa. So I could just as well have defined compositional relevance in terms of having the ingredients needed for positive exemplifications, as in terms of having the ingredients needed for counterinstances.) Now, whatever kind of necessity characterizes the regularities whose obtaining they ensure, laws themselves are surely only contingent: for any law, we surely have to acknowledge that there are possible worlds in which that law does not obtain. Moreover, in acknowledging, for each law, that there are possible worlds in which it does not obtain, we surely have, in particular, to acknowledge that there are possible worlds that are *compositionally relevant* to it and in which it does not obtain. So, in the case of the law of gravity, we not only have to acknowledge that there are possible worlds from which the law is absent, but we also have to acknowledge that there are possible worlds which *contain the relevant sorts of space and matter* and from which the law is absent. But if, for any law, we have to acknowledge that there are compositionally relevant possible worlds from which that law is absent, we cannot avoid also acknowledging that there are compositionally relevant possible worlds in which, in the absence of that law, things occur that are contrary to what it requires. For, without the law (or anything comparable), there would be nothing to prevent such counterinstances from occurring. But if, for any law, we have to acknowledge that there are possible worlds in which there are counterinstances to it, it follows that nomic necessity is never strict. For a necessity is only strict if it excludes altogether the possibility of things being otherwise. Thus it cannot be strictly necessary that bodies behave gravitationally (or that bodies of a certain type behave gravitationally in a certain type of space) if there are possible worlds in which bodies (of the relevant type, in the relevant type of space) sometimes fail to behave in that way.

As far as I can see, there is only one way in which this argument could be challenged, though I do not think that the challenge is effective. It is a familiar fact that, at least typically, the behavioural and causal dispositions of physical objects are in some way grounded on, or sustained by, aspects of their *intrinsic natures*—aspects of what the objects are *like in themselves*, aspects of what they are like *categorically* and *non-relationally*.[5] The brittleness of glass, for example, is in some way grounded on its molecular structure, and the combustibility of wood is in some way grounded on its chemical composition. Now, traditionally, this grounding of dispositions on intrinsic properties is assumed to involve a framework of contingent law. So it is not thought that the molecular structure of a piece of glass, *on its own*, is what makes it brittle, or that the chemical composition of a piece of wood, *on its own*, is what makes it combustible. The assumption is rather that the intrinsic properties of these objects combine with certain contingent laws of nature to sustain the relevant dispositions. Now the only way, I think, in which someone could oppose the view that nomic necessity is never strict necessity would be by insisting that, at least in certain cases, the behavioural and causal dispositions of objects are sustained by their intrinsic properties alone, or perhaps by their intrinsic properties together with certain intrinsic properties of the wider physical context. Thus suppose someone wants to represent the law of gravity as a form of strict necessity—a necessity which imposes a gravitational regularity on all possible worlds which contain the relevant sorts of space and matter. Then what he will have to say, I think, is that there are things about the intrinsic natures of the space and forms of matter that exist in the actual world, such that, as a matter of strict necessity, and without the need for any additional framework of law, their being composed of such matter and located in such a space directly disposes, and indeed obliges, bodies to behave in the relevant gravitational way. And he will then have to say that it is this strict necessitational fact which constitutes the law of gravity.

This, it seems to me, is the only way in which someone could try to represent nomic necessity as, or as in some cases, a form of strict necessity. But, of course, before the approach could be taken seriously, it would need to be given a rationale. And it is here, as I see it, that we encounter the problem. For I just cannot see how the intrinsic properties of physical

---

[5] So, as I use the term 'intrinsic', intrinsic properties are by definition *categorical* properties. Some philosophers use the term in a less restrictive sense, which allows them to think of the intrinsic natures of objects as including dispositional properties.

objects, or of objects and their physical context, could sustain dispositional properties in this way. Take again the case of gravity. We are being asked to suppose that there are things about the intrinsic natures of the space and forms of matter that exist in the actual world which, as a matter of strict necessity, oblige bodies to behave gravitationally. But if the relevant properties really are purely intrinsic—purely to do with what the space and forms of matter are like in themselves, and not directly to do with how the material occupants of space are disposed to behave or causally interact— there seems to be no way of understanding how they could play this sort of role. If the properties are in this way intrinsic, how could there fail to be possible worlds containing the relevant forms of space and matter, but in which bodies are not gravitationally disposed in this way? Of course, gravity is only one case; maybe the champion of strict necessity will hope to fare better with other examples. But if so, the onus is on him to produce them. As things stand in the abstract, there seems to be an objection in principle to the idea that the intrinsic properties of physical objects (or of objects and their wider context) could, on their own, sustain behavioural or causal dispositions—sustain them directly and by strict necessity, rather than with the help of a framework of contingent law.

Perhaps the defender of strict necessity will try to make sense of such sustainment by claiming that, in some cases, it is essential to the *identity* of a certain intrinsic property that it should endow the objects which possess it with certain dispositions—that this property would not be *the property it is* if it did not dispose the things which have it to behave in certain ways or to exert certain kinds of causal influence. Sydney Shoemaker, as I understand him, holds such a view of physical properties in general.[6] But my problem is still that I need to know how this works. I can understand how there can be intrinsic properties which we can only *conceptually identify* by reference to the dispositions that are grounded on them. For example, I think we can only conceptually identify the intrinsic natures of the various types of fundamental particle by reference to the causal powers and sensitivities they sustain (and this does not, of course, mean that such sustainment does not depend on a framework of contingent law). What I cannot understand is how, if the properties are not as such dispositional, the dispositions they sustain could be essential to their *identities*. Shoemaker's reasons for taking

---

[6] Thus see his *Identity, Cause, and Mind* (Cambridge: Cambridge University Press, 1984), ch. 10. Chris Swoyer develops a similar view in his 'The Nature of Natural Laws', *Australasian Journal of Philosophy* 60 (1982), 203–23.

this line seem to be primarily epistemological: he notes that we can only detect the presence of a physical property by its effects on our sensory experience, whether direct effects, by how its presence manifests itself in the object's sensible appearance, or indirect effects, by how its presence affects the presence of other properties which so manifest themselves; and this leads him, by a kind of verificationist route, into supposing that the very identity of a physical property is determined by the empirically relevant cluster of causal powers which its presence sustains. But I just cannot see how the identity of a property can be determined in this way unless the property itself is constituted by powers; and if the property is constituted by powers (which are nothing other than dispositions to exert certain forms of causal influence in certain conditions), then it is not intrinsic in the relevant sense, and so not relevant to the issue at hand.[7]

It seems to me, then, that there is no way of making sense of the suggestion that the intrinsic properties of an object may sometimes, on their own, suffice to endow that object with certain behavioural or causal dispositions. And, in consequence, I can see no way of avoiding the conclusion that nomic necessity is never a form of strict necessity.

V

We have been comparing nomic necessity with logical necessity, and have found two points of difference. The first was to do with the ways in which the two kinds of necessity are discerned: cases of logical necessity, at least of such necessity in its standard form, can be established a priori, while cases of nomic necessity can only be discovered empirically. The second was to do with the relative strengths of the necessities: logical necessity is

---

[7] Recently, some philosophers have argued that laws of nature can turn out to be forms of strict necessity precisely by including powers, and other forms of dispositional property, in their content. So they think that a law to the effect that things of a certain (natural) kind K behave F-wise in circumstances of sort S can turn out to be a form of strict necessity by kind K's being wholly or partly dispositional in character and by the disposition to behave F-wise in S-circumstances being an element or aspect of this character. (Thus see, in particular, B. Ellis and C. Lierse, 'Dispositional Essentialism', *Australasian Journal of Philosophy* 72 (1994), 27–45; B. Ellis, 'Causal Powers and Laws of Nature', in H. Sankey (ed.), *Causation and Laws of Nature* (Dordrecht: Kluwer, 1999), 19–34; and B. Ellis, 'Causal Laws and Singular Causation', *Philosophy and Phenomenological Research* 61 (2000), 329–51.) But strict necessities of this sort would be entirely trivial and, given their triviality, I do not see how they could qualify as laws of nature in any decent sense. (What is not trivial, of course, is that a certain dispositional kind is instantiated.)

strict, excluding the possibility of contrary cases absolutely, while its being nomically necessary that things are regular in a certain way allows for the possibility of situations (for the existence of possible worlds) in which the relevant regularity fails to obtain. It might be thought that these two differences are just different ways of looking at a single difference—that necessity is bound to be of the strict and absolute kind if it can be established a priori, and bound to be of the weaker, qualified kind if it can only be established empirically. But this would be a mistake. It is true, I think, that necessities whose obtaining can be established a priori will always turn out to be of the strict variety. But, as Saul Kripke has shown in his book *Naming and Necessity*,[8] this connection does not hold in reverse. For there are clear-cut cases of necessities of the strongest kind—excluding the existence of possible worlds in which things are otherwise—but where there is no way of establishing them except by recourse to empirical evidence. Kripke's main example is that of identity. There is a single planet, Venus, which is visible in a certain part of the sky in the morning and in a certain part of the sky in the evening. Not knowing that there was only one heavenly body involved, our ancestors called the planet they saw in the morning 'The Morning Star', or, for short, 'Phosphorus', and the planet they saw in the evening 'The Evening Star', or, for short, 'Hesperus'. Later, it was empirically discovered, through the relevant astronomical measurements and calculations, that the planets were one and the same. In other words, it was established empirically that Phosphorus and Hesperus were identical. Now this conclusion could not have been reached in any but an empirical way: no amount of merely rational (armchair) reflection could have revealed that the planet which is visible in the morning is the same as the one which is visible in the evening. But, given that there is only one planet involved, the identity of Phosphorus and Hesperus is something necessary, and necessary in the strongest sense. There is no possible world, of any sort, in which Phosphorus and Hesperus are different; for that would have to be a world in which something was different from itself. So here we have a case of a necessity which is strict and absolute (like the necessity of *bodies being extended* and *2 + 2 being 4*), but which can only be discerned by recourse to empirical evidence—an absolute but a posteriori necessity. Although necessities of this sort are not establishable a priori, and so differ from logical necessities of the standard type, they are often classified as a special subgroup of logical necessities, thereby underlining

---

[8] Oxford: Basil Blackwell, 1980.

the strength of the necessity involved. And, in what follows, I shall classify them in that way myself. In other words, I shall count something as logically necessary if and only if it is strictly necessary, and as logically possible if and only if its negation is not strictly necessary.

Given that strict necessity can be of an a posteriori kind, it follows that what ultimately distinguishes nomic necessity from other forms of necessity is its *weakness*—the fact that it does not exclude contrary possibilities altogether, that it leaves room for possible worlds in which, with the presence of different nomic constraints, states of affairs of sorts that are prohibited in the actual world still sometimes occur. And this now brings us to a crucial question—indeed, for the purposes of my argument, *the* crucial question. Given that, for any law, we have to acknowledge that there are possible worlds in which it does not hold, and in which things do not behave in accordance with it, in what sense does a law qualify as a form of necessity at all? What does it mean to say that it is nomically *necessary* that bodies behave gravitationally, if this allows for the possibility of situations in which, with a different nomological organization in place, such behaviour does not occur? It is here that the issue over the intelligibility of the notion of a law arises. For it is just not clear how there is room for the concept of a necessity of this non-strict sort. On the face of it, it is simply self-contradictory to say that it is necessary that things should be thus and so, but that it is also possible for them to be otherwise.

It might be suggested that we could construe this weak form of necessity as a kind of scope-restricted version of strict necessity. A law-sustained regularity does not extend over *all* possible worlds, and so is not necessary absolutely. But it does, it might be said, extend over all worlds which have the *same basic nature* as our world, and so is necessary in the context of that nature. But the problem is in seeing how we can understand this claim in a way which renders it true, but non-vacuous. If we make it a requirement of a world's sharing the basic nature of our world that it should share its nomological organization, then, of course (at least if we discount the possibility of laws being contravened), the law-sustained regularities in our world will extend to all worlds in the relevant range. But this will be so in a way that is wholly trivial and of no help in illuminating the sense in which the regularities are necessary. On the other hand, if we drop the nomological requirement on sameness of nature—if we decide the question of whether a possible world is of the same basic nature as our world without reference to the sharing of the same laws, or the sharing of the behavioural and causal regularities which these laws prescribe—then there seems to be no way of arranging things so that the relevant regularities *do* extend over the range of worlds in question. How, for example, could we arrange for the gravitational regularity to extend over all possible worlds with the same basic nature as our world if, as we have agreed, there are worlds which have the same intrinsic types of space and matter as our world, but in which, in the absence of a law of gravity, material objects are not subject to the relevant forms of mutual attraction? How could we exclude such worlds from the relevant range—the range of worlds that count as sharing the basic nature of our world—except by reference to the difference in their nomological constitution?

Another suggestion might be that we should alter our conception of the ontological nature of laws. So far, we have been assuming that, although the term 'law' is a noun, signifying a certain kind of entity, the status of laws as entities is only superficial—the product of grammar, rather than a reflection of how things fundamentally are.[9] Thus we have been assuming that for *there to exist a law of a certain type* is for *it to be a law that things are regular in a certain way*, and that for it to be *a law* that things are regular in a certain way is simply for it to be, in the relevant nomic sense, *necessary* that things are regular in that way. And this means that, in so far as we have thought of laws as entities at all, we have thought of them as *abstract* entities, whose whole existence resides in the relevant facts of nomic necessity. But, given the difficulty over the notion of nomic necessity, it might be suggested that we should radically change this view of laws. It might be suggested that we should think of laws, not as abstract entities, which draw their existence from facts of nomic necessity, but as *concrete* entities that govern the world *causally*. So it might be suggested that, instead of taking the law of gravity to be something whose existence consists in the fact that it is nomically necessary that bodies behave gravitationally (or stand in the relevant attractive relationships), we should take it to be something concrete, which causes it to be the case that bodies behave gravitationally (or stand in the relevant relationships). This would still allow us to think of a law-sustained regularity as in a certain sense *necessary*; for if it is *caused* to obtain, it is in that way *made* to obtain, and if it is *made* to obtain, then in that sense it *has* to obtain. But, at the same time, such necessity would be *non-strict*, since there would be compositionally relevant possible worlds in which, in the absence of the

---

[9] Thus see Lecture 3, section I.

relevant kind of law (a law with the relevant kind of causal influence), that kind of regularity did not obtain.

However, although it would solve the problem of non-strictness, it is clear that we cannot construe laws in this way, and that the conception of laws that we have been hitherto assuming is correct. In the first place, if laws were concrete entities, they would have to have intrinsic natures additional to their world-governing role. But the idea of a law having such a nature—for example, of its being a certain type of space-occupying object, with shape and size and internal character—is just a manifest absurdity. It is clearly essential to our conception of a law that its whole nature consists in its world-governing role, as the sustainer of a certain type of regularity. And this can only be accommodated by thinking of a law as something whose existence consists in the relevant fact of nomic necessity. Moreover, given a law which sustains a certain type of regularity, it is essential to the identity of that law that it sustains that regularity. So, given the law of gravity, which ensures that bodies behave gravitationally, there is no possible world in which that same law exists without ensuring that bodies behave in that way. But there is no way of making sense of this fact if we suppose that the relationship between laws and the regularities they sustain is merely causal. Once again, we can only make sense of the situation by retaining our original conception of a law, as something whose very existence consists in the fact that a certain type of regularity is nomically necessary.

We are left, then, with a fundamental problem over how to make sense of the notion of a law of nature. On the one hand, laws (if such there be) are not just regularities of behaviour, but forms of natural necessity. To recognize a law of gravity is to suppose not just that bodies always and everywhere behave gravitationally, but that this is how they *have* to behave—that it is, in some sense, necessary that bodies behave (or attract one another) in the relevant way. On the other hand, we also have to accept that the necessity in question is not a form of *strict* necessity. For we have to accept that, for each law, there are compositionally relevant possible worlds in which it does not obtain, and in which, in its absence, the behaviour it prescribes does not always occur. The difficulty is in seeing how we can provide a satisfactory account of laws on this basis— an account which explains how there can be this special kind of necessity which is both real necessity but not strict. Unless we can provide such an account, then the notion of a law of nature will have to be abandoned as incoherent.

VI

Even in itself, having to abandon the notion of a law of nature would be an unpalatable result. For the recognition of laws seems to be implicit in our ordinary view of the world. Thus we ordinarily take it for granted that there are certain types of event—like water catching fire, or pigs flying, or eggs hitting concrete at 100 mph without breaking—which, while logically possible in the abstract, cannot (barring a miracle) occur in practice; and the recognition of these impossibilities seems tantamount to an acknowledgement that the world is constrained by certain forms of law, prohibiting the types of event in question. Moreover, an implicit acknowledgement of natural law seems to be what underlies our willingness to assent to certain types of counterfactual conditional. Thus we are happy to accept that if I had released this coin a moment ago it would have fallen, and that if I had released a helium balloon into the air it would have risen. And such beliefs presumably rest on the underlying assumption that this is how, in some sense, it is necessary that things of this kind behave in these sorts of conditions.

But, of course, it is not just our ordinary view of the world that is at stake. The reason why we have been focusing on the notion of a law at all is that the recognition of laws has played a crucial role in the solution I have proposed to the problem of induction. If it turns out that we cannot make sense of this notion, then the proposed solution will have to be abandoned, and we shall be no further forward in resisting the sceptic. Nor is this the only cause for philosophical concern. One of the crucial premises on which NES was founded was that hitherto exemplified regularities, when sufficiently extensive, call for explanation; and the claim was then made that the best (most plausible) explanations were ones that involved the postulation of laws. If the notion of a law is deemed to be unintelligible, then the pressure will be on to find some new way of explaining such regularities. For the fact remains that, when a regularity is sufficiently extensive, it would be objectively very surprising if it obtained for no reason.

It is clear that we have reached a critical stage in our investigation. And, in one form or another, the issues which now confront us will occupy our attention for the remainder of the discussion.

LECTURE 6

Armstrong's Theory

I

In the third and fourth lectures, I developed and defended a certain solution to the problem of induction—a solution which I called the *nomological-explanatory solution* (NES), and which involves the recognition of laws of nature, as forms of natural necessity. But we have now seen that there is a prima facie problem over the intelligibility of the relevant notion of a law. The problem arises because the necessity involved in laws—*nomic* necessity, as we termed it—is not a form of *strict*, or *absolute*, necessity. The claim that it is a law of nature that bodies always behave, or attract one another, gravitationally, does not imply the *absolute impossibility* of cases in which this regularity fails: it does not imply that there are no possible situations, *of any kind*, in which bodies do not behave or attract one another in this way. And this is how things stand for law claims quite generally. The way I showed this was by appealing to the fact that laws themselves are only contingent. More precisely, I introduced the notion of *compositional relevance*, whereby a possible world W is compositionally relevant to a law L if and only if the ontological and qualitative ingredients of W suffice for the formation of states of affairs that would be counterinstances to L. I then pointed out that, for any law, we have to acknowledge that there are possible worlds which are compositionally relevant to it but in which it does not obtain, and that, because we have to acknowledge this, we also have, for any law, to acknowledge that there are compositionally relevant possible worlds in which, in its absence, there are the relevant kinds of counterinstance. So, in the case of the law of gravity, we have to acknowledge that there are possible worlds with the relevant sorts of space and matter, but in which this law does not obtain, and in which, in its absence, bodies do not always behave, or attract one another, gravitationally.

Laws of nature, then, are to be conceived of as forms of necessity, but not as forms of *strict* necessity. It is this that creates the problem. For it is just not clear how we can make sense of a necessity which is less than strict. On the face of it, it is simply self-contradictory to say that it is necessary that things should be thus and so, but that it is also possible for them to be otherwise. Unless we can provide an account of the nature of laws which shows us how to get round this problem—how, after all, we can make sense of the non-strictness of nomic necessity—we shall have to reject the notion of a law as incoherent, and, along with it, reject the proposed solution to the problem of induction.

Nor, as we saw, is the viability of NES the only thing which is at stake. In the first place, having to abandon the notion of a law would be unwelcome in itself. For a recognition of laws seems to be implicit in our ordinary view of the world—a view which recognizes that there are certain types of event which, while logically possible in the abstract, cannot (barring a miracle) occur in practice. Moreover, and of more importance philosophically, if we find ourselves debarred from recognizing laws, the pressure will be on to find an alternative explanation of regularity. For the fact remains that many of the regularities that have held good in our experience so far are too extensive to be credibly thought of as coincidental.

For a number of reasons, then, it would be pleasant if a solution to the problem of laws could be found. So far, we have only considered two suggested solutions, namely (i) to think of nomic necessity as a scope-restricted version of strict necessity (as necessity, but in relation to a restricted range of possible worlds), and (ii) to think of laws as concrete entities that govern the world causally. And both these suggestions were found to be unsatisfactory.

II

One further way in which we could try to solve the problem would be by adopting the theory of laws defended by David Armstrong, and it is this possibility that I now want to explore. I indicated at the very beginning of these lectures that Armstrong too accepts the solution to the problem of induction that I have been advocating—a solution which recognizes the existence of laws of nature as forms of natural necessity. So it is of particular interest to see what Armstrong takes laws to be. I shall focus exclusively on the account he offers in his book *What is a Law of Nature?*[1] He has made minor adjustments to this account in his more recent book *A World of States of Affairs*,[2] but, as far as I can see, these do not affect either the substance of his position or the relevance of my main criticisms.

Armstrong's claim is that laws of nature are to be ultimately construed as relationships (the holding of relations) between universals. Thus, given a law that all F-things are G, his claim is that there is a relation R such that the obtaining of this law is to be ultimately construed as the fact that the property of F-ness (a universal) is R-related to the property of G-ness (another universal). To equip them to serve as laws, he takes the relevant relationships to satisfy three conditions. First, he takes each such relationship to be *contingent*—to be something which holds in the actual world, but does not hold in all possible worlds. So, in the case of the law that all F-things are G, and with R as the relevant relation, Armstrong would insist that, while in the actual world F-ness is R-related to G-ness, there are possible worlds in which F-ness and G-ness exist but are not so related. Secondly, he takes the relationships to be ones which logically entail the corresponding regularities. So, continuing with the same example, he would insist that F-ness's being R-related to G-ness logically entails that all F-things are G. (Armstrong eventually comes to qualify this second condition, but this is not something we need to go into.)[3] Thirdly, he takes the relationships to involve something genuinely additional to the corresponding regularities. So he would insist that F-ness's being R-related to G-ness does not reduce to the fact that all F-things are G. (He would also insist, of course, that the respect in which the relationships transcend the corresponding regularities is relevant to the way in which they entail these regularities.) Armstrong does not explicitly address the problem of laws that I have identified. But we can see how his account would equip him to offer a solution. Thus, in the case we are envisaging, it would not, on his account, be *strictly* necessary that all F-things were G. For the relevant relationship between the universals would be only contingent, and indeed would not hold constant through all compositionally relevant possible worlds; and so there would be possible worlds in which, in its absence, things were not regular in that way. But there would still be a clear sense in

---

[1] Cambridge: Cambridge University Press, 1983.
[2] Cambridge: Cambridge University Press, 1997.
[3] I should add, however, that it has nothing to do with making provision for the possibility of supernatural intervention.

which it was *necessary* for F-things to be G. For, granted that the relationship *does* hold, it logically ensures that F-things are always G, and in that sense *imposes* (*forces*) this regularity on the world. Quite generally, each law of nature would consist in a certain relationship between universals, and this relationship, while in itself contingent, would logically oblige things to be regular in the relevant way, and so, in that sense, make the obtaining of the relevant regularity necessary.

If it were acceptable, Armstrong's theory would show us how to make sense of nomic necessity. And, for reasons we have rehearsed, this would be a welcome result.[4] What we must now consider is whether the theory *is* acceptable. I should mention that Armstrong is not the only philosopher who thinks that laws of nature are to be ultimately construed as relationships between universals. In particular, he is joined in this by Fred Dretske and Michael Tooley.[5] Although my own discussion will focus almost exclusively on Armstrong's account, the verdict I shall reach about it will apply to the whole approach.

III

Armstrong's account of laws is advanced in the framework of a realist view of universals, and, of course, he has written extensively in defence of this view in other places.[6] By a 'universal', in this context, is meant a property or relation, such as the property of squareness (the property of being square) and the relation of temporal priority (of being earlier than). To adopt a realist view of universals is to recognize the existence of universals—their existence as *entities*—and to hold that reference to them must feature in the philosophically fundamental description of how things are. It is clear that Armstrong's conception of laws has to be realist about universals in this way. Laws cannot be equated with relationships between universals unless there are universals to stand in these relationships, and

---

[4] For this reason, I do not endorse John Carroll's claim, against Armstrong's approach, that nothing could be gained by giving an account of laws in terms of relationships between universals, rather than thinking of them as fundamental in the form in which they are ordinarily expressed. Thus see his 'Ontology and the Laws of Nature', *Australasian Journal of Philosophy* 65 (1987), 261–76.

[5] See Dretske, 'Laws of Nature', *Philosophy of Science* 44 (1977), 248–69, and Tooley, *Causation* (Oxford: Oxford University Press, 1987).

[6] See in particular his *Universals and Scientific Realism* (Cambridge: Cambridge University Press, 1978) and *Universals: An Opinionated Introduction* (Boulder, Colo.: Westview Press, 1989).

this equation cannot be offered as the *ultimate* way of construing laws unless it represents the way things are to be thought of in the philosophically fundamental account. If we think that the law that all F-things are G is to be ultimately construed as a certain relationship between F-ness and G-ness, then we have to recognize the existence of the entities F-ness and G-ness, and regard their existence as something philosophically fundamental.

This commitment to a realist view of universals is one aspect of Armstrong's position about which I have misgivings. It is not that I am tempted to embrace the opposite extreme of nominalism, which sees reality as entirely composed of particulars. On the contrary, it seems to me self-evident that, in some sense, properties and relations form a crucial ingredient of reality, and one which is not amenable to any form of reductive elimination. Where the realist view causes me misgivings is in its *reification* of universals—in its insistence that the properties and relations which form an irreducible ingredient of reality do so as *entities*. Let us focus on a particular case. It seems to me undeniable that, in a perfectly good sense, material objects have properties of shape, and that this is a fundamental aspect of their nature. But I am also inclined to think that the way in which an object's possession of a shape is to be ultimately understood is not as the concatenation of two entities—the object (which is a particular) and the shape-property (which is a universal)—but rather as one entity (the material particular) being shaped thus and so. In other words, I am inclined to think that, although shape-properties are a fundamental ingredient of physical reality, their presence is to be ultimately understood *predicatively*, rather than *ontologically*—as a matter of objects being, for example, cubic or spherical or ovoid, rather than of their instantiating the entities cubicness or sphericity or ovoidness. And this seems to me the right view to take of properties and relations quite generally. Taking this view does not, I should stress, require one to eschew an ontology of universals altogether. Even if our *fundamental* understanding of properties and relations has to be predicative rather than ontological, there is no objection to treating them as entities for certain purposes. Indeed, I am doing precisely this by the terminology I am employing in the present context—by my very speaking of *properties* and *relations*. My point is only that, in the final philosophical analysis, I am inclined to think that our understanding of the nature of properties and relations has to be in terms of what it is for things to be propertied and related, and that this is something which is captured by the use of predicates rather than by reference to certain kinds of abstract entity. I should also stress that I am not suggesting that the presence of properties and relations in the world is in some way dependent on the existence of the corresponding predicates. Predicates are simply what are needed to express what the presence of properties and relations ultimately amounts to.

I do not have time, in these lectures, for an adequate discussion of the issue of universals.[7] So, although I am inclined to reject Armstrong's realist view in the way I have indicated, I shall put my worries on this score to one side, and confine myself to the question of whether his account of laws is acceptable once the realist framework is in place.

Before we leave the topic of Armstrong's account of universals, there is one further point that I need to mention. Although Armstrong accepts an ontology of universals, and accepts it as something philosophically fundamental, he is quite restrictive about what should be admitted to this ontology. In the first place, he refuses to recognize universals that are uninstantiated—properties which nothing possesses, relations in which no entities stand. So if a certain value of mass (say) is uninstantiated, then, in Armstrong's system, there is no such entity as the property of having that mass. Moreover, he insists that any genuine universal must be, as he puts it, 'something which is strictly *identical*... in all its different instances', by which he seems to mean that different instances of a genuine universal must be, in respect of their being such instances, qualitatively the same.[8] This leads him to reject universals of an essentially negative or disjunctive kind, such as the property of being not square, or the property of being either square or triangular; and, as far as I can see, it would exclude all universals other than ones that are qualitatively determinate. These restrictions on what universals should be recognized are, like the acceptance of a fundamental ontology of universals at all, controversial; and here too I find myself with misgivings about his position, particularly over his insistence on the need for instantiation.[9] But once again, I shall put the issue on one side, in order to focus on the main thrust of his approach to the issue of laws. In a sense, it would be to Armstrong's advantage if he could simply drop the restrictions on the recognition of

---

[7] For a delightful introduction to the issue, and a characteristic attempt to defuse it, see P. F. Strawson, 'Universals', in P. French, T. Uehling, and H. Wettstein (eds.), *Midwest Studies in Philosophy* 4 (1979), 3–10.

[8] *What is a Law of Nature?* 83.

[9] Tooley, it should be noted, though agreeing with Armstrong's rejection of negative and disjunctive universals, does not accept the requirement of instantiation.

universals, since, as we shall see, it would make the development of his theory considerably easier.

IV

Armstrong thinks that laws are to be ultimately construed as relationships (the holding of relations) between universals. So what kind of relationships does he have in mind? And are there, indeed, any relationships at all which would fit the bill?

There is one trivial way of representing laws as relationships between universals which we should take note of and discount at the outset. Any law can be initially formulated by using the nomic operator 'it is a law that' (or 'it is nomically necessary that') followed by a universally quantified sentence expressing the regularity which the law prescribes. Now, given any law thus formulated, we can represent it as a relationship between universals by merely replacing the predicates in the sentence which follows the nomic operator by expressions which speak of the instantiation of the corresponding properties and relations. So a law initially formulated by a sentence of the form:

(1)   It is a law that, for any x, if x is F, then x is G,

which is just a logically precise way of expressing the claim that it is a law that all F-things are G, can be reformulated as:

(2)   It is a law that, for any x, if x instantiates F-ness, then x instantiates G-ness,

which expresses a relationship between the properties of F-ness and G-ness. And the same procedure can be applied quite generally. But it is obvious that this way of representing laws as relationships between universals would be useless for Armstrong's purposes. For Armstrong is not just wanting to equate laws with relationships between universals, but to offer this equation as the philosophically fundamental way of understanding the nature of laws—as the way laws are to be ultimately construed. And this implicitly involves thinking that the move from our initial formulation of laws, using the operator 'it is a law that', to their relevant representation as relationships between universals should shed new light on the question of what laws are. But, in the case of the procedure just envisaged, it clearly does not. For, in this procedure, the concept of a law is just taken for granted; and the move from the initial formulations to the new ones provides only a change in terminology, not in the substance of how laws are to be understood. Indeed, the new formulations are no more than a contrived and longwinded way of saying what was said more straightforwardly and succinctly by the initial formulations, in which there were no explicit references to universals at all.

V

Having dismissed this trivial way of representing laws as relationships between universals, let us now turn to Armstrong's own account. We must begin by taking note of a further restrictive aspect of it.

As they are initially formulated, laws come in a variety of different forms, according to the form of the regularity they prescribe. So there are laws to the effect that anything of one sort is also of another sort; laws to the effect that any event of a certain sort causes an event of another sort in a certain spatiotemporal relation to it; laws to the effect that no event of a certain sort occurs except in such and such conditions; and so on. Since, ostensibly, laws come in this variety of forms, it might seem that Armstrong will have to recognize a corresponding variety of types of relationship between universals to provide their ultimate construal. The types of relationship would vary in response to the number of universals involved and the manner of their (as it were) syntactic arrangement within the prescribed regularity.

Interestingly, however, Armstrong thinks that he can manage with a single type of relationship. Thus, leaving aside the special case of probabilistic laws, he thinks that, despite the superficial variation in form, any genuine law, or at least anything that his system has to treat as such, can be canonically represented as a law to the effect that anything which has one property has another property; and he thinks that, thus represented, each law can be ultimately construed as the holding of a certain dyadic relation between the properties involved—the same dyadic relation in each case. He introduces the 2-place predicate 'N' to signify this relation. In other words, he thinks that any genuine law can be canonically formulated by a sentence of form (1) above, with 'F' and 'G' signifying genuine properties, and that the nomic fact expressed by (1) is to be ultimately understood as:

(3)   N (F-ness, G-ness),

which says that F-ness stands in the relevant N-relation to G-ness. Although he does not say so, I think that Armstrong would also allow for cases in which the relevant F-ness and G-ness were relations rather than (monadic) properties (so that the law prescribes that any entities which are F-related are also G-related), but, for simplicity, I shall ignore this point in my subsequent discussion. Also for simplicity, I shall ignore the way in which Armstrong develops his account to cover probabilistic laws, since, although interesting in its own right, this does not have any bearing on the central issues.[10]

Armstrong, of course, recognizes that, as they are initially formulated, laws do not always exemplify, or at any rate make conspicuous, the form which he regards as canonical. Often, he is able to deal with these cases by simply accepting the initial formulations, but ignoring certain aspects of their syntactic complexity. This, for example, is how he deals with one of the types of law I listed above, where what is prescribed is that any event of a certain sort causes an event of another sort in a certain spatiotemporal relation to it. Any law of this kind would be initially formulated by some such sentence as:

(4)   It is a law that, for any x, if x is F, then there
      is a y such that y is G and x causes y and yRx,

where 'F' and 'G' are predicates signifying the relevant sorts of event, and 'R' signifies the relevant spatiotemporal relation. And this formulation might suggest, contrary to Armstrong's theory, that if the law is to be construed as a relationship between universals, we should think in terms of a 4-place relation holding for F-ness, G-ness, R-ness, and causation. Armstrong's way of getting things into canonical form is simply to treat the expression following the 'then', (i.e. 'there is a y such that y is G and x causes y and yRx') as a single predicate, playing the role of 'G' in (1); and he can then construe the law as the N-relatedness of F-ness to the property which this predicate signifies. So his ultimate representation of the law is as what is expressed by:

(5)   N (F-ness, the property of causing some R-related G-event),

which conforms to the required pattern.

It might seem that, perhaps sometimes with a touch of prior formulational adjustment, this procedure could be applied to all cases where the

---

[10] In fact, this development is open to serious objections. Thus see Bas van Fraassen, 'Armstrong on Laws and Probabilities', *Australasian Journal of Philosophy* 65 (1987), 243–60.

postulated canonical form is not immediately conspicuous in the initial formulation. And, in a sense, this is so. The only trouble is that an unrestrained application of the procedure would conflict with Armstrong's scruples over the recognition of universals. Thus suppose we have what Armstrong speaks of as an *exclusion law*, to the effect that nothing which is of one sort is also of another sort. We would initially formulate this by a sentence of the form:

(6)   It is a law that, for any x, if x is F, then x is not G.

And then it might seem that all Armstrong has to do, to apply his theory, is to read what follows the 'then' not as the denying to x of the property of G-ness, but as the ascribing to x of the property of non-G-ness, so that the ultimate construal is then as:

(7)   N (F-ness, non-G-ness).

But Armstrong has already insisted that there are no such entities as negative universals, and so an appeal to the property of non-G-ness is not an option. There is the same difficulty with laws whose initial formulations involve disjunctions of predicates, such as:

(8)   It is a law that, for any x, if x is F, then either x is G or x is H.

Given his rejection of disjunctive universals, it is not an option for him to appeal to the property of (G-or-H)-ness, as that to which F-ness is supposedly N-related.

Armstrong recognizes that he faces difficulties with these cases, and others besides, and he tries to deal with them in a variety of ways. The most important thing he does, in this connection, is to appeal to a distinction between *underived* laws and *derived* laws. Underived laws are *basic* laws, that hold in their own right. Derived laws are, as Armstrong puts it, 'mere logical consequences of the holding of underived laws'.[11] So if it is a basic law that bodies behave gravitationally, it is a derived law that bodies made of gold behave gravitationally, and a derived law that bodies either behave gravitationally or explode. Since derived laws are mere logical consequences of the underived laws, and have no standing in their own right, it is only the underived laws that Armstrong has to treat as genuine laws for the purposes of his theory—only underived laws that he needs to construe as relationships between universals. So, when faced with cases in which

---

[11] *What is a Law of Nature?* 145.

a law seems to resist construal in terms of his N-relation, one of his options is to look for ways in which the law can be represented as merely derived. For example, in the case of an exclusion law, as formulated by a sentence of form (6), he can hope to find some positive property, H-ness, which logically entails non-G-ness, such that it is a law that all F-things are H. This will allow him to take the basic law to consist in the N-relatedness of F-ness to H-ness, and treat the exclusion law as a mere consequence, and not a genuine law from the standpoint of his theory.

I do not think that Armstrong is entirely successful in his attempts to confine genuine (underived) laws to ones which exemplify the prescribed canonical form, in a way which respects his restrictions on the sorts of universals that he is prepared to recognize. But, for the sake of argument, let us suppose that he is. What we now need to focus on is his account of how, given their exemplification of this form, the laws are to be ultimately construed. As we have seen, his claim is that there is a certain dyadic relation, which he expresses by the predicate symbol 'N', such that each law is to be ultimately construed as the holding of this relation between the relevant universals. In other words, it is the claim that the nomic facts expressed by sentences of form (1) are to be ultimately construed as what are expressed by the corresponding sentences of form (3). The question which now arises is: what is this N-relation supposed to be? What are we to take sentences of form (3) to be saying? All we know so far is that, to play the relevant nomological role, Armstrong requires the N-relation to satisfy the three conditions specified earlier, that each holding of the relation should be something contingent, should entail the corresponding regularity, and should involve something genuinely additional to the obtaining of that regularity.

VI

Armstrong speaks of the relation as one of *contingent* (or *non-logical*) *necessitation*—hence the choice of the symbol 'N' to signify it. But this, in itself, does not take us very far. In what sense can one property contingently necessitate another property, and do so in a way that creates a law?

Armstrong does not try to define 'N': he is prepared to accept it as a primitive in his system. At the same time, he recognizes that, as with any primitive predicate, there has to be some way of making clear what it means—some way of enabling the reader to identify the relation it signifies. And he thinks that this clarification can be achieved by focusing on the occurrence of what he takes to be the same (or essentially the same) relation in a different and more familiar context—that of causation.

The nature of causation is philosophically controversial. Some philosophers, following the empiricist approach of Hume, think that, even as it occurs in particular cases, causation is to be understood in terms of the holding of something more *general*, so that for one item to cause another is, or is partly, a matter of there being some law or regularity concerning the sequential occurrence of items of those types. Other philosophers think that causation is something irreducibly *singular*, so that when one item causes another, that is not to do with how things behave or are constrained *in general*, but is purely to do with how things stand with respect to those particular items. Armstrong thinks that we can at least *understand* the notion of singular causation, and that we can discern in such causation a type of singular *necessitation*. Thus he thinks that we can understand what it would be for one state of affairs to *cause* another state of affairs in this irreducibly singular way, and that we can thereby grasp a sense in which one state of affairs could (by such causing) *necessitate* another state of affairs in an irreducibly singular way. He then claims that, having acquired this notion of singular necessitation in the context of causal relations between particular states of affairs, we can simply transfer it to the domain of universals to give us an understanding of 'N'. To make this transition seem smoother, he equates the relevant universals with *types of states of affairs*. Thus, given the *particular* states of affairs of a's being F, b's being F, c's being F, . . . and so on, there is a *type* of state of affairs of *something*'s being F which they all have in common—a type that we can express by the sentence schema '. . . is F', where the dots mark the place for a designator; and Armstrong decides, for each such case, to identify the property F-ness with this type.[12] With this identification in place, he claims that, just as we can understand what is meant, in the context of singular causation, by saying, of some particular object or event, that the state of affairs of *its* being F necessitates the state of affairs of *its* being G, so, preserving the same necessitational relation, we can understand what is meant by saying that the *type* of state of affairs of *something's* being F necessitates the *type* of state of affairs of *something's* being G, and it is this understanding which gives us our interpretation of sentences of form (3).

---

[12] We must be careful not to confuse this *type* of state of affairs with the *particular* state of affairs expressed by the existentially quantified sentence 'there is something which is F'.

But how exactly is this supposed to work? I am happy to allow Armstrong his equation of properties with types of states of affairs. If there is any problem with this equation, it is, I think, a trivial one; for, whether or not they can be identified, there is no denying that properties and types of states of affairs are sufficiently closely related for the latter to take over the role of the former in Armstrong's theory. I am also happy to allow that we can understand the notion of singular causation, and can discern in it a form of necessitation. Indeed, I think that this notion embodies the right view of causation. But what I still find wholly unclear is how we can simply transfer this form of necessitation to the relevant domain of universals and get something which will serve Armstrong's purposes. Indeed, on the face of it, it seems that we cannot make this transition and end up with something that is even intelligible. For how would it make any more sense to say that the entity F-ness (or the corresponding state-of-affairs type) necessitates the entity G-ness (or the corresponding state-of-affairs type) than to say that the number 4 necessitates the number 7, or that my pen necessitates Australia? If we are to be able to make sense of singular necessitation in the sphere of universals, then we need some further explanation of how it applies. Nor is it any good supposing that what (3) means is not that F-ness *as such* relevantly necessitates G-ness *as such*, but that the *existence* of F-ness necessitates the *existence* of G-ness. For, however we might understand such a necessitation claim, it would not be strong enough for Armstrong's purposes: it would not entail the obtaining of the corresponding regularity, that all F-things are G.

Let us look at how Armstrong himself tries to elucidate the situation:

We may perhaps render 'N (F, G)' ... in words as follows:

Something's being F necessitates that same something's being G, in virtue of the universals F and G

This is *not* to be taken simply as:

For all x, x being F necessitates that x is G

because this would be to fall back, once again, into a form of the Regularity theory. Instead, as the phrase 'in virtue of the universals F and G' is supposed to indicate, what is involved is a real, irreducible relation, a particular species of the necessitation relation, holding between the universals F and G (*being an F, being a G*).... The concept of necessitation involved here is a relation holding between universals, between sorts of states of affairs, types rather than tokens. But, I suggest, it is essentially the same as the singular necessitation which, as we saw in the last section [the section focusing on singular causation], *might* hold between particular states of affairs, between tokens... Transfer in thought the concept of necessitation from the sphere of particular states of affairs, taken simply as particular, to the sphere of sorts or types of states of affairs, that is universals. Instead of a's being F necessitating it to be the case that a is G, without the benefit of law, we have instead something's being F necessitating that something to be G, where a type of state of affairs (the universal F) necessitates a type of state of affairs (the universal G).[13]

This account of the situation is, seriously confused. One slight awkwardness, which I mention in passing, is Armstrong's use of the letters 'F' and 'G' sometimes as predicate symbols and sometimes as names of properties. To be consistent, he should have reserved these letters for use as predicates, and used the terms 'F-ness' and 'G-ness' when he wanted to refer to the properties they signify. Still, this is only a terminological point and does not reflect any underlying confusion in his thought. Nor, indeed, is there ever any difficulty, when he uses the letters, in discerning which of the two roles they are intended to play. Where the confusion occurs is in the way in which he tries to set out the content of the necessitational claim as it applies to F-ness and G-ness. He wants this claim to be understood as ascribing, as he puts it, a 'real, irreducible relation' to F-ness and G-ness, or, what amounts to the same thing, to the corresponding types of states of affairs. But when he tries to spell out what this involves, we find him offering such formulations as:

(9)   Something's being F necessitates that same something's being G...

and

(10)   Something's being F necessitates that something to be G.

The crucial point here is his anaphoric use of the demonstrative terms 'that', or 'that same', in front of the second 'something'. To serve Armstrong's purposes, the phrases each side of the word 'necessitates' have to refer to types of states of affairs—in effect, to the universals F-ness and G-ness. But with the inclusion of the demonstrative on the right-hand side, this reading becomes impossible. The point of the demonstrative is to indicate that it is the *same* thing that is being envisaged as the something which is F and the something which is G. But if the terms of the necessitation

[13] *What is a Law of Nature?* 96–7.

relation are types of states of affairs—universals—the notion of its being the *same* something involved in the two cases makes no sense: there is no particular something featuring in the first type and available for re-featuring in the second. The only way in which we can make sense of the demonstrative is by interpreting (9) and (10) as meaning either

(11) For any x, if x is F, then the state of affairs of x's being F necessitates the state of affairs of x's being G

or

(12) It is necessary that, for any x, if x is F, then x is G.

And neither of these interpretations will serve Armstrong's purposes. Proposition (11) just asserts a regularity about instances of singular necessitation, and does not imply the obtaining of a general law. (Armstrong himself explicitly rejects this interpretation in the passage cited, when he says 'This is *not* to be taken simply as ... '.) Proposition (12), in contrast, *can* be interpreted as asserting the obtaining of a general law; for we can take the necessity involved to be nomic. But this would not advance us one iota towards an account of laws as relationships between universals, since no universals are even referred to. Indeed, with the necessity as nomic, (12) would just be a terminological variant of (1), and we would be no nearer to *any* kind of understanding of the nature of laws.

VII

Armstrong fails to provide any adequate account of his N-relation. He specifies certain conditions which this relation has to satisfy to play the nomological role assigned to it (so that N-relationships have to be contingent, to entail the corresponding regularities, and to involve something more than the obtaining of these regularities), but he does not tell us anything which enables us to know what the relation is. Nor, I think, can we form a conception of anything which it might be. The only way, as far as I can see, in which we can represent a law of the relevant form as a relationship between universals is by employing the trivial mode of representation noted and discounted at the outset, in which sentences of form (1) are transformed into sentences of form (2); and, for reasons already made clear, this would be useless for Armstrong's purposes.¹⁴ Nor, of course, would anything be gained if we were to liberalize Armstrong's approach and allow for a range of different types of relationship between universals, to cover the varying forms of law that initially present themselves. If we cannot think of a suitable type of relationship to play the nomological role in the case which Armstrong regards as canonical, there is no prospect of being able to think of suitable types for other cases either. In each case, the trivial way of representing the laws as relationships between universals would be the only one available.

The fact that we cannot *think* of any suitable types of relationship does not, of course, entail that such relationships do not exist. And this, it might be suggested, gives Armstrong a line of escape. For perhaps he could just dig his heels in and insist that it is indeed relationships between universals that constitute the real nature of laws, even though we cannot specify them. Moreover, it might seem that Armstrong could appeal to an analogy here. In physics, we can identify various types of supposedly fundamental particle by their distinctive powers and sensitivities. But we cannot specify the intrinsic natures of the particles—the natures on which their powers and sensitivities are nomologically grounded—nor even conceive of what these natures might be.¹⁵ So why should not Armstrong say, analogously, that we can identify the relevant relationships between universals by the nomological roles they play, but that we cannot specify what these relationships are, or might be, in themselves? Why should he not claim that there *is* a nomological relation that meets the requirements of his theory—a relation that can hold between universals and whose holding satisfies the conditions of contingency, entailment, and transcendence already specified—but concede that its identity, like the natures of the particles, lies beyond the reach of our knowledge and conception?¹⁶

---

¹⁴ Michael Tooley has suggested (*Causation*, 123–6) that, in the case of a law that anything which is F is G, we could take the relevant relationship to consist in the fact that the universal F-ness only exists as part of the conjunctive universal (F and G)-ness. But I cannot understand what he has in mind. Perhaps he means that F-ness is not an ontologically basic entity, but rather something which derives its existence from the existence of (F and G)-ness. But I do not understand how F-ness could be ontologically derivative in that way. Nor, for that matter, do I understand how such derivativeness would create the relevant law.

¹⁵ For a detailed elaboration of this point, see my *The Case for Idealism* (London: Routledge & Kegan Paul, 1982), ch. 4.

¹⁶ Before he makes the suggestion referred to in n. 14, Tooley seems, in *Causation*, to be sympathetic to this approach.

But we only need to reflect, for a moment, on the two cases to see that they are quite different. In the case of the particles, we know that the relevant entities must have intrinsic natures in order to exist at all; and even though we cannot specify these natures, or conceive of what they might be, there is no difficulty in understanding how particles possess them. But, in default of our being able to think of any types of relationship which could play the role of laws, we simply have no reason to suppose that such relationships exist. Nor, indeed, can we even understand how they would be possible. Apart from the trivial mode of representation already dismissed, we can no more understand how a law could turn out to be a relationship between universals than how it could turn out to be a relationship between numbers, or, for that matter, between garden gnomes. There is no denying, of course, that laws are distinctively concerned with universals, in a way that they are not concerned, except *per accidens*, with numbers or gnomes. Thus the law that all F-things are G is distinctively concerned with the properties of F-ness and G-ness. But this is just the trivial point that laws are concerned with the properties and relations that feature in their content (feature in the regularities that they render nomically necessary), and can be explicitly represented as such when they are formulated along the lines of (2).

VIII

As far as I can see, then, Armstrong's whole approach fails, and there is no interesting way in which laws of nature can be construed as relationships between universals. And this, of course, brings us back to the original problem. We would like to be able to recognize the existence of laws of nature, both because this is in line with our ordinary view of the world, and, more crucially, because it meets our philosophical needs. But before we are entitled to do this, we need to be able to offer some account of what a law is, and in particular of how, without paradox, it can qualify as a form of non-strict necessity. At present, we have no idea how to do this; and the worry is that we may have to reject the notion of a law as incoherent.

LECTURE 7
The Scenario without Laws

I

We are finding it difficult to make sense of the notion of a law of nature. As I am here construing them, laws are not just regularities in the workings of the world, but forms of natural necessity. So the law of gravity is not just the fact that bodies always behave or attract one another gravitationally. It is something whose existence, or obtaining, consists in the fact that it is in some way naturally necessary that bodies behave or attract one another in that way. It is the nature of this necessity—*nomic* necessity—that creates the problem. The necessity is not a form of strict necessity: it does not exclude absolutely the possibility of things being otherwise. For even where it is a law that things are regular in a certain way, we must still acknowledge that there are compositionally relevant possible worlds in which that law does not obtain, and in which, in its absence, things are not regular in that way. The difficulty is in seeing how the law can be a genuine form of necessity at all without being strict. On the face of it, it just seems self-contradictory to say that it is necessary that things should be thus and so, but also possible for them to be otherwise.

We have tried various ways of getting round this problem without success. We considered the suggestion that we might think of nomic necessity as a scope-restricted version of strict necessity—a version which coincided with strict necessity, but with respect to a restricted range of possible worlds. We also considered the suggestion that we should abandon our view of laws as abstract entities, which draw their existence from the relevant facts of nomic necessity, and construe them instead as concrete entities that govern the world causally. Finally, I devoted the whole of the last lecture to a detailed examination of the account of laws offered by

David Armstrong—an account which construes laws as the holding of relations between universals. None of these approaches proved satisfactory, and we are no further forward in being able to show how the notion of a law can be understood.

So should we just conclude that this notion is incoherent? Well, for the moment, I do not want to commit myself to a final verdict on this. Rather, what I want to do in the present lecture is to address an issue which *would* arise, if we *were* to accept this negative conclusion. It may seem perverse to address this further issue while it is merely hypothetical. But, in fact, addressing it will help us to reach a conclusion about the issue of laws itself, as we shall eventually see.

If we conclude that the notion of a law is incoherent, we shall obviously have to abandon NES as our solution to the problem of induction, since this solution explicitly involves the recognition of laws. But there is also a further consequence. Underlying NES was the claim that hitherto exemplified regularities, when sufficiently extensive, call for explanation, or, at least, that it would be hugely surprising if no explanation were available, and this is something that we are still assuming to be correct. If we are not allowed to explain these regularities by an appeal to the presence of laws, then the pressure will be on to find a different way of explaining them. The issue I want to address is how, if at all, an alternative mode of explanation can be plausibly developed. It should be stressed that what we are looking for here is not an explanation of the specific content of the regularities, but of the phenomenon of regularity which they exemplify. This is not to say that their specific content may not call for explanation too—for other reasons. But it is only the phenomenon of regularity itself which presently concerns us. Thus, for each regularity, the question at issue is not 'Why, without laws, have things been, in our experience, regular *in just that way?*' but 'Why, without laws, have things been, in our experience, to that extent regular *at all?*'

Put like this, the issue of explanation is concerned with the obtaining of regularities within the domain of the cases *examined*—the cases covered by our *past experience*. In one sense, this restriction is crucial. For until we have a solution to the problem of induction, we have no grounds for believing that what has held good for the examined cases will also hold good for the unexamined; and so it is only regularities within the examined domain that present themselves as data for explanation. But it is also true that, for the specific purposes of our present investigation, the restriction is not relevant. What we are trying to discover is whether there is a satisfactory way of explaining regularities once an appeal to laws has been excluded; and, in pursuing this question, it is of no consequence whether we think of the regularities to be explained as confined to the examined cases or as holding universally. Since it will be simpler to represent the regularities as universal, this will tend to be my practice in the ensuing discussion.

II

To explain regularities by an appeal to laws is to explain them in purely *natural* terms—in terms of factors that lie within the natural realm. One of the main things that I want to try to establish, in this lecture, is that, once we exclude an appeal to laws, no purely naturalistic explanation, at least with any claim to plausibility, is available. It is true, of course, that many of the regularities in nature can be scientifically explained in terms of other such regularities which are more fundamental. Thus the fact that unsupported stones fall is just a consequence of a more fundamental gravitational regularity (the regularity that we are assuming to be captured by Newton's equation), together with certain facts about the nature of stones and the nature of the wider situation in which instances of unsupported stones occur. Likewise, the fact that petrol ignites when it is exposed to flame is a consequence of certain more fundamental regularities about chemical reactions, together with the relevant facts about the chemical composition of petrol and what is involved in its exposure to flame. And this will be the pattern of things in the case of almost all the regularities that are conspicuous at the level of ordinary observation. These will be amenable to scientific explanation in terms of more fundamental regularities, together with a suitably penetrating account of the types of object and situation involved. But what is at issue, of course, is the explanation of the regularities that cannot be explained in terms of others—the regularities that are physically *basic*. And it is at this point, it seems to me, that the resources for naturalistic explanation prove inadequate. It might be suggested that perhaps there are no basic regularities in that sense. For could we not envisage that each type of physical entity is composed of other more elementary types of entity, and that any regularity about certain types of entity is potentially explicable in terms of regularities about the types of entity that compose them? Well, I am not sure that this idea really makes sense. But even if it does, it would still leave a crucial issue of explanation. For the fact that any specific regularity was in principle explicable in terms of others would not mean that the overall regularity of the world was self-explanatory. Moreover, this residual issue of explanation would suffice for the development of my argument. However, for simplicity, I shall work on the assumption (which I in any case regard as, at the very least, very plausible) that there *are* basic regularities and that all other regularities are explicable in terms of them.

Once we have excluded an appeal to laws, there are, as far as I can see, only two ways in which we might think of trying to explain the basic regularities in purely natural terms. I shall consider these ways in turn.

One suggestion would be that we should try to explain the regularities by supposing that the types of physical object which feature in them are endowed with appropriate dispositions—dispositions to behave and causally influence things in the relevant (regularity-exemplifying) ways. Thus it might be suggested that we should try to explain the regularity of gravitational behaviour (or gravitational attraction) by supposing that bodies are endowed with an overriding disposition to behave gravitationally (or to exert and be subject to the relevant forms of attractive force). Normally, we would take the dispositions of objects to be dependent on laws of nature: the laws, together with the intrinsic properties of the objects, would be thought of as logically ensuring that the objects are disposed to behave or causally influence things in the relevant ways. In the present context, we have to think of the relevant dispositions as autonomous. For the whole point of the appeal to them is to meet an explanatory need that arises when an appeal to laws has been excluded. What we must now consider is whether the appeal to such dispositions would be successful in meeting this need.

One potential source of difficulty for the dispositional proposal is that it is not clear what sense we can make of the notion of an autonomous disposition. Clearly, if they are to be equipped to play the explanatory role assigned to them, such dispositions cannot just consist in facts about instances of behaviour and causal influence that actually occur. Thus if the overriding disposition of a body to behave gravitationally is to explain *why* it behaves gravitationally, then this disposition cannot just consist in the fact that the body does, in practice, always behave in this way. Rather, the disposition will have to have a *modal* character: it will have to consist in the fact that the body is, in some way, *obliged* to behave in that way. And this point will extend to any other disposition which is marked out to play the relevant kind of explanatory role. But given the difficulties we have encountered over providing a coherent account of the modal character of *laws*, we can expect to encounter analogous difficulties over making sense of the modal character of *dispositions*. Indeed, an autonomous disposition could itself be represented as a kind of law—a law which is restricted in its scope to the behaviour of a particular object. Thus, given any body, instead of speaking of it as having an autonomous overriding disposition to behave gravitationally, we could equally well speak of there being a law that this body always behaves in that way. And when a disposition is represented in that nomological form, the problem over making sense of nomic necessity applies to it directly.

But even if we could make sense of the modal character of the relevant dispositions, there is a quite different reason why the dispositional proposal fails. And this is simply because the putative explanations it envisages do not explain what needs to be explained. They do not explain what needs to be explained, because they only account for the behaviour and causal influence of objects *taken separately*, and not for why the separate modes of behaviour and causal influence collectively exemplify a *regularity*. And the reason why they do not explain the latter is that they do not explain why different objects of the same intrinsic type have the same dispositions. Thus take again the case of gravity. The regularity to be explained is that all bodies (in relation to other bodies) behave gravitationally, and the explanation offered is that all bodies are *disposed* to behave (in relation to other bodies) gravitationally. But even if this succeeds in explaining, for each body, why *it* behaves gravitationally, it does not explain, or purport to explain, why different bodies have the same gravitational disposition, and so does not explain why, in the relevant respect, different bodies behave in the same (generically gravitational) way. And this means that the sense of puzzlement that attaches to unexplained regularity, and which underlies the need for explanation, remains, in the present case, almost entirely undiminished. In fact, the situation for the dispositional proposal is even worse than I have so far represented it. For, as well as offering no explanation of why different objects of the same intrinsic type have the same behavioural and causal dispositions, it does not even offer an explanation of why a single persisting object of constant intrinsic type has the same dispositions at different times. And so it does not even offer explanations of the regularities concerning particular objects. Thus if B is a particular body, the proposal assigns a gravitational disposition to B at all times of its existence; but it does not offer an explanation of why B is, in this respect, uniform in its dispositions over time, and so does not, in any way that provides what was needed, explain why B is regular in its gravitational behaviour over time.

III

The other way in which we might try to find a natural but non-nomological way of explaining the basic regularities would be to look for something in the natural realm that *causally* accounts for them. Some philosophers would rule out the possibility of such an explanation a priori, on the grounds that it makes no sense to suppose that there could be instances of causation without the backing of covering laws.[1] But I do not think that they are right. The only way I can see of trying to give their view a rationale would be by offering a nomologically reductive account of causation—an account which claims that causal facts are ultimately constituted by the obtaining of laws, together with certain non-causal properties of the causally related items and conditions involved. Thus, for the case where the causally related items are events, it might be claimed that when an event x causes an event y, there are types A, B, and C, and some temporal or spatiotemporal relation R, such that the fact of x's causing y is wholly constituted by, in combination:

(1) the fact that x is of type A;
(2) the fact that y is of type B;
(3) the fact that the conditions in which x occurs are of type C;
(4) the fact that x is R-related to y;
(5) the fact that it is ensured by law that any A-type event occurring in C-type conditions is R-related to some B-type event.

In other words, x's causing of y may be held to be reducible to the fact that it is ensured by law that any event of x's type, occurring in the relevant conditions, stands in the relevant temporal or spatiotemporal relationship to some event of y's type. There is a strong echo here of the constant-conjunction view of causation defended by Hume, though Hume himself did not recognize any sort of natural necessity, and thought of laws of nature as mere regularities.[2]

---

[1] For example, see Donald Davidson's 'Causal Relations', *Journal of Philosophy* 64 (1967), 691–703 (reprinted in Davidson, *Actions and Events* (Oxford: Oxford University Press, 1980)), though I am not sure that Davidson would regard laws as forms of natural necessity.

[2] See Hume's *A Treatise of Human Nature*, Bk. 1, Pt. 3, sect. 14. The constant-conjunctive view, of course, only covers *one* of Hume's two definitions of causation—the definition that represents causation as an *objective* relation, which applies to events independently of our inferential propensities.

As I see it, the main objection to this account, and anything else along the same general lines, is that it does not do justice to the inherent directionality of the causal relationship and the essential asymmetry which this entails.[3] Thus, as we actually conceive of it, the causal relationship assigns contrasting ontological roles to cause and effect. The cause, to qualify as a cause, has to be *ontologically prior*, to be *responsible for the occurrence of* the effect; the effect, to be the effect, has to be *ontologically dependent*, to *owe its occurrence to the occurrence of* the cause. And this ontological directionality makes the relation of cause and effect necessarily *asymmetric*, so that it is logically impossible for there to be a case in which both x is the cause of y and y is the cause of x.[4] But, although central to our actual concept, this inherent directionality in the causal relationship has no place in the sort of reductive accounts envisaged. For, as construed reductively, the obtaining of the causal relationship would involve nothing more than the fact that the sequential occurrence of the relevant items is law-governed in the appropriate way, and this in itself would not confer an ontological direction on the sequence: it would not render one of the items in any way *responsible for* the occurrence of the other. It could still be insisted, of course, that, in so far as the reductive approach fails to do justice to our concept of causation, the concept itself is unintelligible and needs to be purged of the factors that resist reductive treatment. But I cannot see what could justify such a view. Any attempted justification would presumably have to invoke some radically empiricist criterion of intelligibility, of the kind I mentioned in Lecture 5, and claim that our concept of causation can be shown to be unintelligible by this standard.[5] But, as I stressed in that earlier context, I do not think that there are any good grounds for accepting such a criterion, however it is developed;

---

[3] Another forceful objection, which I shall not go into, is that, in certain types of case, the reductive approach cannot provide an adequate account of the uniqueness of causal pairings—of the fact that when two simultaneous events, E1 and E2, of the same type respectively cause two further simultaneous events, E3 and E4, of the same type, there is something that makes it correct to say that E1 is the cause of E3, and not of E4, and that E2 is the cause of E4, and not of E3. Thus consider my example of the two metal spheres presented in section III of my 'In Self-Defence' (in G. Macdonald (ed.), *Perception and Identity* (London: Macmillan, 1979)), and again in my *Ayer*, Pt. III, sect. 7.

[4] Note that this *ontological* directionality in causation is not the same as its *temporal* directionality. It is true, I think, that causes have to precede their effects (or at least cannot follow them), and that a crucial part of the reason for this is that the cause has to be ontologically prior. But the two forms of directionality are distinct.   [5] See Lecture 5, sect. III.

and, once again, I would appeal to my discussion of this issue elsewhere.⁶ I should add that, even if such a criterion were acceptable, I do not see why our concept of causation would be in difficulties. For I think that, contrary to what is normally assumed, we do, in certain situations, have direct experience of something causal. Thus it seems to me that when we try to lift something heavy, or when someone pushes against us in a crowd, we can feel the relevant form of causal pressure—the downward pressure of the heavy object, and the pressure of the other person's body against ours. And I do not see why the availability of these experiences should not allow the concept of causation to meet whatever requirements of respectability the empiricist may seek to impose.⁷

I do not think, then, that, when laws are rejected, we can exclude the possibility of causation a priori. And so we have at least to consider the suggestion that there might be a natural way of explaining the basic regularities in causal terms. Even so, it is hard to see how such an explanation could be plausibly envisaged. We need to begin by reminding ourselves of what is needed if the explanation is to be successful. Even if we could do it, it would not suffice to explain a regularity in the required way if, in the case of each occasion in the history of the universe that offered the formal opportunity for a counterinstance, we were to show how the relevant event of exemplification causally resulted from some physical event or state of affairs that preceded it. For, as with the problem we encountered in the dispositional case, this would not explain the phenomenon of regularity as such: it would not explain why all the events that were caused to occur on these different occasions happened to conform to the common pattern. Take a by now familiar analogy. Suppose a coin is tossed a hundred times and comes up heads on each occasion. As I have stressed, such a consistency of outcome calls for explanation; for it would be hugely surprising if it turned out to be merely coincidental. Now suppose we look into the situation and fail to discover anything that has imposed a constant bias in favour of the heads outcome. At the same time, we are able, in the case of each individual toss, to explain, in ordinary scientific terms, how the heads outcome came to occur as a result of the particular set of forces operating on the coin in the conditions that obtained. In one sense, the sum of these explanations for each particular outcome would amount to an explanation

---

⁶ In *Ayer*, Pt. I.

⁷ For a fuller discussion of these cases, and a defence of the view that they afford a direct experience of causal pressure, see Armstrong, *A World of States of Affairs*, 211–16.

of the total outcome, since it would cover all the events that collectively constituted that outcome. But, obviously, it would not explain the uniformity exemplified by the total outcome in the relevant way. It would not help to remove our puzzlement as to how it came about that the forces exerted in each case conspired to produce the *regularity*. In the same way, what we need, if we are to explain a basic regularity of nature, is not just a way of separately accounting for the various events or states of affairs that collectively constitute it, but something that will remove our puzzlement as to how these different items, and the ways they have come about, collectively conspired to be thus regular. This, after all, was why we turned to laws of nature in the first place, and how we were able to appeal to the explanatory role of laws to solve the problem of induction. Laws, if there are such things, are, quintessentially, factors that impose regularity: if we could recognize them, they would, for each relevant regularity, entirely answer the question of why that regularity obtains. Now that we are looking for a substitute, we have to make sure that it is equipped to play a similar explanatory role, though it will obviously have to play it in a different way.

Appealing to a law explains why the corresponding regularity holds because a law imposes a regularity *as such*—imposes it *as a regularity*: the obtaining of the law just consists in the fact of its being nomically necessary that things are regular in the relevant way. In order to provide a natural explanation of a regularity in *causal* terms, what we would presumably need to find is some natural factor which, like a law, imposes a regularity *as such*, except that, in this case, the imposing would be a form of *causing*. So, in the case of gravity, what we would need to provide, to explain why things are gravitationally regular, is not an account of how the different instances of gravitational behaviour (or gravitational attraction) are separately caused, but an account of how there is something in the natural realm which, independently of the precise form which the regularity takes (the precise character of the various instances of behaviour or attraction which exemplify it), causes it to be the case that bodies always and everywhere behave gravitationally (or stand in the relevant forms of attractive relationship). But, as far as I can see, there is no remotely plausible way in which explanations of this kind could be developed. And here the point is not just that there is no direct empirical evidence to suggest that regularities are ever brought about by natural factors in that kind of way. It is also that that kind of causation would be wholly out of keeping with all that we empirically know about how the world works. It might be suggested that, without moving too far away from empirically accredited forms of causal theorizing, we could think of the regularities as causally sustained, as regularities, by aspects of the global structure of the world—aspects that create a kind of global field of causal influence. For example, it might be suggested that the gravitational regularity is causally sustained, as a regularity, by the nature of physical space and the forms of matter located in it. But the only remotely plausible way we could think of this as working would be to suppose that it is aspects of the structure of the world *at a time* that causally dispose things to behave in the relevant regular ways *at that time*. And this would not provide an explanation of the obtaining of the regularities *through time*. To explain the latter, we would need to add something which explains why the relevant aspects are conserved over time and why they dispose things to behave in the same regular ways at different times. And I cannot think of anything in the natural realm that we could turn to here other than laws of nature—laws that would make it naturally necessary for the aspects to be conserved and naturally necessary that things behave in the relevant ways in response to their presence.

IV

We cannot envisage a satisfactory causal explanation of the basic regularities in natural terms. Nor, as we saw earlier, can we explain them by an appeal to autonomous dispositions. As far as I can see, there are no further non-nomological options for naturalistic explanation available that are worthy of serious consideration. The question we must now consider is whether we can do better if we allow ourselves to appeal to *non-natural* factors. Can we find a satisfactory way of explaining the regularities by reference to things that lie *outside* the natural realm? Presumably, if we can, the explanation will have to be a *causal* one; and presumably the non-natural cause or causes that are cited will have to be *concrete*. It is true that some philosophers have suggested that the ultimate reason why there is an orderly universe is simply that it is good that there should be, which would mean that what is responsible for the orderly character of the universe, and maybe also for its existence, is something purely abstract.[8] But I find it hard to take this suggestion seriously. Even if it were *logically possible* for the

---

[8] Thus see John Leslie, *Value and Existence* (Oxford: Basil Blackwell, 1979), and Hugh Rice, *God and Goodness* (Oxford: Oxford University Press, 2000).

abstract fact of goodness to affect things in this way (which I doubt), there is not the slightest reason to suppose that it *does*. For there is absolutely no evidence that anything ever occurs merely in response to the fact that it would be good for it to do so. All our evidence suggests that if goodness ever has an influence on things—an influence in the direction of its own instantiation—it has it via the good intentions of personal agents who strive to achieve it. If we did not firmly believe this, the world would no doubt be in a vastly worse state than it already is.

We are looking for a way of explaining the regularities in terms of some concrete cause or causes that lie outside the natural realm. And, of course, we are looking for a mode of explanation which meets our explanatory requirements—one which, for each regularity, genuinely accounts for the phenomenon of regularity it exhibits. As far as I can see, there is only one approach that is now available. This would be to suppose that what causes the regularities is a source of agency of a *personal* kind—some being or group of beings who are endowed with a rational mentality and who bring about the regularities deliberately. So to the question 'Why are things thus regular?', the answer, in each case, would be 'Because this being or these beings have deliberately made them so'. Explanations of this personal kind are, of course, commonplace and uncontroversial in the realm of *human* affairs. The reason why there is a house in a particular place is that people have built it with the intention of producing just such an object. The reason why a certain light comes on whenever a certain switch is pressed is because people have deliberately wired things up so as to ensure such a connection. Constructing this kind of explanation around the postulation of a *non-natural*—*supernatural*—personal agent, or agents, is, in an obvious sense, more speculative: it takes us beyond the realm of what we can directly verify. But, given what we have already excluded, I cannot see any alternative. Of course, we could always suppose that what accounts for the regularities is something beyond our comprehension. Perhaps what imposes the regularities on the world are things or states of affairs of which we can form no conception, and which causally operate in ways that are beyond our imagining. But I take it as obvious that, in this area, as in others, we should at least *aim* to construct an explanation within the limits of our understanding, and only turn to the suggestion that the explanation may be incomprehensible as a last resort. And, within these limits, I cannot see what option is available other than the approach envisaged—the approach of supposing that there is a being or group of beings outside the natural realm, who are equipped with a rational mentality and a power of intentional agency, and who bring about the regularities deliberately. Let us refer to this as the *personal-agency* approach.

But it may now be asked: is the personal-agency approach itself a real option? What initially allows it to pass as such is that, as we noted, we can represent it as a redeployment of a mode of explanation that is familiar and uncontroversial in the realm of human affairs. But it might well be thought that, as well as being more speculative *epistemologically* (which is inevitable), this redeployment is problematic *conceptually*—that it is not, in the last analysis, something that is fully *intelligible*. The supposed problem stems from the fact that human persons are normally assumed to be entities with corporeal natures—entities which, whatever their other endowments, have shape, size, and material composition—while a supernatural personal being would have to be something outside the physical universe, and so devoid of corporeal properties or location in physical space. If this corporealist conception of human persons is correct, the gulf between the human and the non-natural cases might well seem too great to allow us to use the personal mode of explanation familiar in the context of the first as a model for a similar mode of explanation in the context of the second.

There are two aspects to this. In the first place, it might be thought that we cannot detach our understanding of what it is for something to be a personal being, or indeed a mental subject of any kind, from the physical context in which this understanding has evolved. There are a number of ways in which this point can be developed. For example, it might be claimed that we cannot detach our understanding of what mentality is from the behavioural criteria by which, in the human case, we gauge its presence and character in third-person perspective. Or again, it might be claimed that it is only when we take a mental subject to be a corporeal entity that we can provide an adequate account of its individuality and its identity through time. Or yet again, it might be claimed that if we try to envisage a mental subject which lacks corporeal properties, we lose our grip on how it can qualify as a substantial thing. And, in each of these cases, the basic claim can assume a number of more specific forms according to the details of the argument that underlies it. The common factor in all these positions, and what makes them relevant to our present concerns, is the insistence that we can no longer retain our understanding of what it is for something to be a mental subject—a subject of mental states and activities—when we try to envisage such subjects existing in a wholly non-corporeal form.

The second aspect is that, even if we can achieve an understanding of how a mental subject could be wholly non-corporeal, there is still the question of whether we can intelligibly think of a non-corporeal subject as capable of acting on the physical world, and so as able to play the explanatory role envisaged. In the human case, as ordinarily construed, there seems to be no problem here. For if human subjects have corporeal natures, then action *on* the physical world is action *within* it; and even if the nature of such corporeal action is, in some respects, obscure, there will presumably be no obstacle in principle to understanding how a corporeal subject is equipped to perform it. In contrast, if a subject lies outside the physical world, and thus lacks any capacity for corporeal action, it might well seem that there is no intelligible mechanism by which it could bring about some physical event or state of affairs.

It is not difficult to see how there might be thought to be these problems for the explanatory approach envisaged. But, in my view, the problems are illusory. The reason why I think this is that I think that, even in our own case, the entities that form the ultimate subjects of mental states and activities are themselves wholly non-physical—devoid of corporeal properties or location in physical space. This, of course, is the *Cartesian* view of the human person, and it is one for which I have argued in detail in my book *The Immaterial Self*.[9] My argument turns on the defence of three crucial claims. The first is that all items of mentality, like thoughts, perceptions, sensations, and beliefs, are to be ultimately understood as the token states, acts, or activities of persisting subjects. (This stands in contrast with the Humean view of the mind, which construes such items as ultimately subjectless.)[10] The second is that we can only intelligibly suppose that the ultimate subjects of human mentality are corporeal entities if we combine this with a suitably reductive account of the mentality itself—an account which enables us to understand the occurrence of this mentality as ultimately consisting in, or constituted by, something physical. The third is that all such reductive or materialist accounts fail, the most obvious example of this failure being that they do not do justice to the subjective character of conscious experience. This is not the place in which to rehearse the arguments I offer in support of these claims, nor to rehearse the ways in which I try to deal with objections to the Cartesian conclusion to which they lead.

---

[9] London: Routledge, 1991. For a more recent and more succinct presentation of the argument, see my 'A Brief Defence of the Cartesian View', in K. Corcoran (ed.), *Soul, Body, and Survival* (Ithaca, N.Y.: Cornell University Press, 2001), 15–29.

[10] Thus see Hume, *A Treatise of Human Nature*, Bk. 1, Pt. 4, sect. 6.

In the context of these lectures, I shall simply have to assume that, on both counts, I have been successful, and that we can now take the Cartesian view to be correct. I should perhaps add that although, from the standpoint of my own philosophy of mind, an appeal to the Cartesian view provides the most natural and clear-cut way of defending the intelligibility of the personal-agency approach, I am not ruling out the possibility of there being other ways of doing this, and, in particular, ways that would be available to those who do not share my view of the human case.

Granted the correctness of the Cartesian view, the non-physical character of the supernatural being or beings that feature in the personal-agency approach is not as such problematic. But it might still be objected that we are no better equipped to understand how the relevant being or beings could have a causal influence on the physical world. There are two distinct ways in which this objection could be developed. On the one hand, it might be argued that, once we accept the Cartesian view, then, even in the human case, we can no longer understand how the subject is able to exert a causal influence on the physical world, or, indeed, how there can be psychophysical causal relations in either direction. On the other hand, it might be argued that, even if we can make sense of psychophysical causation in the human case, this is only because the relevant subjects, though non-physical in themselves, are *embodied*, and that embodiment would not be a feature of the supernatural being or beings postulated to account for the regularities. But neither of these lines of objection is effective. With respect to the first, I have shown in *The Immaterial Self* that, contrary to what is commonly supposed, the Cartesian has the resources to make perfectly good sense of two-way causal relations between the non-physical subject and the body.[11] And, with respect to the second, it cannot be that it is by reference to embodiment that we are able to make sense of such causal relations, since it is precisely in terms of the capacity of the subject to exert certain kinds of causal influence on the body and the capacity of the body to exert certain kinds of causal influence on the subject that embodiment (in the Cartesian system) has to be defined. This is not to deny that the way in which we would have to think of the supernatural being or beings as acting on the world is very different from the way in which we act on it ourselves. We can only act on the world by acting on our own bodies, whereas the postulated being or beings are not thus restricted. Moreover, whereas the being or beings would be capable of *intentionally*

[11] *The Immaterial Self*, ch. 6.

bringing about physical effects *directly*, it is an aspect of our embodiment that, whenever we intentionally perform some physical action, what we directly bring about is some event in the brain (for example, the firing of certain motor neurons); and the bringing about of this brain event is standardly unintended, and not even something of which we are aware. But these differences do not, as far as I can see, create any problems for the personal-agency approach. Once it has been accepted that the ultimate subjects of human mentality are wholly non-physical, and that there is no conceptual difficulty in recognizing causal relations from the non-physical subject to the body, I cannot see how we can avoid concluding that the personal-agency approach is at least intelligible, and needs to be given serious consideration.

There is one other thing that I should make clear. In *The Immaterial Self*, I not only defended the Cartesian view of human persons, and showed how we can make provision for causal interaction between the non-physical subjects and the bodies to which they are attached, but I also argued that these subjects enjoy a freedom of will (a freedom of intentional agency) of a strong libertarian kind—a kind which logically excludes the possibility of their choices of action being causally determined by prior events and conditions.[12] Although this argument was only directly concerned with the case of the *human* mental subject, the considerations to which it appealed would apply to personal agents in general—to any mental subject with the capacity for intentional action. So they would apply, in particular, to any supernatural being or beings envisaged under the personal-agency approach. From now on, then, I shall take it for granted that any such beings enjoy a freedom of will of the relevantly strong libertarian kind.

V

If we are looking for a non-nomological explanation of the basic regularities, then, as far as I can see, the personal-agency approach is the only one available, or, at least, the only approach which falls within the limits of our understanding and which has any prospect of acceptability. It does not follow that the approach should now be endorsed. For one thing, we have not yet established, or been forced to conclude, that a nomological explanation would be inappropriate. We have identified a serious prima

---

[12] *The Immaterial Self*, ch. 8, sect. 4.

facie problem for the notion of a law of nature, conceived of as a form of natural necessity. But, as things presently stand, we are still leaving open the possibility that a solution will be found. And if a solution is found, and the notion of a law becomes available, then an explanation by appeal to the presence of laws will presumably be the most natural procedure. In any case, even if we are eventually obliged to reject the notion of a law, it does not automatically follow that the personal-agency approach should be accepted. For it could still turn out that, although it is intelligible, there are special reasons which render this approach implausible; and this implausibility might be sufficiently great to balance or outweigh the fact that it would be hugely surprising if the regularities have occurred for no reason and that we do not have any alternative way of explaining them.

The personal-agency approach is the only non-nomological explanation of the regularities available. But the approach itself can be developed in a number of different ways—ways which relate to the number of the supernatural beings involved, their attributes, the manner in which they bring about the regularities, and how the bringing about of the regularities relates to the existence of the physical universe whose workings these regularities characterize. Before we try to reach a final verdict on the correctness of the approach, I want to focus on the different options and see whether considerations of relative plausibility, and perhaps sometimes of intelligibility, will enable us to narrow down the range of possibilities that we need to take seriously. Maybe we shall be able to identify a quite specific proposal to which we can restrict our attention. This matter will form the agenda for the next lecture.

One final point. In addressing the question of the relative merits of different versions of the personal-agency approach, we are obviously moving into an area of religious significance. For, in its doctrinal aspects, religion is primarily to do with having certain beliefs about the existence and nature of some supernatural being or group of beings, and about its, or their, relationship to us and our world. It goes without saying that, in the present context, we are trying to evaluate the different options in a purely *philosophical* way—a way that is sensitive to rational considerations alone. So it is crucial that we should not allow prior religious convictions, or for that matter *anti*-religious convictions, to bias our judgement. I, in particular, have to be very careful here. For I come to the philosophical issue with a prior commitment to a specific set of religious doctrines, namely those of the Christian faith in its orthodox form, and it would be disingenuous of me to pretend that I am indifferent as to whether the conclusions we reach will turn out to lend support to those doctrines or to undermine them. I am not ashamed of that commitment. But, in conducting the philosophical investigation, I need to try to put it on one side, and judge things on their philosophical merits alone.

LECTURE 8

The Theistic Account

I

There is a problem over whether we can make sense of the notion of a law—the problem of understanding how laws can involve a form of necessity which is non-strict. If the notion of a law is abandoned, we shall be prevented from offering a nomological explanation of the basic regularities in nature. In the previous lecture, I considered the question of whether a satisfactory alternative explanation was available. What I tried to establish was that the only alternative with any prospect of acceptability was to appeal to the intentional agency of some supernatural personal being or group of beings—a mode of explanation that I referred to as the *personal-agency approach*. So to the question 'Why are things thus regular?', the answer in each case would be 'Because this being or these beings have deliberately made them so'. I also made it clear that, as I see it, the intentional acts of these beings, as of any personal being, would have to be free in a strong libertarian sense—a sense which logically excludes the possibility of their being causally determined by prior events and conditions.

Some philosophers will regard the personal-agency approach as unintelligible. They will either insist that we cannot make sense of there being personal beings outside the physical universe, on the grounds that we can only make sense of mental subjects as *corporeal* entities. Or they will insist that, even if we can make sense of there being personal beings who are non-physical, we cannot understand how such beings could have a causal influence on the physical world. But, as I indicated, both these objections are, in my view, misconceived. The reason I think them so is that I think that, even in the case of human persons, we should take the ultimate subjects of mentality to be wholly non-physical—in accordance with the Cartesian view—and that, notwithstanding their non-physical character, there is no difficulty in understanding how there can be lines of causation from such subjects to the relevant human bodies, and vice versa. These points are not ones that I have time to defend in these lectures. But, as I have made clear, I have defended them in detail in my book *The Immaterial Self*, and, for the purposes of the present discussion, I am content to rely on the arguments I presented there.

I have called the personal-agency approach an *approach* because there are a number of different ways in which it can be developed. What I want to do in this lecture is to set out some of the options, and try to assess their relative plausibilities. Not all the relevant issues will be considered at this stage. But what I shall try to show, in this phase of the discussion, is that, whatever further details we need to add, the most plausible form of explanation, and indeed the only form with any prospect of acceptability, is one which, at least in broad outline, accords with the requirements of Judaeo-Christian theism—an explanation constructed around the postulation of a being conceived of along the general lines of the Judaeo-Christian God. What this involves will emerge presently.

II

It is not easy to identify a comprehensive set of criteria of plausibility that can be invoked to guide our investigation. But there are two points which I take to be clear. The first is that, in aiming at plausibility, we should develop the explanatory account in a way that avoids unnecessary complexity. So if H1 and H2 are explanatory hypotheses, both of which cover what needs to be explained, but H1 offers a simpler explanation than H2, then, in that respect, we should regard H1 as preferable to H2. When I speak here of the simplicity of an explanation, I am, of course, thinking of what the relevant hypothesis postulates, not the manner of its formulation. I am thinking of such factors as ontological economy and explanatory tidiness.[1] The second point is that, in aiming at plausibility, we should

---

[1] The importance of simplicity, in adjudicating between rival explanatory hypotheses, has been much stressed by Richard Swinburne. Thus see his *The Existence of God* (Oxford: Oxford University Press, 1979), ch. 3, and his *Is There a God?* (Oxford: Oxford University Press, 1996), ch. 2. As I see it, considerations of simplicity can only help in such adjudication in cases where the rival hypotheses share a common approach. (Thus see my *The Nature of Perception* (Oxford: Oxford University Press, 2000), 235–8.) This condition is clearly satisfied in the present case, where the rival hypotheses in question are all versions of the personal-agency approach.

try to develop the account in a way that avoids, or at least minimizes, residual sources of puzzlement. So if H1 and H2 are explanatory hypotheses, both of which cover what needs to be explained, but the situation postulated by H1 is more puzzling than that postulated by H2, then, in that respect, we should regard H2 as preferable to H1. There are different sorts of puzzle that can be involved here. One sort that will be of particular relevance to our discussion is that which arises when something in the postulated situation calls for explanation, but no satisfactory explanation is available.

Applying these two points, I think we can already see the need to restrict the development of the personal-agency approach in four ways.

First, and most obviously, we need to confine our attention to explanatory accounts which take the personal source of agency to be a *single* being, rather than a *plurality* of beings. The regularities to be explained—at least as they have been revealed in our experience so far—form a uniform system across a unitary space and time. To envisage a plurality of beings as causally involved, with the various ways in which they would need to work in harmony to produce the unified outcome, would be a clear case of making things significantly more complex than they need to be; and, on that score alone, it would be much less plausible than an account that assigns the causal role to a single being. It also seems to me that the situation of a plurality of causally relevant beings does not offer such a satisfactory *terminus* of explanation—that it would be puzzling if there were nothing further that accounted for their existence and for the harmonization of their roles. But, even if a further layer of explanation can be envisaged, recognizing it would inevitably involve us in additional complexity, and so only serve to underline the merits of the single-being alternative.

Secondly, having opted for a single relevant being, we ought to think of him as the causal source, not merely of the regularities, but of the whole physical universe. Once again, this is partly a matter of avoiding unnecessary complexity. For obviously the overall account is going to be much simpler—explanatorily tidier—if we suppose that the being's responsibility for the regularities is just an aspect of his creative responsibility for the whole universe which they characterize. But it is also again—and I think in this case more crucially—a matter of avoiding a source of puzzlement. If the being is responsible for the basic regularities of the universe, he is responsible for determining the systematic ways in which it develops over time, and this development constitutes the form of its continuing existence. But it is hard to think of the being as having this control over the *form* in which the universe continues to exist without also having control over its continuing existence *altogether*. And once we grant that he is fully responsible for its continuing existence, and is so with respect to each moment in its history, the only point where we could think of his responsibility for its existence as failing would be with respect to its initial creation. But it would be very strange if the being had responsibility for the existence of the universe at every moment in its history apart from the first.

Thirdly, given that we are taking the relevant being to be the creator of the whole physical universe, we should also take him to be the creator of human persons too. If we were to think of such persons as corporeal entities, there would, of course, be no other option here: the creator of the physical universe would *have* to be the creator of human persons, since they would be ingredients of that universe. But, even on the Cartesian view, whose truth I am now assuming, each non-physical human subject is embodied by a particular biological organism. And, given that these organisms are created by the supernatural being, by far the most plausible conclusion, because it yields by far the simplest, tidiest, overall explanatory account, would be that he is responsible for creating the non-physical subjects as well, and for arranging for their functional attachment to the relevant organisms in the appropriate (embodiment-securing) way.

Finally, we should take the creative being to be *causally primitive*, by which I mean that there is nothing else which is responsible for causing him to exist or causally sustaining any phase of his existence. This, again, is to avoid unnecessary complexity. But, in the present instance, the case for avoiding the relevant complexity assumes a particularly sharp form. Given that the being is causally prior to the existence of the physical universe, the only way, as far as I can see, in which we could envisage him as failing in causal primitiveness—envisage him as *causally derivative*—would be by supposing his existence to be causally initiated or sustained by some other supernatural being. But to postulate this causally prior being would not only increase the complexity of the overall account (and, of course, *any* theory that represents the being as causally derivative is bound to do that), but would do so in a way that was, from any standpoint, totally gratuitous, since there is nothing that we could hope to gain by postulating the pair of beings that we could not achieve, more simply, by postulating only one. The only way in which we could try to represent the two-being hypothesis as offering some advantage would be by claiming that the existence of the original being calls for explanation, and that the agency of the additional being is equipped to do the explaining. But we only need to reflect on the situation of the additional being to see that there is no advantage here at all. If we think of the existence of this being as itself calling for explanation, then postulating him to account for the existence of the original being has, in its overall effect, achieved nothing, since the same explanatory challenge remains. And if we think of his existence as not calling for explanation, we cannot suppose that there was any call to explain the existence of the original being in the first place. But if the complexity of the two-being scenario is, in this way, gratuitous, the only rational course is to postulate a single being, who both plays the requisite creative role with respect to the universe and human persons, and does not causally derive his existence, or any phase of his existence, from anything else.

When these four restrictions are put together, the explanatory account that emerges is this: the personal source of agency that causally underlies the basic regularities takes the form of a single supernatural being, who is causally primitive, and who is responsible for creating the whole physical universe and the human persons who live their embodied lives within it. I shall refer to this as the *basic account*. My claim, then, is that, if we want to develop the personal-agency approach in a way that is at all plausible, we need to confine our attention to theories which conform to this account—that only such theories offer any prospect of proving ultimately acceptable.

III

This endorsement of the basic account, in relation to other ways of developing the personal-agency approach, brings us significantly closer to the conclusion that I am aiming to establish, that the most plausible form of explanation, and indeed the only form with any prospect of acceptability, is one which, at least in broad outline, meets the requirements of Judaeo-Christian theism. For certainly Judaeo-Christian theism insists that there is a supernatural and causally primitive personal being, God, who is the creator of both the universe and the human persons embodied within it. But, of course, Judaeo-Christian theism insists on much more than this. In particular, it includes a quite distinctive conception of the supernatural being involved. If we were trying to capture in a single idea what is so distinctive about this conception, we might say that it represents the being as someone of unsurpassable greatness; and, of course, this transcends—hugely transcends—anything that is implicit in the basic account.

This Judaeo-Christian conception of the supernatural being has a number of aspects. But there are three, in particular, which I regard as fundamental, and as essential to any account that could claim to be, even in broad outline, Judaeo-Christian in its approach.

The first aspect is that, under the Judaeo-Christian conception, there is no temporal limitation on the extent of the being's existence. This can mean different things to different Judaeo-Christian theists. The almost universal view among ordinary believers is that God is sempiternal—that he exists in time, and that his existence stretches infinitely in both temporal directions. But, against this, a number of theologians have insisted that to locate God in time is, in itself, an unacceptable limitation on the form of his being—that it is something incompatible with his unsurpassable greatness; and, as they see it, the lack of a temporal limitation is simply a consequence of the fact that God's existence is timeless. Given the nature of our investigative concern, this second view can, it seems to me, be set aside. For I do not think that we can make sense of the notion of a personal being existing outside time; indeed, I do not think that we can make sense of the notion of any kind of concrete entity existing outside time. The only way, I think, in which we could make sense of the timeless view of God would be by conceiving of God as an *abstract* entity, such as goodness or love or being. And since we are only interested in the options available in the framework of the personal-agency approach, such a conception is not relevant to our present discussion.[2] As for the claim that locating God in time in some way undermines the traditional view of his greatness, this too seems to me misconceived, though it is not a matter that I want to discuss here.[3] The only point I would stress, in this connection, is that, in recognizing God's existence as temporal, we do not have to think of time as something which is ontologically more fundamental than God. We can recognize time as the essential form of God's existence, but also as something which does not, and cannot, exist without him. I should also point out that, in taking God's existence to be in time, I am leaving open the

---

[2] In chapter 4 of his *Eternal God* (Oxford: Oxford University Press, 1988), Paul Helm tries to show that we can, after all, make sense of the view that God is both a personal being and timeless. But it seems to me that the most he succeeds in showing is that, if we suitably restrict the psychological attributes that we ascribe to God, this view does not involve any clear-cut contradiction. He does not, to my mind, succeed in giving us any proper understanding of how it would be possible for there to be a personal being outside time.

[3] But see Richard Swinburne, *The Christian God* (Oxford: Oxford University Press, 1994), 137–44.

option of taking his time dimension to be different from ours, though, for simplicity, this is something I shall ignore in my future discussion.

The second aspect is that, in so far as his attributes are ones which, in their generic form, admit of degrees, the Judaeo-Christian God is conceived of as possessing them to the highest degree. And, granted that we are taking God's existence to be temporal, this means his possessing them to the highest degree *at all times*. In particular, and this will suffice for the present, his rationality is taken to be, at all times, perfect, and his power and knowledge are taken to be, at all times, limitless, apart from limitations imposed by logic alone. What, precisely, these logical limitations are is a complicated matter, and to some extent controversial, and I shall not try to provide a comprehensive account of the situation here.[4] But, at least in the case of his power, some points are clear. Thus obviously we cannot think of God as having the power to bring about things that are logically impossible (such as the existence of an object that is both a cube and a sphere), or that it would be logically impossible to *bring about* (such as the occurrence of an uncaused event). Nor, presumably, can we think of him as having, at any time, the power to affect what has already happened.

The third aspect is that, in addition to his power and intellectual endowments, the Judaeo-Christian God is conceived of as, at all times, morally good, and his goodness, like his rationality, is taken to be perfect. Thus he is conceived of as morally perfect in all his actions, and as morally perfect in the attitudes and traits of character that his actions reflect.

As I have said, I regard these three aspects of the Judaeo-Christian conception of God as fundamental, and ones that have to be preserved in any account which could claim to be, even in broad outline, Judaeo-Christian in its approach. What we must now consider is how they fare with respect to plausibility. I have already argued that our only chance of developing the personal-agency approach in a plausible way is by adopting the basic account. We must now try to see whether, within the framework of that account, there are also grounds for taking the postulated being to be of the Judaeo-Christian type in these further respects. I shall claim that there are such grounds—grounds which, as in the case of the basic account, ultimately stem from the need to avoid unnecessary complexity and residual sources of puzzlement.

---

[4] For a good detailed discussion of the issues, see Richard Swinburne, *The Coherence of Theism* (Oxford: Oxford University Press, 1977), chs. 9 and 10.

IV

Let us start, then, with the issue about existence. On the Judaeo-Christian conception, the supernatural being is not subject to any temporal limitation on the extent of his existence; and, as I have indicated, I am taking this to mean that he is sempiternal—that he exists in time, and that his existence stretches infinitely in both temporal directions.

Now to see why there are good grounds for accepting the Judaeo-Christian view, let us focus on the opposing position, which takes the temporal extent of the being's existence to be limited. There are two forms of limitation that we need to consider: first, a limit on the extent of the being's existence in the direction from later to earlier, and I shall speak of this as a limit on the *E-extent* of his existence; and second, a limit on the extent of his existence in the direction from earlier to later, and I shall speak of this as a limit on the *L-extent* of his existence. I shall begin by considering the first form of limitation. And I shall treat the claim that such a limitation obtains as equivalent to the claim that there is a time when the being starts to exist. Strictly speaking, these claims are not equivalent. For there is the formally available option of supposing that there is a time t, such that the being exists at all times after t, or at all times after t and before some later time, but that he does not exist either at, or at any time before, t. And, granted that time is a continuum, this would imply that, although his existence is limited in its E-extent, there is no time when it begins. But, though formally available, I doubt if this option is coherent; and, even if it is, it is one that we can conveniently ignore.

Now it would surely be very hard to suppose that the being starts to exist at a certain time without also supposing that there is something that causally accounts for this—something that is responsible for bringing him into existence at that time. It is not that I want to rule out altogether the possibility of events occurring without a cause; nor do I even want to say that, if an event occurs without a cause, the fact of its doing so is bound to be puzzling. But there would, surely, be something very puzzling about the fact of a personal being coming into existence without a cause; and the idea of this happening in the case of the supernatural being in question—a being with the creative role we are envisaging—strikes me as absurd. It might be objected that I should not assume that if the being *starts* to exist at a certain time, he *comes into existence* at that time. For this presupposes that there is a stretch of time prior to his existence; and, if time itself could have a beginning, this may not be the case. But even if we were to suppose that time and the being start together, this would not, as I see it, alter the dialectical situation. The being's starting to exist would still cry out for a causal explanation. The only difference would be that there would also be a call to account for the beginning of time itself.

It is very hard to suppose that the being starts to exist without there being something that causally accounts for this. But, within the framework of the basic account, no such causal explanation is possible, since the being of this account is characterized as causally primitive. Nor was the insistence on causal primitiveness arbitrary. As I said, the only way I could see in which we might envisage the being as failing in such primitiveness was by envisaging his existence as causally initiated or sustained by a further supernatural being. And, as we saw, the case against such an ontological expansion was particularly clear-cut, since the extra complexity involved would be not only avoidable, but gratuitous: there is nothing that we could hope to gain by recognizing such a pair of beings that we could not achieve, more simply, by recognizing only one. This is so, of course, irrespective of whether we suppose there to be a limit on the E-extent of the existence of the causally prior being himself. If we suppose that there is such a limit, the issue of how to account for the start of *his* existence remains. If we suppose there is not, the same option was already available for the being of our original theory.

Granted the difficulty of supposing that he starts to exist without a cause, the only rational course, as I see it, is to take the E-extent of the original being's existence to be unlimited. This still leaves the option of envisaging his existence as limited in its *L*-extent—its extent in the direction from earlier to later. But this too, I think, should be rejected. For the same kind of problem that arises for the supposition of a *start* to the being's existence arises for the supposition of its *coming to an end*. Once again, it would be very puzzling if such an event occurred without there being something that causally accounted for it. Once again, as far as I can see, the only type of cause that we could plausibly envisage would be the agency of a further being—a being who has control over the life span of the original being and decides to terminate it at a certain point. And, once again, the postulation of this additional being would just involve us in gratuitous complexity. For if we take the L-extent of *his* existence to be limited too, the issue of causal explanation recurs, while if we take it to be unlimited, we cannot suppose that there was any need to envisage a limitation in the case of the original being. It also seems to me that, once we have accepted that the being's existence is unlimited in its E-extent, this, in itself, makes it hard to think of it as coming to an end. For it would surely be hard to think of his existence as stretching infinitely into the past without supposing that this fact reflects something very far-reaching about his ontological nature, and that, in particular, what it reflects is something that would also ensure his existential permanence. Interestingly, this further point does not hold in reverse. There is no special difficulty about envisaging a being who will endure for ever as having had a beginning—though, of course, as in the case at hand, there may be a separate difficulty about how the envisaged beginning is to be explained.

It seems to me, then, that, given the need to avoid unnecessary complexity and residual sources of puzzlement, we cannot plausibly envisage a limitation on the extent of the being's existence in either temporal direction. So I conclude that, on this issue, there is a strong case for endorsing the Judaeo-Christian view that the being is sempiternal.

V

As well as taking the being to be sempiternal, Judaeo-Christian theism insists that, in so far as his attributes are ones which, in their generic form, admit of degrees, the being possesses them, and possesses them at all times, to the *highest degree*. So he is, at all times, perfect in his rationality and moral goodness; and, apart from the restrictions imposed by logic, there are never any limitations on the extent of his power and knowledge. I want to try to show that we should endorse the Judaeo-Christian view on these points too. There are four distinct issues to be considered, respectively concerning the being's power, knowledge, rationality, and goodness, and I shall look at each in turn. In one respect, the case of moral goodness stands apart from the others. Power, knowledge, and rationality are attributes that we *have* to ascribe to the supernatural being within the framework of the explanatory approach we are pursuing; and, in their case, it is only the maximal form of their possession which is at issue. But, in the case of moral goodness, the issue is not only whether there is a case for taking the being to possess this attribute *in its maximal form*, but also whether he should be thought of as possessing it *at all*. I shall leave discussion of this issue until last. Of the other three issues, I shall begin by looking, in some detail, at the case of power; and this will enable me to deal more briefly with the issues of knowledge and rationality in the light of what emerges.

The Judaeo-Christian view is that, within the limits of what is logically allowable, the being's power is, and is at all times, limitless. And, as with the issue over existence, the best way of bringing out why there are good grounds for endorsing this view is by focusing on the alternative. So, for the sake of argument, let us, for the moment, suppose that this view is false. In particular, to give us a concrete point of focus, let us suppose that there is a limitation on the being's power to create types of physical universe, so that, within the domain of types that are logically available, there are some that he is able to create and others that he is not. And, to keep things simple, let us provisionally assume that we are thinking of this as the situation at all times. The pressing question is now: what accounts for the limitation? For it surely cannot be just a brute fact—a fact without explanation—that the being's creative power extends to certain types of universe but not to others. There must surely be something else—something about his nature or the circumstances of his existence—that is responsible for putting the limitation in place. Certainly, if the limitation obtained for no reason—without anything causally underlying or in any other way accounting for it—the situation would be deeply puzzling. It would be puzzling in the same sort of way as it would be if, as in the kinds of case envisaged in Lecture 4, the scope of a law were restricted to a particular period or region or group of bodies, without there being any qualitative factor which the restriction reflected.

In the human sphere, limitations on what a subject can intentionally bring about typically stem from the properties of his body and his physical environment. If he can move his hands, but cannot waggle his ears, this difference is due to the neuro-muscular arrangements within his body. If he has the power to lift a bicycle but not a car, this is because of the limits of his muscular strength and the differing weights of the two types of object. Even in a case where the limitation merely concerns the subject's capacity to affect his own mentality—like, say, an inability to imagine sounds above a certain pitch—it is natural to assume that there is some kind of underlying neural mechanism which is involved in the activity and whose properties account for the limitation. But the supernatural being of our theory is not embodied, and so is not subject to the limitations that embodiment might impose. Nor can we form a conception of anything else in the supernatural realm that we could think of as playing an analogous role—some form of non-physical apparatus whose operations we could think of as mediating the exercise of his intentional agency, and whose structure we could think of as restricting the range of its achievable types of effect. Indeed, ever since the personal-agency approach was introduced, we have taken it for granted that, for a *supernatural* personal agent, the basic way of intentionally bringing things about is causally direct: the agent simply wills something to happen and it happens, without any intervening causal process between the volitional act and its intended effect. Of course, the fact that we cannot form a conception of a mediating apparatus does not entail that nothing of that sort exists. But, as I have already stressed, we should only think of postulating something beyond the reach of our understanding if there is no viable alternative.[5] And, in the present instance, there is the viable, and indeed much simpler, alternative of denying the limitation altogether.

Another suggestion might be that, in addition to his psychological nature as a mental subject, and the psychological attributes and capacities that he possesses as such a subject, we should think of the being as having an underlying nature of a non-psychological kind. For we could then suppose that it was some aspect of this underlying nature that was causally responsible for endowing him with his capacity for intentional agency and for fixing the limits of what it can achieve. But this suggestion, too, seems to me misconceived. Once again, there is the point that we cannot form any conception of what the supposed underlying nature might be, and we should avoid postulating things beyond our understanding, if we can. But there is also something else. As I mentioned last time, the reason why I accept a Cartesian view of the ultimate subjects of human mentality is that the only way in which we could intelligibly suppose such subjects to be corporeal entities would be by combining this with a suitably reductive account of the mentality they possess—an account which enabled us to understand this mentality as ultimately consisting in, or constituted by, something physical; and, as I see it, all such accounts fail.[6] But if I am right about this, then an exactly analogous point would count against thinking of the supernatural being as having an underlying nature that was non-psychological. The only way in which we could intelligibly suppose the being to have such a nature, and yet also be equipped to be a mental subject, would be by taking his mentality to be in some way reducible to—to consist in or be constituted by—states of affairs that pertain to that nature. And the same considerations that exclude reduction in the human case would exclude it in this case too. Indeed, it is ultimately in these terms that the point applies to the human case itself. For the reason why there

---

[5] See Lecture 7, sect. IV.   [6] See Lecture 7, sect. IV.

is a problem in understanding how corporeal entities could be the ultimate subjects of human mentality is that corporeal nature is itself non-psychological, and so contains nothing which helps us to understand how something that possesses it could also have psychological attributes in an irreducible form.[7]

If we cannot appeal to an analogue of embodiment, and if we exclude the possibility of the being's having an underlying non-psychological nature, then, as far as I can see, there are only two remaining suggestions as to how we might try to account for the envisaged limitation. The first would be to take the limitation to be something imposed by another supernatural being. The second would be to take it to be something which the being imposes on himself. Assuming that we have to exclude the possibility of backward causation, it will be, in the case of both suggestions, technically much simpler if we begin by dropping the provisional assumption that the limitation holds at all times, and think of it as limited in its past extent. For, by thinking of it as thus limited, we can envisage an earlier vantage point from which it could be imposed by a single forward-looking act. It is not that it would be *impossible* to make sense of the suggestions if we took the limitation to be sempiternal: formally, at least, there would be the option of thinking of such a limitation as imposed in an infinite and non-starting series of temporal stages.[8] But things will certainly be more straightforward if we take the limitation to have a beginning, and think of it as imposed by a single act at an earlier time.

But, whatever view we take of the temporal extent of the limitation, it is clear, I think, that neither of the two suggestions would yield an acceptable outcome. The objection to the first is already familiar. For, as with other cases of this sort, it would involve us in gratuitous complexity. Thus if we take the further being's power to be itself limited, we face the same explanatory challenge over again; while if we take his power to be unlimited, we cannot think that there was any reason to recognize the limitation in the case of the original being. Either way, there are no benefits that we

---

[7] Or, at least, corporeal nature is not psychological in any way that would be relevant to the present issue. Interestingly, such is our ignorance of the intrinsic nature of physical space and its occupants, that, even within the framework of physical realism, it is possible to envisage the physical world as something purely mental. Thus see my *The Case for Idealism*, Pt. II.

[8] For example, we could suppose that there is an infinite sequence of times $t_1, t_2, t_3, \ldots$, spaced out at equal temporal intervals, with each t_n later than t_{n+1}, such that, at t_1, there is an imposing of the limitation for all times later than t_1, and, at each t_{n+1}, there is an imposing of the limitation for the period from t_{n+1} to t_n. This series of impositions would collectively cover all times.

could hope to secure by postulating a pair of beings that are not available, in a simpler form, if we postulate only one. The second suggestion has the merit of avoiding the ontological complexity of the two-being approach. But its problem is that we cannot envisage any remotely plausible reason why the being should choose to limit his power in this way. Having a power does not oblige one to use it. So what would the being stand to gain by forgoing some of the power that he would otherwise possess? It surely cannot be that he would find the possession of unlimited power burdensome, or that, with so many options, he would be spoilt for choice.

Neither of the suggestions considered yields an acceptable outcome, and, as far as I can see, there are no further explanatory options available. So I think we are forced to conclude that there is no plausible way of accounting for the envisaged limitation, or at least none that would not—like the postulation of a further being—merely serve to show that it was more rational to reject the supposition of the limitation in the first place. Since such a limitation would call for explanation—since it would be deeply puzzling if it turned out to be just a brute fact that the being's creative power extended to certain types of universe but not to others—the rational conclusion to draw is that the limitation does not hold. But, obviously, the same considerations that apply to this case would apply, in the same way, to other forms of limitation on power that we could envisage—for example, a limitation on the being's power to create other types of supernatural being, or on his power to create types of embodied person. So, as I see the situation, there is a strong case for concluding that, apart from the limitations imposed by logic, the being's power is, in all respects, limitless, and limitless at all times: in other words, a strong case, once again, for endorsing the Judaeo-Christian view of the matter.

VI

Having defended the Judaeo-Christian view of the being's power, I want now to turn to the issues of his knowledge and rationality. And, given our findings with respect to power, I think I can here afford to be brief.

With respect to the first issue, we need to begin by noting that the kind of knowledge that concerns us is *direct* knowledge, rather than knowledge possessed on the inferential basis of other knowledge. For it is unlimited *direct* knowledge that is ascribed to the Judaeo-Christian God. Thus the Judaeo-Christian position is not that God directly knows certain things, and can then reach warranted conclusions about all other matters by inference, but that, within the limits of what logic allows, all facts are directly evident to him, and directly evident to him at all times. What we have to decide is whether this is a further area in which, in developing our explanatory theory, we should model things on the Judaeo-Christian view.

Well, with the resolution of the issue of power in place, I think it is clear that we should.

To begin with, the same considerations that supported the Judaeo-Christian position in the case of the being's power will also serve to support it in the case of his knowledge. Thus any limitation we might envisage on the scope of his direct knowledge would call for explanation: a situation in which some facts were directly evident to the being and others were not would be puzzling, unless there was something that accounted for the difference. And, as far as I can see, there is no form of explanation available that would be both satisfactory in its own terms and would leave things satisfactory from the standpoint of the overall account. Thus, given his lack of embodiment, or anything analogous, and given that we cannot make sense of his having an underlying non-psychological nature, the only forms of explanation I can envisage are, as in the earlier case, that the limitation is imposed by another being and that it is imposed by the being on himself; and, in the same way as in that earlier case, neither of these options would yield something that is ultimately acceptable—the first because it involves a gratuitous increase in ontological complexity, the second because we cannot envisage a plausible motive for the self-denying ordinance. But if any limitation would call for explanation, and if there is ultimately no satisfactory way of dealing with the explanatory challenge, the rational conclusion to draw is that, within the limits of what is logically allowable, the extent of the being's direct knowledge is, like the extent of his power, at all times limitless.

In any case, once we have accepted the Judaeo-Christian view of the being's power, we are, in effect, already committed to accepting the corresponding view of his knowledge. For if the being has unlimited power, subject only to the restrictions of logic, then, subject to those same restrictions, he has the power to make the facts directly accessible to him in any area he chooses. And if he has this power, it would be strange if there were certain areas where he chose to keep himself in ignorance.

Granted an acceptance of the Judaeo-Christian view of the being's knowledge, we can also quickly vindicate the Judaeo-Christian view of his rationality.

Rationality can be divided into two types: *intellectual* rationality (or rationality of *thought*) and *practical* rationality (or rationality of *action*). Any flaw or deficiency in the being's intellectual rationality would involve some limitation on his capacity for a certain kind of direct knowledge, namely the direct knowledge of truths that are in principle recognizable by the light of reason alone. So if we suppose the being to be unlimited in his possession of direct knowledge, within the limits of what is logically possible, then we must suppose him to be perfect in his intellectual rationality as well. But if he is perfect in his intellectual rationality, and has complete knowledge, on any occasion, of the rational merits of each possible course of action, it is hard to see what could ever prompt him to *act* in an irrational way—to do what, all things considered, reason prescribes he ought not to do. There is, of course, in the sphere of human behaviour, the phenomenon of *akrasia*, or *weakness of will*, in which the insistence of some desire, or the anticipated pleasure of its satisfaction, beguiles a person into doing something which he knows to be irrational. But however this phenomenon is to be understood—whether it is to be thought of as the wilful rejection of the prescriptions of reason or as a failure to pay sufficient attention to them at the moment of decision—it is very hard to think of it as afflicting a being with the other attributes that we are now assuming to be in place. Given his possession of these other attributes—unlimited power and knowledge, and perfect rationality of thought—it is surely safe to assume that the being is perfect in his practical rationality too.

VII

I have tried to show how we can defend the Judaeo-Christian view with respect to the unlimited character of the being's existence and with respect to the maximal form of his power, knowledge, and rationality. But, as I have stressed, it is also fundamental to Judaeo-Christian theism that the being who has created us and our universe is morally good, and perfect in his goodness. I want now to consider whether we should accept this further aspect of the Judaeo-Christian position.

I am going to begin by making a crucial assumption. In taking the supernatural being to be morally good (morally perfect), Judaeo-Christian theism is assuming, in line with what we ordinarily believe, that morality is objective. It is assuming that questions of what is morally good or bad, and what is morally right and wrong, have objective answers—answers whose truth is logically independent of our own moral views and evaluative attitudes. Now, in addressing the issue of the being's moral goodness, I too am going to make this common-sense assumption of objectivity. It is an assumption which I believe to be correct, and to be philosophically defensible, but it is not something that I can hope to argue for here.

Granted the objectivity of morality, do we, then, have grounds for taking the supernatural being to be morally good? And do we have grounds for taking him to be perfect in his goodness? Well, assuming that we already have grounds for taking him to be both perfectly rational and relevantly unlimited in knowledge, it seems to me that we do. The crucial point is that, on questions of how one should act, the claims of morality are rationally overriding. Thus if there is something which one knows that one morally ought to do, then, whatever other considerations may count against doing it, it is something which, all things considered, it would be rational for one to do. And if there is something which one knows that one morally ought not to do, then, whatever other considerations may count in favour of doing it, it is something which, all things considered, it would be rational for one not to do. These principles are, as I see it, constitutive of our conception of the moral ought: they are what distinguish it from other forms of ought, such as those that are merely relative to one's desires, and those that are internal to the rules of a game. But once we accept that moral considerations are rationally overriding, it follows automatically that if the being is perfect in his rationality and relevantly unlimited in his knowledge, he will also be perfect in his moral dispositions. For if he is relevantly knowledgeable, he will, in particular, have an unerring capacity to discriminate between what is morally right and what is morally wrong. And if he possesses this capacity, and is also perfect in his rationality, he will be wholly and unshakeably disposed to do the things he morally ought to do and to refrain from doing the things he morally ought not to do. But a being who is thus disposed must be a being who is morally perfect in all his actions, and morally perfect in the disposing attitudes and traits of character that his actions reflect. In other words, he must be a being who, like the Judaeo-Christian God, qualifies as perfect in his moral goodness.

If this reasoning is sound, then the case that has already been made out for accepting the Judaeo-Christian position on the being's knowledge and rationality turns into an equally strong case for accepting its claim with respect to moral goodness. But there is also, I think, an independent reason why we should find this latter claim congenial. For it enables us to fill a crucial lacuna in the explanatory approach we are envisaging.

On this approach, we are trying to account for the regularities in nature by postulating a supernatural being who deliberately creates the physical universe and the human persons embodied within it. But if this mode of explanation is to be plausible, then we have to be able to envisage a plausible reason why the postulated being should choose to perform this creative work—a reason that both does justice to the character of what has been created and is consonant with the being's own nature, in so far as we can gauge it. Now what makes the claim of moral goodness independently congenial is that it allows us to envisage such a reason. For if the being is morally good, and good to perfection, then not only is he the sort of being who would want things to go well for other personal beings that exist, but he is also the sort of being who, out of his generosity of spirit, would want there *to be* other personal beings for whom things go well. And so, focusing on the opportunities for significance and fulfilment that human life makes available, we can see his moral goodness as giving him a reason for creating embodied personal beings of our sort, located in our sort of universe. Admittedly, along with its opportunities for significance and fulfilment, human life also leaves ample room for disappointment and suffering; and it may be wondered why a being of perfect goodness and unlimited power should so arrange things. The full answer to this would make a long story—much longer than I could hope to cover here, and, indeed, a story that would take us much more deeply into Christian theology than would be appropriate to my purposes in these lectures. But the basic point is that, unless it left room for disappointment and suffering, human life would not offer the opportunities for the relevant kinds of significance and fulfilment. And it is not implausible to suppose that the intrinsic value of these good things is such that, in order to ensure their availability, it would be rational for a being of perfect goodness to allow for the bad things too.

VIII

We have seen that the only plausible way of developing the personal-agency approach is by adopting the basic account, which takes the personal source of agency to be a single supernatural being, who is causally primitive, and who is the creator of the physical universe and the human persons embodied within it. And I have additionally tried to show how, if we are to develop this account in a plausible way, we need to think of the supernatural being involved as satisfying, in certain basic respects, the requirements of Judaeo-Christian theism. Specifically, we need to think of the being as sempiternal, as perfect in rationality and moral goodness, and as unlimited in power and direct knowledge, except for limitations imposed by logic alone. Someone who both accepts the basic account and takes the relevant being to satisfy these further conditions can be reasonably described as believing in the existence of a God of a broadly Judaeo-Christian type. And when the basic account is developed in this way, I shall speak of what results as the *theistic account*. What I have tried to show, then, is that, if we want to pursue the personal-agency approach at all, the theistic account is the only version of this approach with any prospect of acceptability.

The question of whether we *should* pursue the personal-agency approach remains open. I have argued that, if we are looking for a non-nomological explanation of the regularities in nature, this approach is the only one available—the only one that falls within the limits of our understanding and has any claim to plausibility. But I have not yet settled the issue of whether the explanation has to be non-nomological—of whether the notion of a law of nature is incoherent. And, although I have tried to counter the claim that the personal-agency approach is unintelligible, I have not yet excluded the possibility of there being other objections to it, and ones which might outweigh the prima facie need to find an explanation of the regularities.

On this last point, however, there is only one line of objection that I can think of, and I want to close the present discussion by considering it.

I have been putting considerable stress on the fact that one way in which an explanatory theory can show itself to be unacceptable is by postulating some state of affairs which itself calls for explanation, when no satisfactory explanation is available. But it might seem, at first, that *any* version of the personal-agency approach is bound to incur that sort of problem, simply on account of its supernatural ontology. Maybe we can reduce the *extent* of the problem by developing the approach in the theistic way proposed. But it might still seem that, however the approach is developed, it will leave us with a pressing but unanswerable why-question over the existence of the supernatural being or beings it postulates, or at least of those of them that it takes to be causally primitive.

There are two things that I want to say about this. My first, and main, point is that if the personal-agency approach does face a problem here, it is not one which in any way detracts from its plausibility, since it is a problem that would arise, in exactly the same way, on any alternative approach. For wherever we decide to locate the terminus of explanation, there is the possibility of raising the same kind of why-question with respect to the ontological ingredients of the reality envisaged; and I cannot see how, with a different reality, that question could turn out to be less pressing, or its unanswerability less worrying, than in the case of the personal-agency approach itself. Thus suppose we decide to stay within the bounds of a naturalistic ontology; and, for the sake of argument, let us assume that there is no longer any problem about postulating natural laws to account for the natural regularities. Then, even without the special issue over the explanation of the regularities, we can still raise the question of why there is a physical universe at all; and, with supernatural explanations excluded, this question will have no answer. Nor can I see why the unanswerability of the why-question here would be less problematic than in the case of a supernatural ontology. But unless the personal-agency approach can be shown to face a *distinctive* problem here, or, at least, one that does not affect *all* the available alternatives, there is no challenge to its plausibility, and so no grounds for rejecting it.

My second point focuses on an intriguing possibility, though not one that I can here explore in any detail. The fact that there is no *distinctive* problem for the personal-agency approach does not, of course, mean that there is no problem *at all*. But if there is, one way in which we might think of responding to it would be by supplementing the theistic account with a further claim that may be thought to be implicit in the Judaeo-Christian view, namely that the relevant being is someone whose existence is strictly necessary—someone who could not have failed to exist, someone who exists in all possible worlds. For if we limit the supernatural ontology to a single being, and take this being's existence to be strictly necessary, the ontological why-question has an immediate answer: the relevant being exists simply because he *has* to exist. The reason why the claim of necessity may be thought to be implicit in the Judaeo-Christian view is that, granted that God is causally primitive, to think of his existence as merely contingent seems tantamount to thinking of it as just a fluke. And such a thought may well seem to be at odds with the Judaeo-Christian understanding of God's greatness.

I find this approach to the issue of the residual why-question attractive, but I shall not try to reach a verdict on it here. The only point I would stress—for there is sometimes confusion on this matter—is that accepting the necessity of the being's existence in the relevant sense would not commit us to accepting that his existence can be established a priori, for example by some version of the Ontological Argument. We could take the being to exist in all possible worlds, but still insist that the only way of establishing his existence, or making out a case for accepting it, is by appealing to certain forms of empirical evidence—evidence such as is provided by the existence of the physical universe, or by the presence of the regularities that have featured so prominently in my own discussion.

LECTURE 9
God and Laws

I

There is a problem about how to make sense of the notion of a law of nature, and, over the last two lectures, I have been exploring the situation in which we would find ourselves if we abandoned this notion as incoherent. In particular, I have focused on the issue of how we should try to explain the basic regularities in nature if nomological explanations are excluded. The conclusions for which I have successively argued are: first, that the only form of non-nomological explanation with any prospect of acceptability is that provided by the *personal-agency approach*, in which the regularities are taken to be brought about through the intentional agency of a supernatural personal being, or group of beings; and, secondly, that, within the framework of this approach, the only form of explanation with any prospect of acceptability is that provided by the *theistic account*, which appeals to the agency of a single supernatural being, conceived of along the general lines of the Judaeo-Christian God. Specifically, the theistic account postulates a being who is causally primitive, who is the creator of the physical universe and the human persons embodied within it, who is sempiternal, who is perfect in his rationality and goodness, and who possesses unlimited power and knowledge, save for the limitations imposed by logic alone.

I said at the outset of these lectures that one of my aims was to provide an argument for the existence of God—a God of a broadly Judaeo-Christian type. We can already identify one form which such an argument could take. We have agreed that, when sufficiently extensive, natural regularities call for explanation, and we have seen that there is a problem over making sense of the notion of a law. Well, suppose we decide that this latter problem is insoluble and that the notion of a law is incoherent. Granted that the regularities cannot be explained by appeal to laws, and that the only non-nomological form of explanation with any prospect of acceptability is that provided by the theistic account, we must acknowledge a strong prima facie case for accepting this account, and thereby accepting the existence of a God of the relevant type. Thus derived, the case is still only *prima facie*, because the fact that the theistic account is the only explanatory account with any *prospect* of acceptability does not ensure that there is no other consideration which decisively counts against it. However, if I have been successful in my defence of the intelligibility of the personal-agency approach, and if I am right in insisting that there is no special implausibility attaching to its supernaturalist ontology, I cannot see what form such a counter-consideration could take.

Once we reject the notion of a law, then, and so exclude nomological explanations of the relevant regularities, a powerful argument for the existence of a God of the relevant type becomes immediately available. What still has to be decided is whether this notion *should* be rejected. The problem which threatens it is clear enough; and we have not yet been able to solve it. But the final verdict on this issue is one that I have explicitly left open.

The reason why I have left this issue open is that there is a possible account of the nature of laws that we have not yet considered. But, to prepare the way for the consideration of this new account, there is something else that we need to take note of first.

II

The theistic account is the only version of the personal-agency approach that we need to take seriously. But there remain a number of different ways in which this account can be developed. For our purposes, the most important issue here concerns the *method* by which the God it postulates creates the physical universe and endows it with its regularities. To keep things relatively simple, and allow the main aspects of the issue to stand out clearly, let us provisionally work on the assumption that, whatever his method, this God (if he exists) is responsible for creating the physical universe *in all its details*, leaving nothing to occur which he does not, in some way, causally determine. This is an assumption that we may eventually want to modify, but it is best to leave any modification until after the options available on the simpler scenario have been clearly identified. I think we can also safely assume that the method of creation will be of a unitary type. This need not mean that there is no variation in how the method applies to different portions or aspects of the universe. But it does mean that any such variation must reflect some underlying unitary strategy—a strategy that could not be implemented without things varying in that way. Nothing else, I think, would be consistent with the being's perfect rationality.

With these assumptions in place, there are just three ways in which we could envisage the relevant God as creating the physical universe. The first possibility would be to think of him as directly creating the whole universe by a single act. In other words, we could think of him as forming a conception of the type of universe he wants to create—a conception which covers its entire spatiotemporal extent and every detail of its content—and then, by a single volitional act, causing this type to be instantiated. This would be the theoretically simplest, most straightforward, account of the creation. The second possibility would be to think of God as directly creating the whole universe, but in a piecemeal way—by a set or series of volitional acts rather than by a single act. This, of course, covers a multitude of more specific options, according to how the division into pieces is effected. The main option would presumably be for God to create the universe in temporal stages, so that—on the assumption that the universe has a beginning—there would be an act of creating its history from t_1 to t_2, an act of creating its history from t_2 to t_3, an act of creating its history from t_3 to t_4, and so on, with t_1 as the time when the universe begins, and $t_2, t_3, t_4, \ldots$ as a sequence of subsequent times occurring at regular intervals. (This would still, of course, leave an infinite range of still more specific options according to the interval length selected.) The third possibility, put roughly, would be to think of God as directly creating the universe in its initial state—the universe as it was at t_1—and making provision for its subsequent history by prescribing the systematic ways in which its state at any given time is to give rise to its states at subsequent times. On this account, unlike the first two, God does not create the whole of the universe *directly*. What he creates directly is just its initial state, along with the prescribed modes of transition for the succession of states through time, and he then leaves all the subsequent history to unfold in response—each event or state of affairs that subsequently occurs occurring, as it were, in obedience to the original prescription, in the light of the currently prevailing conditions.

I said that this was the third possibility *put roughly*. And the reason for the qualification is that, in this case, there are two respects in which the way I have characterized the method of creation needs to be refined.

In the first place, in its present form, the characterization represents God as making provision for the subsequent history of the universe by assigning certain types of continuation to certain types of momentary state. But this is too restrictive. For, without affecting the basic method of creation, we need to leave room for the possibility that God may, or may in some cases, wish to make the way in which the universe continues from a time depend not just on its state at that time, but also on aspects of its immediately preceding history. So, to achieve precision, I need to characterize the method of creation in a slightly more complicated way. Instead of saying that what God directly creates is the universe in its initial state, I need to say that what he directly creates is the universe in its initial state *or in some small initial phase*; and instead of saying that what he prescribes are the systematic ways in which the state of the universe at any given time is to give rise to its states at subsequent times, I need to say that what he prescribes are the ways in which the state of the universe at any given time, *or the series of its states over any given relevantly short period*, is to give rise to its states at subsequent times. This said, I shall, for ease of expression, continue to employ the simpler characterization in much of what follows, leaving the refinement in question to be understood.

Secondly, the way in which I have characterized the relevant method of creation suggests that the direct fixing of the initial state (or phase) of the universe and the prescribing of the modes of transition cover the *whole story* of creation—that every element of what physically occurs or obtains (and we are provisionally assuming that every such element is in some way brought about by God) is determined by these two factors alone. But, in fact, we ought to think of these factors as constituting only the *main part* of God's creative work—a part which is responsible for determining the basic structure of the universe, and indeed the greater part of its detailed content, but which also leaves room for further ways in which God may operate to affect things. The reason why we need to leave room for such additional creative acts will emerge in due course (I shall deal with this in Lecture 10). For the time being, it will be convenient to put the matter on one side, and proceed as if the two factors already identified were the only ones involved.

Of the three possible accounts of the method of creation, the second one is, I think, considerably less plausible than the first. In as much as it represents God as directly creating every part and aspect of the universe, it is, in effect, just a more complicated version of the first, and it is hard to see what reason God could have for preferring to operate in this more complex way, when the simpler mode of operation is available. (Given his limitless power and rationality, it obviously cannot be that God is incapable of creating everything by a single act, nor that he finds it intellectually easier to take things a step at a time.) Nor is this the only problem. For, by dividing the work of creation into discrete parts, the second account is also liable to impose awkward limits on the operation of causality within the physical realm. Thus, in the case of the main version of the account, in which we represent God as creating things in temporal stages, we have a situation in which the relevant successive phases in the history of the universe are not, as we ordinarily assume, causally related: its history from t_n to t_{n+1} does not causally give rise to its history from t_{n+1} to t_{n+2}, since the latter, like the former, is directly brought about by God. Admittedly, we could envisage a revised form of the temporal-stages procedure, in which God brings about each relevant phase, apart from the first, by causing the preceding phase to cause it. This would preserve the piecemeal nature of the creation—each phase being brought about by a separate act of divine volition—but would avoid the internal breaks in the operation of physical causality. But, even with this revision, the gratuitous complications of the account still leave it distinctly implausible. And, in one respect, the revision seems to make it more contrived. For, given that God is dealing with the phases one at a time, it is hard to see what purpose he could have in delegating the causing of each one to its predecessor—other than to make our ordinary beliefs about physical causation correct.

There is a strong case, then, for eliminating the second account and leaving the first and third as the only serious options. But, at present, reaching a verdict on the relative merits of the different accounts is not what concerns me, and I am content to leave the second one in play. What I want to do now is to draw attention to a particular aspect of the way in which the third account differs from the other two. It is an aspect that will be of crucial importance to our subsequent discussion, when we come to consider, once again, the issue over the problem of laws.

Our reason for focusing on the theistic account in the first place—as a version of the personal-agency approach—was that we were looking for a non-nomological way of explaining the basic regularities in nature: a way that is available even when the notion of a law is taken to be incoherent. All three accounts of the method of divine creation provide such an explanation—an explanation in terms of the causal agency of God. But the explanation offered by the third is of a quite different kind from that offered by the first and the second, and gives the causing of the regularities a quite different place in the overall scheme of creation. On the first two accounts, God brings about the regularities by directly causing the instantiation of a determinate type of universe in which they hold. The causing of the regularities does not itself play any creative role: it is just an aspect of the causing of something bigger. In effect, God arranges for the obtaining of the regularities by directly fixing all the relevant items of content in the universe in ways that conform to them, and so in ways that collectively ensure that the regularities hold. On the third account, as we have seen, God creates the universe by directly creating its initial state and prescribing the relevant modes of transition. But, in prescribing these modes of transition, he is, in effect, prescribing for the universe its basic forms of regularity, since it is precisely such forms of regularity that define the systematic ways in which how things are at any time gives rise to how they subsequently become. So, in contrast with the first two accounts, the causing of the regularities is here given a creative role. The regularities are imposed on the universe *as regularities*, leaving open all the details of how things conform to them, and their imposition is then what, in combination with the conditions obtaining at each subsequent time, is responsible for fixing the relevant items of content in a conforming way. Thus, instead of directly creating the whole universe in a way that ensures the obtaining of the regularities, God prescribes the regularities for the universe at its first moment of existence, and leaves this prescription to be what keeps its subsequent history to its regularity-exemplifying path.

When I speak, in this context, of God as *prescribing* certain modes of transition or certain forms of regularity, I am speaking, of course, metaphorically. We are not to suppose that God literally issues a command or instruction, which reality then obeys. (The only genuine commands or instructions that we can think of God as issuing are ones that are addressed to other personal beings, such as ourselves.) All we are to suppose is that God intentionally causes it to be the case that the universe develops along the relevant lines—in accordance with the relevant modes of transition, and so in conformity to the relevant forms of regularity. Even so, the metaphor of prescription reflects an important aspect of the situation. For, in intentionally causing the universe to develop along the relevant lines, God is not bringing about any specific form of subsequent history. He is merely doing something which is designed to combine with the state of the universe at any time to determine its history (or perhaps certain aspects of its history) from that point. And so what he is doing is, in its functional role, equivalent to laying down a set of rules to which the subsequent history of the universe is obliged to conform. In that respect, the causing involved has a kind of prescriptive force, which it lacks in a case where God just forms a conception of a determinate type of physical state of affairs and directly brings about its instantiation.

You may already be getting some inkling of how the difference between the causal explanation of the regularities on the first two accounts and their causal explanation on the third could be thought relevant to the issue over the problem of laws.

III

The problem over the notion of a law, as we have seen, concerns the nature of the necessity involved in laws. If it is a law of nature that bodies always behave gravitationally, it is in some sense necessary that they behave in this way. But the necessity involved—*nomic* necessity—is not a form of *strict* necessity: it does not exclude altogether the possibility of bodies behaving differently. In particular, it leaves room for the possibility of worlds in which, with different laws in place, bodies are not constrained to behave gravitationally and do not always do so. The problem is in understanding how we can make sense of a necessity of this kind. On the face of it, it is just self-contradictory to say that it is necessary for things to be thus and so, but is also possible for them to be otherwise.

So far, we have not been able to find a solution to this problem. But, as I indicated, there is a possible account of the nature of laws that we have not yet considered. It will be helpful if we begin by reminding ourselves of a suggestion that we noted, but rejected, when the problem of laws was first introduced, back in Lecture 5.

The suggestion in question was that we should think of laws as *concrete* entities that sustain regularities *causally*. So, instead of thinking of the law of gravity as something whose existence consists in the relevant fact of nomic necessity—the fact that it is nomically necessary that bodies behave gravitationally, or stand in the relevant attractive relationships—it was suggested that we should think of it as a concrete entity which causes it to be the case that bodies behave gravitationally, or stand in the relevant relationships. This would render a law-sustained regularity in a certain sense *necessary*; for if a regularity is *caused* to obtain, then in that way it is *made* to obtain, and if it is *made* to obtain, then in that sense it *has* to obtain. At the same time, the necessity involved would not be *strict* necessity; for there would be the possibility of worlds in which, in the absence of this kind of causal necessitation, things were not regular in the relevant way. In these two respects, then, the suggestion gave us what we were looking for. But we also found that, in its basic features, the suggestion was clearly unacceptable. Thus if we were to think of laws as concrete entities which imposed regularities causally, we would be obliged to think of them as having intrinsic natures that were additional to their regularity-imposing role. But it is essential to our conception of a law that its whole nature consists in its role *as a law*—as the sustainer of a certain type of regularity. Moreover, given a law which sustains a certain type of regularity, it is essential to the identity of that law that it sustains that type of regularity. But there would be no way of making sense of this if we supposed the relationship between laws and the regularities they sustain to be merely causal. On both these counts, we recognized that, if there are laws at all, we must take them to be not concrete entities that control the world causally, but abstract entities whose existence consists in the relevant facts of nomic necessity.

This is going over ground we have already covered. But the reason why I am focusing on these points again is that there is something important here that we failed to notice. What we failed to notice is that there is a way of preserving what is attractive in the rejected suggestion, while discarding what is objectionable. For we could accept that a law is something whose existence consists in the relevant fact of nomic necessity, but still construe nomic necessity as causal necessitation. All we would need to do is insist that what does the necessitating is something other than the law itself. In other words, we would need to say that, wherever it is a law that things are regular in a certain way, then (i) there is something which causes, and thereby causally necessitates, things to be regular in that way, (ii) the fact that there is something which causally necessitates things to be regular in that way is what renders the regularity nomically necessary (so that the fact of nomic necessity is to be construed as the fact of causal necessitation), and (iii) the law itself is not the thing that does the causal necessitating, but something whose existence consists in the fact of such necessitation. In this way, we would still be able to make sense of the non-strictness of nomic necessity, since we would not have to think of a regularity that was causally necessitated in the actual world as obtaining in all possible worlds. But we would avoid the unacceptable construal of laws as concrete entities that control events causally.

This new account of the nature of laws is looking promising. But, to give it a chance of proving ultimately acceptable, we need to refine it in a certain respect. It is at this point that the distinction drawn earlier—in relation to the alternative accounts of creation—becomes crucial.

As we saw, there are two quite different ways in which, in the framework of the theistic account, we can think of God as causing the basic regularities. On the one hand, we can think of him as ensuring the obtaining of the regularities by directly fixing all the relevant items of content in the universe in a way that conforms to them. This is the situation envisaged by the first and second accounts of creation, in which God is represented as directly creating the universe in its entirety. On the other hand, we can think of him as imposing the regularities on the universe *as regularities*, in a way that leaves open all the details of how things conform to them, so that this imposition is then what combines with the conditions obtaining at different moments in the history of the universe to determine the specific form which the conformity takes. This is the situation envisaged by the third account of creation, in which God directly creates the initial state of the universe and prescribes the modes of transition to control its subsequent development. Now, at the moment, we are not concerned with the question of the nature of the causal agent—of the thing that is ultimately responsible for bringing about the regularities: in the framework of the theistic account, we take this to be God, but that is not what presently matters. What does matter is the distinction between the different ways in which we can envisage the regularities being caused. For it is only if the regularities are imposed on the universe *as regularities*—caused in a way that leaves open all the details of how things conform to them—that the causing yields the kind of necessity required for laws. There are two aspects to this.

The first and most obvious point is that we only have to reflect on our ordinary conception of a law to see that the necessity involved only covers the obtaining of the relevant regularity, and does not include anything more specific about the way in which things conform to it. Thus the law of gravity, if it exists, makes it necessary, in the relevant sense, that bodies always and everywhere behave, or attract one another, gravitationally, but it does not, on its own, ensure anything more specific about the sorts of gravitational behaviour or attraction that occur. The detailed ways in which the gravitational regularity gets exemplified on any occasion depend not just on the law, but also on the nature of the conditions obtaining on that occasion. So the details of how bodies attract one another at any time depend, in part, on what bodies exist at that time, and on their masses and distance relations; and the ways in which these attractive relationships dispose the relevant bodies to behave depend on still further aspects of the current situation. It follows that if the causing of a regularity is to constitute the obtaining of a law, it must, in the fashion of a law, impose the regularity *as a regularity*. It must necessitate the obtaining of the regularity, but in a manner that leaves open all further details about how this obtaining is concretely realized.

The second point emerges when we consider the relationship between laws and counterfactual conditionals. Laws, if they exist, are not forms of *strict* necessity: the regularities they sustain do not hold through all possible worlds. Even so, the obtaining of a law does have consequences for how things would turn out, or would have turned out, in certain kinds of counterfactual situation. For example, if there is a law of gravity, then not only does this ensure that bodies always *do* behave or attract one another gravitationally (or do so apart from any cases of supernatural intervention). It also ensures such things as that if I *had* released this coin a moment ago, it *would have* fallen, and that if the earth and the sun *were* at this moment closer, the force of attraction between them *would be* correspondingly greater. For, in cases like this, the counterfactual supposition merely envisages some change in the detailed content of the actual world, without disturbing the constraints that flow from its laws. But the causing of a regularity will only have consequences for the outcomes in counterfactual situations if it is a causing of a regularity *as a regularity*. If a regularity is brought about by directly fixing each relevant item of content in the universe in a way that secures conformity, this does not set any constraint on how things would turn out (would have turned out) in any non-actual case. It is only when a regularity is causally imposed on the universe *as a regularity*, without determining anything about the specific form of its holding, that the causing comes to embody a sort of *rule*, which sets a restriction on the range of things that are *capable* of happening, and thereby carries consequences for the outcomes in the relevant kinds of counterfactual situation.

In both these respects, then, we can see that if we want to be able to think of the causal necessitation of a regularity as yielding a law, we need to stipulate that the causation involved be an imposing of the regularity *as a regularity*. With this refinement in place, the account that now emerges of the nature of laws is this:

1. For there to exist a law of nature is for there to be a certain type of natural regularity such that it is necessary, in the relevant nomic sense, that things are regular in that way.
2. For it to be necessary, in this nomic sense, that things are regular in a certain way is for there to be something which causally imposes this regularity on the universe *as a regularity* (i.e. in a way that leaves open all the details of how things conform to it).

I shall refer to this account of the nature of laws as the *causal account*.

Have we at last found, in the causal account, a satisfactory theory of the nature of laws—one that meets our intuitive requirements of what a law should be, and does so in a way that eliminates the problem of coherence that has dogged us for so long? It seems to me that we have. On the one hand, the imposing of a regularity on the universe *as a regularity* creates a necessity of just the right kind. Thus the imposing of the regularity constrains things to behave in the relevant conforming way, and in that sense makes it *necessary* for things to behave in that way. It does this, moreover, in a way which, in the fashion of a law, leaves open all further details about the nature of this conformity. And, crucially, while having the right sorts of consequences for counterfactual situations, the necessity it creates is non-strict, since there is the possibility of worlds in which, in the absence of the relevant constraint, the regularity does not hold. On the other hand, I can think of no other way in which the required form of necessity could be secured. The difficulty all along has been over making sense of the non-strictness of nomic necessity; and the only way I can see of overcoming this difficulty is by understanding such necessity in the causal terms envisaged. Of course, this way of construing nomic necessity is only available if it is coherent to suppose that causation can occur without a prior framework of law, and, as we saw in Lecture 7, there are those who would claim that this is *not* coherent. But I have already indicated why I think that these philosophers are mistaken.

The fact that we have at last found a satisfactory account of the nature of laws does not, of course, entail that there *are* any laws: it just means that we are now in a position to suppose that there are without incurring the charge of incoherence. Whether we should recognize the existence of laws is something that I shall consider presently. But, first, I want to return to the issue of the existence of God, and consider how our conclusion about the nature of laws affects the situation.

IV

Now that we know how to make sense of the notion of a law, I can no longer think of endorsing the argument for theism envisaged earlier. For this argument depended on the assumption that the notion of a law is incoherent and that nomological explanations of the basic regularities are excluded. However, our very way of making sense of the notion of a law makes a new argument available, and it is this argument that I believe to be successful.[1]

The argument is simple. Suppose, for the sake of argument, that there *are* laws. Then, given the causal account, it follows that, for each law, there is something which causally necessitates the corresponding regularity in the relevant way—something which imposes that regularity on the universe *as a regularity*. But now what should we envisage as the agent or agents of these instances of causal necessitation? Well, exactly the same considerations that left the theistic account as the only serious option for explaining the obtaining of the relevant regularities when an appeal to laws was excluded will now leave the theistic account as the only serious option concerning the source of the necessitation. In other words, we shall be rationally warranted in concluding that it is God—the God of the theistic account—who creates the laws by imposing the regularities on the world as regularities.

This means that, whatever view we take of the existence and explanatory role of laws, the need to explain the basic regularities leads us, in one way or another, to a theistic conclusion. If nomological explanations are excluded, there is a strong case for explaining the regularities by appeal to the agency of God. And if nomological explanations are accepted, there is a strong case for concluding that it is God's imposing of the regularities that creates the relevant laws. Either way, there is a strong case for accepting the existence of God.

I should perhaps add that I do not regard this as the *only* strong argument for the existence of God. For, in addition to the phenomenon of regularity, there are a number of other things that I think can only be adequately explained in theistic terms. In particular, I think that it is only by appealing to the creative agency of God that we can satisfactorily account for the existence of non-physical human subjects and their embodiment by human

---

[1] I first put forward an argument along these lines in my 'Regularities, Laws of Nature, and the Existence of God', *Proceedings of the Aristotelian Society* 101 (2000–1), 145–61.

organisms. And I think that it is only by appealing to the values and purposes of God that we can understand how morality can be (as I believe it to be) objective. But these are not matters that it would be appropriate to pursue here. What gives the argument I have presented its special place in our discussion is that it arises out of considerations that are independently central to our investigative concern.

V

Let us assume that we find the argument presented persuasive, so that we now accept the truth of the theistic account and the existence of the God it postulates. In accepting the truth of the theistic account, we are accepting that God is the creator of the physical universe. What we have not yet decided is the method by which he performs this creative work, and it is to this issue that I now turn. I shall continue to work with the provisional assumption that God is responsible for creating every detail of the universe. And I shall also continue to take it for granted that God will use a method of creation of a unitary type in the sense explained.

We have already seen that, within the framework of these assumptions, there are just three methods of creation that we can envisage. The first is to think of God as directly creating the whole universe, in all its extent and with all its content, by a single act. The second is to think of him as directly creating the whole universe by a set or series of acts. The third is to suppose that he directly creates the universe in its initial state, and makes provision for its subsequent history by prescribing the systematic ways in which its state at any given time is to give rise to its states at subsequent times. We have noted that the second account of creation is considerably less plausible than the first: if God wants to create the entire universe directly, it is hard to see why he should divide the work of creation into a set of acts, when he could achieve the same end more simply by a single act. But what I shall now try to show is that, whatever their comparative plausibilities, both these accounts should be rejected in favour of the third.

We have already seen how this third account differs from the other two with respect to the causing of the basic regularities and the place of this causing in the overall scheme of creation. For whereas these other accounts represent God as arranging for the obtaining of the regularities by directly fixing all the relevant items of content in the universe in a way that secures conformity, the third account represents him as imposing the regularities on the universe *as regularities*, and leaving this imposition to be what combines with the conditions obtaining at subsequent times to fix the items of content in an appropriate way. We also know, from the causal account, that it is only where regularities are imposed on it as regularities that the universe comes to contain laws. So we know that it is only on the third account of creation that we are entitled to recognize the existence of laws. This is one of things that makes the distinction between the third account and the other two accounts of particular interest.

In one way, the fact that the third account is the only one that allows for the existence of laws already puts it in a favourable light. As we noted when the problem of laws was first identified, a recognition of laws seems to be implicit in our ordinary view of the physical world. Thus we ordinarily take it for granted that there are certain types of event—like pigs flying or eggs hitting concrete at 100 mph without breaking—which, while logically possible in the abstract, cannot (barring a miracle) occur in practice; and the recognition of these impossibilities seems tantamount to an acknowledgement that the world is constrained by certain forms of natural law. In as much as we would be reluctant to abandon this aspect of our ordinary view of the world, we are, in this respect at least, bound to find the third account attractive. At the same time, we can hardly appeal to this point as providing rational grounds for thinking that the third account is correct. We could only do so if we could first provide rational grounds for thinking that our ordinary view is correct. And, at present, it is quite unclear what such grounds would be. Presumably, our ordinary view can be adequately explained as a response to the presence of the relevant forms of regularity, and such an explanation says nothing about how these regularities have been brought about, or whether the view is true.

However, there is a further point which I see as more telling. Just as it is part of our ordinary view of the world that some types of event and states of affairs are naturally impossible, so it is also part of our ordinary view that material objects have *dispositions*—dispositions to behave in certain ways, or to exert certain kinds of causal influence, in certain types of condition. So we think of a crystal glass as *fragile*, meaning that it is disposed to break when it is subjected to certain kinds of impact, and we think of arsenic as *poisonous*, meaning that it is disposed to cause death or biological damage to certain kinds of organism when ingested. Notice that the presence of a disposition does not depend on there being occasions when the disposition is exercised; nor, when there are such occasions, is the presence of the disposition exhausted by the totality of events that occur on them.

Thus if something is fragile, it is so even if it is never subjected to the kind of impact that would make its fragility manifest. And its fragility has consequences for its behaviour in merely counterfactual situations, as well as in actual: it entails that if the object *were* about to be subjected to the relevant kind of impact, it *would* be about to break, and that if it *had been* subjected to such an impact, it *would have* broken—or, at least, it entails that these are the naturally probable outcomes.

Now if we think of God as creating the universe by the method of the third account, there is no difficulty in seeing how such dispositions would be generated. For, on this account, God imposes certain regularities on the universe *as regularities*, and thus endows it with laws, and these laws would then, together with the intrinsic natures of the objects in question, yield dispositions in the standard way. So the fragility of a crystal glass would be secured by the molecular structure of the glass, together with whatever laws are relevant to the behaviour of things with that structure. But it would not, it seems to me, be possible for God to endow material objects with dispositions if his mode of creation conformed to one of the first two accounts—the accounts which represent him as creating the entire universe *directly*.

Thus let us focus on the case of a particular crystal glass, and let us suppose that God wants to create the universe in a way that renders this glass fragile. How can we think of him as achieving this end under either of the first two accounts of creation? *Ex hypothesi*, he cannot achieve it by creating the appropriate *laws*—laws which, together with the intrinsic nature of the glass, dispose it to behave in the relevant way in the relevant types of condition—since neither of these accounts allows for the creation of laws. But nor, as far as I can see, do these accounts leave God with any other effective procedure. The problem turns on the point, already stressed, that dispositions are not just to do with what actually happens, but also with what would happen, or would have happened, in certain types of merely possible situation. Thus let t be some time occurring within a period when God has decided that the glass is to rest safely in a certain sideboard, out of harm's way. In order to ensure that the glass is in a state of fragility at t, he has do something which ensures that had the glass been subjected to the relevant kind of impact at t, it would then have broken. But if he creates the entire universe (throughout its history and in all its details) directly, the only way in which God could ensure the truth of this counterfactual conditional would be by ensuring that, had he decided to create the universe in a way which made the antecedent of this conditional true (i.e. made the counterfactual situation of impact actual), then he would also have decided to create it in a way which made its consequent true as well (i.e. made the outcome of breaking actual). In other words, the only way in which God could ensure the truth of the counterfactual conditional *about the glass* would be by ensuring the truth of a corresponding counterfactual conditional *about himself*.

Now I am not sure whether there is a way in which God could ensure the truth of this sort of counterfactual about himself. As far as I can see, the only possibility would be to envisage him as starting by forming a generic plan of the sort of universe he wants to create—a plan which would include the specification of certain forms of regularity, but without specifying the details of their exemplification—and then see his adoption of this plan as involving his acquisition of certain creative dispositions, which transcend the content of his actual creative act or acts. So, on this account, what would allow us to envisage it as true of God that, if he had decided to create the universe in a way that included the relevant event of impact, he would also have decided to create it in a way which included the relevant event of breaking, is that we could envisage his overall commitment to ensuring that the universe exhibits the relevant forms of regularity as disposing him in the appropriate way. But even if this makes sense (and I have doubts about whether God could bind the content of his hypothetical acts of creation in this way), it clearly does not allow God to endow the glass, at the relevant time, with a genuine disposition. For the only disposition involved is the one that characterizes *God*, and this makes no difference, in any respect of substance, to how things are *with the glass*.

Take an analogy. Suppose I am a magician—a *real* magician—who can cast spells. In particular, I have the power to cast a spell on this coin which, though not altering its intrinsic (categorical) nature, ensures that it will jump into the air whenever it is touched by a feather. Now if I exercise this power, I give the coin itself a genuine disposition: although I do not alter its intrinsic nature, I dispose it to behave in a distinctive way in a certain type of circumstance, and thereby affect how things are with it. But if, instead of casting a spell on the coin, I simply resolve to keep it constantly in view, and, again by magic, to make it jump in the air on any occasion when I see it touched by a feather, then I do not give the coin itself a disposition. I do not alter the ongoing state of the coin in any way; I simply dispose myself to operate on it in a certain way whenever the relevant condition obtains. In the same way, we cannot think of God as making the glass fragile at t, if all he does to ensure the truth of the relevant counterfactual conditional about it is to acquire a certain creative disposition with respect to it—a disposition which ensures that he would have decided to bring about the breaking had he decided to bring about the impact.

It seems to me, then, that neither of the first two accounts of creation, which represent God as creating the entire physical universe directly, would allow us to envisage him as endowing material objects with dispositions. So, if we are to retain our ordinary belief in such dispositions, these accounts have to be rejected. It also seems to me that, whatever flexibility we might have with respect to our belief in natural impossibilities, our belief in physical dispositions is not one that we could afford to relinquish. For if we did, we could no longer preserve an acceptable account of the nature of the external reality and our relationship to it. Thus if we denied their possession of dispositions, we could no longer think of material objects as having powers to affect our senses; and, without their possession of such powers, there would be nothing in our relationship to such objects which equipped us to perceive them. Moreover, with the rejection of physical dispositions, we could no longer recognize the existence of any of the types of material object that feature in our ordinary and scientific beliefs. For all these types (trees, stones, houses, ... molecules, atoms, electrons, ...) are ones which we conceptually identify, and indeed can *only* conceptually identify, in part by reference to the dispositions of their instances, whether their dispositions to certain forms of sensible appearance or their dispositions to behave and interact in certain ways in the physical domain. The upshot is that if we were to abandon our belief in physical dispositions, we would have to abandon our belief in a physical universe altogether—or at least in a universe that we could still regard as *our world* in any recognizable sense. And, whatever forms of sceptical hypothesis it might be appropriate to entertain in other contexts, it is clear that the existence of a physical universe that qualifies as our (perceptually and conceptually accessible) world is something presupposed by the terms of our present discussion.

Since a non-dispositional account of the physical universe is not an option, we must take God's method of creation to be that of the third account. We must conclude that God creates the universe by directly creating its initial state, and by making provision for its subsequent history by prescribing the systematic ways in which its state at any given time is to give rise to its states at subsequent times. This will ensure that God imposes certain regularities on the universe as regularities, thereby creating laws; and the creation of laws will, in the standard way, furnish material objects with their dispositions.

VI

Our original reason for focusing on the theistic account was that it offered a way of accounting for the regularities in nature that avoided a (potentially problematic) appeal to natural laws. We can now see that, when properly construed and developed, the nomological and theistic modes of explanation coincide. If we decide to explain the regularities by postulating laws, we have to construe the obtaining of each such law as the causal imposing of the corresponding regularity on the universe as a regularity; and the only plausible account of what does this imposing is theistic. If we decide to explain the regularities by appeal to the agency of God, we have to develop this theistic explanation in a way that yields an acceptable account of the nature of the universe; and we can only do this by representing God as bringing about the regularities in a way that suffices for the creation laws. So a nomological approach, correctly pursued, eventually leads us to theism, and a theistic approach, correctly pursued, eventually leads us to nomism. By either route, the need to explain the regularities leads us to a recognition of God as lawmaker.

LECTURE 10

Completing the Picture

I

In the previous lecture, I tried to do three things.

First, I tried to show how we can make sense of the notion of a law, as a form of natural necessity. The problem threatening this notion turned on the point that the necessity involved in laws—*nomic* necessity—is not a form of *strict* necessity. Thus the claim that a certain regularity is nomically necessary allows for the existence of possible worlds in which that regularity does not obtain; and it seems self-contradictory to say that it is necessary for things to be a certain way if there is the possibility of them being otherwise. The solution I offered was embodied in what I called the *causal account* of the nature of laws. On this account, the existence of a law consists in the fact that a certain regularity is causally imposed on the universe *as a regularity*, that is, in a way that leaves open all further details concerning the way that things conform to it. Such causal imposing of a regularity makes the obtaining of the regularity necessary in just the right sense—a sense that explains how things are constrained to be regular in the relevant way, but also allows for the existence of possible worlds in which, in the absence of the relevant form of causal imposing, the regularity does not obtain.

Secondly, in fulfilment of the promise I made at the outset of the lectures, I offered an argument for the existence of God—a God of a broadly Judaeo-Christian type. Specifically, I argued for the truth of what I called the *theistic account*, which postulates the existence of a supernatural personal being, who is causally primitive, who is the creator of the physical universe and the human persons embodied within it, who is sempiternal, who is perfect in his rationality and goodness, and who, apart from any limitations imposed by logic, is limitless in his power and knowledge. My argument rested on two initial assumptions, which I took to be already established. The first was that, when sufficiently extensive, natural regularities call for explanation, and do so simply in virtue of the phenomenon of regularity they exemplify. The second was that, even within the domain of cases already examined, nature exhibits regularities that are extensive to the relevant degree. With these assumptions in place, I then focused on alternative ways in which an explanation of the regularities might be sought. One option was to seek to account for the regularities without an appeal to laws. Drawing on what had been established in Lectures 7 and 8, my claim with respect to that option was that, if nomological explanations are excluded, the only plausible explanatory approach available is to suppose that the regularities have been brought about through the intentional agency of some supernatural personal being, or group of beings, and that the only plausible way of developing this personal-agency approach is by accepting the theistic account, as specified. The other option was to offer an explanation of the regularities by an appeal to laws—laws which, either on their own, or in conjunction with certain standing conditions, require things to be regular in those ways. But, by the causal account, any claim that a certain regularity holds as a matter of law becomes the claim that it is causally imposed on the universe as a regularity. And my claim then was that the same considerations that oblige us to accept that the only plausible non-nomological explanation of the regularities is that provided by the theistic account also oblige us to accept that, if certain regularities are causally imposed on the universe as regularities, only the theistic account offers any plausible story of how such imposing is achieved. So, overall, my claim was that whichever explanatory option we pursue, we are brought to the conclusion that it is only the theistic account that offers a plausible mode of explanation.

Thirdly, having offered an argument for the existence of the relevant type of God, I argued for a specific account of the way in which he creates the physical universe. Thus I tried to show that we should not think of God as creating the *entire* physical universe, in its full spatiotemporal extent, *directly*. Rather, we should think of him as directly creating the universe in its initial state (or in some small initial phase), and making provision for its subsequent history by prescribing the systematic ways in which its state at any given time (or the series of its states over any given relevantly small period) is to give rise to its states at subsequent times. The reason why we have to adopt this second account of creation is that it is the one that allows us to preserve our common-sense belief that material objects have dispositions; and the preservation of this belief is essential if we are to retain an acceptable view of the nature of the universe and our relationship to it. The account allows us to preserve this belief because the prescribing of the modes of transition for the newly created universe is equivalent to the imposing of certain regularities on it as regularities, thereby creating laws; and the laws thus created will then combine with the intrinsic properties of material objects to endow them with dispositions in the standard way. In contrast, if we think of God as creating the entire universe directly, the closest we can come to envisaging him as endowing objects with dispositions would be to envisage him as creating the universe in the framework of certain prior creative policies (policies which ensure that had he decided to create things differently in one respect, he would also have decided to create them differently in another); and his adoption of these policies would, at best, endow *him* with certain dispositions, rather than assign dispositions to the objects he creates.

So, if my arguments have been successful, we now have (i) a proper understanding of the nature of laws, (ii) strong grounds for accepting the existence of a broadly Judaeo-Christian type God, and (iii), within the framework of the assumption of God's existence, a knowledge of the method by which he has created the physical universe and endowed it with its laws. With these results secured, the bulk of what I was aiming to achieve in these lectures is now in place. All that remains to be done, in this final lecture, is to fill in certain details that will serve to complete the picture, or come as close to such completion as I can hope to achieve in the present context.

II

I want to begin by briefly returning to an issue that I raised at the end of Lecture 3, in the wake of my introduction and advocacy of the nomological-explanatory solution to the problem of induction. The issue is somewhat peripheral to my main concerns. But it is nonetheless an interesting one, and, in one important respect, the conclusions that are now in place enable me to make some further progress with it. I shall start by summarizing the issue as it arose in that earlier context.

At the level of particle physics, many of the regularities that empirically present themselves as basic are of a statistical kind—regularities about the relative frequency of certain types of event in certain types of condition—and, like other extensive regularities, they call for explanation. But what sort of explanation should we offer? If we accept that these regularities are indeed basic, and if, in line with the approach of NES, we want to account for them nomologically, it seems that our only course, at least in many cases, will be to accept the existence of probabilistic laws, which assign appropriate degrees of natural probability to the occurrence of the relevant types of event in the relevant types of condition. For example, if we want to account for the statistical regularities characterizing radioactive decay, it seems that our only course will be to suppose that, for each radioactive substance, there is a function f from lengths of period to probability degrees such that, for any period length d, it is a law that, for any atom of that substance, existing at any time, the probability of its nucleus decaying within a period of length d from that time is f(d). The trouble is that the notion of such law-imposed probabilities might well be thought incoherent. If it is a law of nature that, whenever conditions are of a certain sort, there is a certain degree of probability of a certain type of outcome, then, given any instance of such conditions, we not only have to recognize the relevant fact of probability, but also have to think of this fact as a fundamental ingredient of the situation. And it may well be wondered whether we can make sense of there being facts of probability that are fundamental in this way. Of course, it is possible that the relevant regularities are not basic after all: there could be underlying physical factors that are empirically concealed. So it is possible that the real basic regularities, if only we knew of them, would turn out to be nomologically unchallenging. But it would be awkward if we had to appeal to this possibility to avoid the problem. On the face of it, there should be a way of handling things within the framework of what the empirical evidence seems to indicate.

This is how I left things in the earlier discussion. On the central issue of whether we can make sense of natural probability in a fundamental form, I reached no verdict. Nor, indeed, am I going to reach a definite verdict on it now. My inclination is to say that the notion of such probability is indeed incoherent. But I do not, at the moment, have anything I can here appeal to other than a raw intuition. And even this intuition only has the force of how things on balance strike me, rather than of how (as Descartes would have put it) they clearly and distinctly appear.

The point that I now want to make—and it is one that importantly alters the dialectical situation—is that, with our account of the nature of laws in place, and with our recognition of the role of God as lawmaker, a further explanatory option becomes available. For we can envisage God as creating laws which (a) are not probabilistic (in that they do not explicitly assign probabilities of outcome to types of condition), and so do not require a recognition of facts of probability as fundamental ingredients of the world, but (b) play the same organizational role as probabilistic laws, and so are equipped, in the same way as such laws, to account for statistical regularities that are basic. The point is that, because God is a personal being, endowed with rationality, he can deliberately impose rules for the occurrence of certain types of event in certain types of condition which, though not as such probabilistic, succeed in ensuring that everything behaves *as if* there were certain degrees of probability of the occurrence of those types of event in those types of condition.

To illustrate, suppose that God wants to create a law which, while not as such probabilistic, ensures that everything behaves as if processes of a certain type P have a probability of j/k of terminating in events of a certain type E, where j and k are positive integers, with j less than k. (You may find it easiest to focus on a concrete example of j/k, such as 3/4 or 5/8.) And, to keep things simple, let us assume that, at the time when he creates the initial state of the universe, and independently of anything he may know about the extent or circumstances of the occurrence of P-processes in its subsequent history, God is in possession of a method, M, which will suffice, and which he knows will suffice, to order whatever P-processes occur in a discrete series according to their spatiotemporal location. So he knows, in advance, that, for any positive integer n, if there turn out to be at least n P-processes, there will be a unique nth P-process relative to M. Let D be the set of integers from 1 to k. Then we can envisage God as creating the relevant law by (i) mentally selecting an infinite series, S, of numbers drawn from D, with the different members of D randomly distributed over the positions in S, or distributed in a way that simulates randomness for all practical purposes,[1] and then (ii) prescribing that, for any integer n, if there are at least n P-processes, the nth such process relative to M is to terminate in an E-event if and only if the nth item in S is no greater than j. We know that the proportion of the members of D that are no greater than j is j/k.

---

[1] In the present context, the relevant practical purposes are, of course, those that feature in the example, i.e. the purposes of enabling God to create a law that will play the organizational role of a probabilistic law. In allowing the distribution to be merely a simulation of randomness, I am allowing for the case in which God identifies S by means of an algorithm, thereby avoiding the need for a separate act of selecting a number for each place in S.

(For example, if j is 5 and k is 8, D will be the set of the eight integers from 1 to 8, of which the first five will be no greater than 5.) So, since the members of D are randomly (or quasi-randomly) distributed over the positions in S, we can see that, by making this prescription, God ensures that everything behaves as if P-processes have a law-imposed probability of j/k of terminating in events of type E. The regularity which the prescription imposes on the universe is not one about probabilities, but one that consists in a certain correlation between the occasions in which P-processes terminate in E-events and the makeup of S; and since S is fixed in advance, the outcome in the case of each P-process is fully determined by the imposing of this regularity and the position which the P-process has in the ordering defined by M. Even so, the effect of imposing this regularity is to create a law whose organizational role, in terms of the functioning of the universe, is equivalent to that of the corresponding type of probabilistic law, which assigns a j/k probability of E-termination to P-processes. We might appropriately speak of the sort of law thus created as a *virtual* probabilistic law.

The crucial point, in the present context, is that the availability of such virtual probabilistic laws offers the prospect of a further way of explaining the statistical regularities that we encounter in particle physics. For if these laws replicate the organizational role of genuine probabilistic laws, they are also equipped to play the same explanatory role. So if, for example, we want to explain the statistical regularities that characterize the phenomenon of radioactive decay, but think that it is illegitimate to assign the explanatory work to *genuine* probabilistic laws, we can look to the *virtual* variety to do the job instead. In this way, whatever the outcome of the issue over probabilistic laws, we have the prospect of being able to offer a satisfactory account of the situation. Admittedly, the case I have focused on, as a hypothetical example of the creation of a virtual probabilistic law, is of an especially simple type, designed to make the creative procedure particularly straightforward. Things would be more complicated if, say, the probability value involved were irrational, or if the relevant domain of processes were non-denumerable. But if the specific procedure envisaged for this simple case is effective, I assume that, with technical refinements, something along the same general lines could be developed for more complex types of case as well. And, although I cannot claim to have any special competence in this area, I assume, in particular, that something along these lines could be applied to the relevant phenomena of particle physics.

III

I want now to turn to a quite different topic, though again one which relates to something mentioned in our earlier discussion.

The account of creation we are accepting is one that represents God as directly creating the physical universe in its initial state, or perhaps in some small initial phase, and as making provision for its subsequent history by prescribing certain modes of transition for the succession of its states. Let us refer to this as the *evolutionary* account. I choose this label because, although God is represented as the ultimate creative source, the universe is left to achieve its subsequent history by an internal process of causal development, whereby each bit of its history causally evolves out of what immediately precedes it in the framework of the initial prescriptive package.

There are just two creative factors that explicitly feature in the evolutionary account: the direct fixing of the initial state or phase of the universe and the prescribing of the modes of transition. But I made it clear, when I first introduced the account, that we should not understand it as implying that these factors cover the *whole story* of creation. What I have not yet indicated is why we need to leave room for something more—for additional ways in which God acts to determine what takes place in the universe—and it is this matter that I now want to consider. I shall speak of the two factors already identified as the *core* factors. And, for simplicity, I shall assume that God wants to arrange things so that, at any time, the only direct sources of physical influence on how the universe is to continue are contained within the current state of the universe, and do not include aspects of its preceding history.

As I see it, there are three reasons why we should not insist on the core factors covering the whole story of creation. I shall start with the two most obvious.

The first reason concerns the role of human mentality. In defending the coherence of the personal-agency approach, I made clear my commitment to a Cartesian view of human persons and my acceptance of causal interaction between the non-physical mental subjects involved and the human organisms that embody them. But, if I am right about this, we have to accept that there are occasions when non-physical human mentality has a direct causal influence on what takes place in the physical world; and so this form of causal influence is something for which we have to make provision in our account of creation. It follows that, in adopting the evolutionary account, in which we think of God as directly creating the initial state of the universe and prescribing certain modes of transition for its successive states, we cannot think of these acts of creation and prescription as the only creationally relevant factors. Rather, we have to think of God as additionally doing something to bring about the existence of the relevant mental subjects and to ensure their functional attachment to the relevant organisms. There is still the question of the precise way in which God achieves this result. Does he, for example, create the subjects individually (by a separate act of creation for each) or by putting in place some general subject-generating law? And what precisely does he do to secure the appropriate forms of functional attachment of subjects to organisms? But these are not matters that we need to resolve in the present context. All we need to recognize is that, by creating the subjects and securing their embodiment, God is arranging for a special source of causal influence on the physical world, and that his doing so is something additional to what is covered by the two core factors.

The second reason why we should not insist on the core factors covering the whole story of creation concerns the nature of the modes of transition. By prescribing these modes, God is requiring the subsequent history of the universe to be regular in certain ways, and this causal imposing of the regularities *as regularities* suffices to create certain laws. Now let us, just for the moment, ignore the fact, stressed above, that what takes place in the physical world is partly affected by non-physical human mentality. In fact, just for the moment, let us adopt the false, but simplifying, assumption that, apart from *God's* creative role, the physical universe is a closed system, which is not affected by anything outside it. Given this assumption, we can envisage the situation in which, when added together, the laws created by God's prescriptive package form a fully deterministic system—a system which, when applied to the total state of the universe at any time, determines a unique and fully specific mode of continuation. But while we can envisage this situation, there is nothing in the conception of the evolutionary account which obliges us to do so. We could equally suppose that there are cases where all that the laws collectively determine, with respect to the state of the universe at a particular time, is a certain range of modes of continuation, each of which is left as a permissible outcome. For example, we could suppose that, combined with the physical conditions obtaining at a certain time, the laws restrict the movement of a certain particle to a certain range of directions, but do not assign any particular direction to it from within that range. But if there are cases where there is a range of different types of outcome which the laws leave open, then there are opportunities for God to determine the actual outcome *directly*—by additional acts of intentional causing. And so, in allowing for the possibility of such cases, we are allowing for the possibility of a further respect in which there is more to God's creation of the universe than the fixing of its initial state and the prescribing of the relevant modes of transition. Nor is the situation altered when we drop the simplifying assumption. For even when we allow for the fact that human mentality exerts a causal influence on the physical world, we can still envisage cases in which the physical and psychological conditions obtaining at a certain time, together with the physical and psychophysical laws, do not fully determine how things will physically continue, and in which, in consequence, there is room for God to fix the outcome directly.

Two things should now be noted in connection with this. First, in order to envisage this sort of failure of determinism in the system of laws created, we do not need to suppose that any of the laws involved is probabilistic. It is true, of course, that if there were probabilistic laws, they would introduce an element of indeterminism into the system. But even if none of the laws is probabilistic—and, as we have seen, there is an issue over whether we can make sense of such laws—it could still be the case that some of them do not impose a fully specific constraint on the course of events, merely requiring that, whenever certain kinds of condition obtain, some event from a certain range of types occurs. Or it could be that, although each law imposes a fully specific constraint in its own terms, the laws do not collectively cover all physical properties, so that there are certain aspects of the behaviour of the universe over time on which they impose no constraint at all.

Secondly, although the failure of determinism would provide an *opportunity* for God to fix the relevant outcomes directly, there is nothing that would *require* him to do so: he would equally have the option, in each case, of leaving the specific outcome to chance, so that, within the range of what is nomologically permissible, there is nothing, at any point, which causes or encourages things to turn out one way rather than another. And, indeed, if God has set up the system from the outset to be non-deterministic, we can expect leaving things to chance to be his standard policy. Of course, if we allow for cases in which God leaves the outcome to chance, we have to drop the assumption that God is (in one way or another) responsible for bringing about every detail of what physically occurs—an assumption which I provisionally adopted when the different options with respect to the method of creation were first introduced.[2] But, in any case, I think that we need to drop this assumption for a different reason. For since I believe that human subjects (as *all* personal agents) are endowed with a capacity for free choice in a strong, contra-deterministic, sense—a sense which precludes the causal determination of our choices by prior events and conditions—I think that there are certain aspects of the physical universe for which we ourselves are ultimately responsible, or are so, at least, within the framework of the God-created laws that give our choices of action their efficacy.[3]

IV

I have covered the two most obvious reasons why, in adopting the evolutionary account of creation, we should not insist that the two core factors—the fixing of the initial state of the universe and the prescribing of the modes of transition—form the whole story of creation. The third reason, to which I now turn, is less obvious, but more interesting.

We have been assuming that when God prescribes a certain mode of transition for the newly created universe, everything that subsequently physically occurs conforms to it. And, indeed, if the prescribing is without qualification, this assumption cannot be disputed. For to speak of God as *prescribing* a certain mode of transition is just another way of saying that he *intentionally causes* the subsequent history of the universe to conform to it; and if he prescribes this mode *without qualification*, then he causes this history to conform to it in *all instances* and *without exception*. But what I think we need to acknowledge is that God's prescribing of the modes of transition might not be unqualified in this way. For it might be that what he prescribes, in the case of each mode, is not that things are to conform to it *in all instances*, but that things are to conform to it in all instances *apart from* those where he subsequently decides on a different outcome. If God attaches this qualification to his prescribing, then, even in cases where the prescribed modes assign a definite type of outcome to the course of events on a particular occasion, he leaves himself the freedom to overrule what is thus provisionally determined and get things to turn out differently. And so, in acknowledging the possibility that God leaves himself such freedom,

---

[2] See Lecture 9, sect. II.
[3] For my account of human freedom of choice, see my *The Immaterial Self*, ch. 8, sect. 4.

we are acknowledging a further area where the core factors may not constitute the whole story of creation—where God's creative work with respect to the physical universe may involve something additional to his direct creation of its initial state and his prescribing of the modes of transition.

The reason why we need to accept the evolutionary account of creation, rather than one which represents God as creating the entire universe directly, is, as we saw, that it is only the evolutionary account that allows us to think of God as creating laws, and thereby endowing material objects with dispositions. In now claiming that God might prescribe the modes of transition in the qualified way envisaged, I am implicitly assuming that his doing so would not prevent the creation of laws. And this assumption seems to me to be clearly right. For, even if the prescribing were thus qualified, it would still succeed in imposing certain regularities on the universe as regularities, in a way that causally obliged certain forms of behaviour in all instances where there was no additional act of divine intervention, and this imposing would still satisfy the requirements for the existence of laws under the causal account that we have embraced.

There are two ways in which we might think of representing the nomological situation that would emerge if the modes of transition were prescribed in the envisaged way. On the one hand, we might represent the resulting laws as purely physical in their subject matter—as exclusively concerned with the ways in which certain types of physical condition give rise to certain types of physical outcome—but also think of them as laws that God has the capacity to override. So, in the case of gravity, we might represent the law as of the standard type—a law that requires bodies to behave, or attract one another, gravitationally—but take its nomic force to be sufficiently weak to allow God to suspend its efficacy whenever he chooses and bring about a non-gravitational outcome instead. On the other hand, we might represent the resulting laws as unbreakable—as laws that do not even allow their creator to override them—but build the possibility of divine intervention into their content. So, in the case of gravity, we might think of the obtaining of the law as logically excluding the occurrence of counterinstances, but take what is required by the law to be not that bodies behave gravitationally, but that bodies behave gravitationally except in cases where God decides otherwise. Of these two ways of representing the nomological situation, the second is the one that is strictly correct under the terms of our causal account of laws. For, if God prescribes the modes of transition in the qualified way envisaged, the regularities whose obtaining he thereby causally ensures (the regularities he thereby imposes on the universe as regularities) must be correspondingly qualified in content. And, under the causal account, it is these regularities that are thereby rendered nomically necessary. Nonetheless, for ordinary purposes, it is certainly more natural and more convenient to formulate the laws in terms that restrict their subject matter to natural phenomena (so that the law of gravity stays as the law that bodies behave, or attract one another, gravitationally), and represent cases of divine intervention as ones where God is overriding the requirements of the laws, rather than exploiting a permissiveness in their content. And, so long as we know the true nature of the situation—that what God initially causes to obtain explicitly leaves room for the cases of subsequent intervention—there is no objection to looking at things in this way.

It is in these terms that I can now clear up an issue that I raised some time ago, but put on one side. Nomic necessity, as I have constantly stressed, is not a form of *strict* necessity, since it does not exclude altogether the possibility of things being otherwise. The most obvious way in which it falls short of strictness turns on the fact that laws themselves are only contingent and do not even hold constant through all possible worlds which have the sorts of ingredient that are relevant to them. So, for any law, there are compositionally relevant possible worlds in which things fail to conform to the law simply because the law is not present to ensure such conformity. It was exclusively on this point that our discussion of the problem of laws focused. But, as I mentioned when I first introduced the problem back in Lecture 5, there is another way in which nomic necessity might be thought to fall short of strictness.[4] For it might be thought that, as well as not holding through all compositionally relevant worlds, it makes sense to suppose that laws are sometimes contravened. More specifically, it might be thought that, although it makes no sense to suppose that a law is contravened when nature is left to its own devices (when there is nothing other than its own conditions and laws to influence what takes place within it), it does make sense to suppose that there is some supernatural source of agency with the power to interfere in the workings of nature and override the constraints of law on any particular occasion. At the time when I mentioned this point, I left it open as to whether the notion of such contravention was in fact coherent. This issue can now be resolved. Under the terms of the causal account, the notion of the contravention of a law

---

[4] See Lecture 5, sect. IV.

does not, strictly speaking, make sense, since if a regularity is causally imposed on the universe, there is no logical room for counterinstances: if it is caused to be the case that all Fs are G, then all Fs are G. But once we accept that it is God who is the causal agent, we can see how he can fashion the content of what he imposes in a way that leaves room for cases in which he subsequently intervenes; and, if they occur, such interventions will produce physical outcomes that are out of line with the ways in which the universe normally functions, and which differ from the outcomes that the imposing would have produced if the interventions had not occurred. Such interventions would at least amount *in spirit* to overridings of the laws of nature; and, as I have already said, for ordinary purposes, it is more natural and convenient to think of them in this way.

The fact that the account of creation we have endorsed allows us to envisage God as retaining the freedom to intervene—the freedom directly to bring about outcomes that deviate from what his initial prescriptions and the current state of the universe would otherwise determine—will be a welcome result to traditional Judaeo-Christian theists, who believe that God actually does intervene in this way. Thus such theists believe that, on occasions, God intervenes quite dramatically, to bring about outcomes that are *conspicuously* contrary to the normal ways of working of the universe. These dramatic interventions are the ones that carry the title of 'miracles', and cover such putative events as Jesus's turning water into wine and his raising of Lazarus. And they also believe that, as part of his ongoing pastoral care of his human creatures, God sometimes intervenes in less conspicuous ways, doing things that do not, at least to the casual observer, suggest that there is any unusual source of influence at work. Such interventions might occur, for example, in response to petitionary prayer, where the prayer is for some type of outcome (like a good night's sleep or calmness before an examination) which could well come about, in circumstances not noticeably relevantly different from the ones that obtain, through the operation of natural factors alone.

But there is also a further and metaphysically deeper reason why our being able to envisage God as retaining the freedom to intervene is helpful to the religious tradition. The orthodox view, in both Judaism and Christianity, is that, quite apart from cases of intervention, God is constantly at work in sustaining the universe and controlling events within it. At first sight, this view might seem to be in radical conflict with the evolutionary account we are accepting, where the main elements of creation consist in God's fixing of the initial state of the universe and his prescribing of the modes of transition. For, on this account, it seems that, once it has come into existence, the universe is, for the most part, left to run its own affairs. However, if we suppose that God prescribes the modes of transition in the qualified way—leaving himself the freedom to determine outcomes directly whenever he chooses—then, in a sense, the orthodox view is preserved. For in the cases where God refrains from subsequent intervention, he is deliberately allowing things to follow their preordained course, and in that sense is exercising direct control over what happens. So, when one billiard ball strikes another and the second ball moves in the normal way, the first movement brings about the second movement in accordance with the modes of transition already prescribed. But, granted that this prescribing was relevantly qualified, then the second movement only occurs because it has, at the time of its occurrence, God's blessing: it occurs because God decides that, in this case, the normal ways of working are to apply. Quite generally, granted that God has the freedom to intervene whenever he chooses, then, whatever he decides with respect to any occasion—whether he uses this freedom to bring about something anomalous, or deliberately allows things to follow their preordained course—he exercises direct control over everything that happens in the universe throughout its history.

The fact that we are able to develop the evolutionary account in a way that is congenial to traditional theism does not, of course, entail that we should do so. But, even from a purely philosophical standpoint, the supposition that God leaves himself the freedom to intervene in the way envisaged is, I think, very plausible. Obviously, he would have nothing to lose by giving himself this freedom, since possessing it would not oblige him to use it. And, on the face of it, he would also have something to gain. For, granted that he cares about what takes place in the physical world and about the character of our lives within it, it would presumably be advantageous for him to be in a position where he had the power to change the preordained course of events if it conflicted with his purposes. It might be suggested that God could ensure *in advance* that everything conformed to his purposes, simply by fixing the initial state of the universe and the modes of transition in the appropriate ways. But, given that the course of events is partly dependent on how human beings themselves choose to act, and that such choices are made freely (in a way that precludes causal determination by prior events and conditions), there is bound to be a severe limit on what he can ensure by those means alone; and the likelihood is that, whatever initial state and modes of transition he selected, a capacity for subsequent intervention would be of use.

V

Since Lecture 5, we have been focusing on the topics of laws of nature and the creative role of God. And we have seen how these topics come together. Thus we have seen how laws have to be construed as the causal imposing of regularities on the universe as regularities, and how God must be thought of as creating the universe by a method that imposes regularities on it in just that way. I want to conclude by briefly looking again at the topic that dominated our discussion in its first phase. This topic was the problem of induction; and what, in particular, I want to consider is how, if at all, the nomological-explanatory solution I proposed to this problem is affected by the conclusions that we have now reached about laws and God. The basic idea of the solution was that (i) when they are sufficiently extensive, hitherto exemplified regularities call for explanation, (ii) the appropriate way of explaining them is by appeal, wholly or partly, to the existence of laws, and (iii) at least in a significant range of instances, the best (most plausible) nomological explanations available are ones which allow us to deduce that the regularities will continue to hold for the unexamined cases, or will do so subject to the continued holding of certain standing conditions.

In one respect, the situation for NES has clearly improved. At the end of Lecture 5, we left it facing a major problem, namely the difficulty of making sense of the notion of a law; and the account of laws that has now emerged shows how that difficulty can be overcome: it shows how laws can qualify as forms of natural necessity and yet the necessity involved be non-strict. But there are also respects in which both the nature of NES and its underlying rationale have now to be adjusted in response to the theistic outcome. One minor point, which need not detain us, is that if we think that God creates laws in the qualified way envisaged above, so that he prescribes that the universe is to conform to certain regularities *except* in those instances where he subsequently decides on a different outcome, then the deductive move from the nomological explanation to the extrapolative conclusion has to be subject to a further qualification—in effect, to a *Deo volente* clause. This will not undermine the effectiveness of the NES procedure, since we can safely assume that God would not have created laws (imposed regularities as regularities) unless he intended to leave the world to follow its law-ordained course in at least the vast majority of cases.

But there is also a more fundamental way in which the theistic outcome affects the situation, and it is on this that I want to focus. In the original form of NES, regularities were to be explained by appeal to laws, as forms of natural necessity, and the nomological character of the explanations was left as something irreducible. But we now know that the existence of laws must be ultimately understood in terms of the causal agency of God: laws exist, but they are simply what get created by God's causal imposing of certain regularities on the universe as regularities. So, in the ultimate explanation of the regularities, the concept of law disappears and it is only God's acts of intentional causing, and the policies and purposes they reflect, that explicitly feature. This raises the question of whether the shift from the irreducibly nomological to the theistic mode of explanation makes any difference to the final step in the NES account, where it is argued that, in a significant range of instances, the most plausible forms of explanation available are ones that sustain the drawing of an extrapolative conclusion. In its original—irreducibly nomological—context, the central issue here was whether we are justified in postulating laws that are fully universal in scope, in preference to ones that are restricted to some particular period, or region, or set of objects. For, by choosing suitably restricted laws, we could, as we saw, explain the hitherto exemplified regularities without providing any basis for inferring their holding for the relevant unexamined cases. Thus, in the case of gravity, we could account for the hitherto exemplified regularity of gravitational behaviour by supposing it to be a law of nature that, up to the present time, bodies behave gravitationally, while not committing ourselves as to whether there is a stronger law of gravity which covers the future as well. And obviously the acceptance of this explanation would not help to justify the belief that the regularity will continue. My argument against these scope-restricted forms of nomological explanation was that, if we take them as the explanatory terminus, they leave us with a serious puzzle—the puzzle of trying to understand why the fundamental necessities of nature should be discriminatory in the relevant way. Why, for example, in the case envisaged, should a certain moment have this unique significance in the structure of the universe that bodies are gravitationally constrained in the period up to it, but not thereafter? What we now need to consider is what happens to this issue, and the way I tried to deal with it, when we look at things in the new—theistic—perspective.

Well, it becomes, of course, the issue of whether we are entitled to suppose that, in deciding to impose regularities on the universe, God selects ones that are fully universal in scope, in preference to ones that are subject to the relevant kinds of restriction. And there is no denying that this is a quite different issue from the corresponding one about laws prior to their theistic interpretation. In the latter case, the issue was of a somewhat rarefied kind: it was a matter of whether we should think of a certain kind of singular bias in the content of the laws as inherently puzzling. In arguing that we should, I claimed that the notion of generality was already built into the notion of a natural law, and that the gratuitous inclusion of a singular restriction in the content of our nomological theories would run counter to the grain of nomological explanation. In the new context, the issue becomes much more concrete. It changes from an issue of nomological metaphysics to one of divine psychology. Does our knowledge of the mind of God make it rational to suppose that he would set a premium on nomological uniformity? Does it, for example, entitle us to think that he would wish to avoid an arrangement in which bodies behaved gravitationally up to a certain time, but not thereafter, or in which they behaved gravitationally in one part of the universe, but not in another?

Well, given that the God whose existence we are now assuming conforms to the requirements of the theistic account, it seems to me that it does. There are two points to be made here.

In the first place, the God of the theistic account is perfect in his rationality. But if such a God were to restrict the scope of the regularities he imposes on the universe, he would surely need a positive reason for so doing. For to restrict their scope without reason would be to act capriciously—to discriminate between different items on no basis—and such capriciousness would surely have no place in the psychology of a perfectly rational being. But it is hard to think of anything that might give God such a reason—any purpose that might be served by his imposing different nomological constraints on different periods or regions or groups of objects. So, simply from our knowledge of his rationality, our expectation must be that the scope of the regularities he has imposed is not restricted, and that the system of laws he has thereby created is uniform over different parts and phases of the universe.

Secondly, while it is hard to think of how God might have a reason for wanting to restrict the scope of the regularities, it is not hard to identify something that gives him a special reason for ensuring nomological uniformity, or at least for doing so in respect of that portion of the universe whose events and conditions could have some practical relevance to human life. For since the God of the theistic account is morally perfect, we know that he must be benevolently disposed towards his human creation. And if he is benevolently disposed towards us, he will surely want to give us the kind of stable and predictable environment needed for our survival and basic well-being. But he could only do this if, amongst other things, he ensured that, at least in so far as it was liable to affect us, nature worked in a fundamentally uniform way. Of course, ensuring nomological uniformity would not be enough, on its own, to provide all that is required for our survival and well-being. For the *content* of the uniform system has to be of an appropriate kind too. But that does not alter the point that uniformity is needed.

It seems to me, then, that the transformation of the original *nomological*-explanatory solution into the new *theological*-explanatory one preserves our resources for meeting the sceptical challenge; and perhaps it even increases them. Given his perfect rationality, we know that God would not restrict the scope of the regularities he imposes on the universe without reason, and it is hard to think of how a reason for restriction might arise. And, given his perfect goodness, we know that, at least within the domain of things that could affect us, he has a special reason to avoid restriction, so that he can provide the kind of stable and predictable environment on which our existence and well-being depend. It remains, of course, a matter for empirical investigation as to what the God-imposed regularities are; and, here, there is no infallible method of finding the answers: given any hypothesis that is plausible in the light of present evidence, new evidence could show it to be mistaken. But at least we are justified in believing that, under the control of a rational and benevolent God, the world is organized in a way that is conducive to the success of the empirical enterprise—a way that, by its fundamental uniformity, is designed to allow us to gauge how things stand with respect to the unexamined cases from how they have turned out in our experience so far. And that is all that is needed to defeat the sceptic.

Bibliography

Armstrong, D. *A World of States of Affairs*. Cambridge: Cambridge University Press, 1997.
—— *Universals: An Opinionated Introduction*. Boulder, Colo.: Westview Press, 1989.
—— *Universals and Scientific Realism*. Cambridge: Cambridge University Press, 1978.
—— *What is a Law of Nature?* Cambridge: Cambridge University Press, 1983.
Ayer, A. J. *The Central Questions of Philosophy*. London: Penguin Books, 1974.
—— *Probability and Evidence*. London: Macmillan, 1972.
—— *The Problem of Knowledge*. London: Penguin Books, 1956.
Black, M. *Problems of Analysis*. London: Routledge & Kegan Paul, 1954.
—— 'Self-supporting Inductive Arguments', *Journal of Philosophy* 55 (1958), 718–25.
Blackburn, S. 'Hume and Thick Connexions', *Philosophy and Phenomenological Research* 50 (suppl. vol., 1990), 237–50.
—— *Reason and Prediction*. Cambridge: Cambridge University Press, 1973.
Braithwaite, R. *Scientific Explanation*. Cambridge: Cambridge University Press, 1953.
Carroll, J. 'Ontology and the Laws of Nature', *Australasian Journal of Philosophy* 65 (1987), 261–76.
Cartwright, N. *How the Laws of Physics Lie*. Oxford: Oxford University Press, 1983.
Davidson, D. 'Causal Relations', *Journal of Philosophy* 64 (1967), 691–703. Reprinted in *Actions and Events*. Oxford: Oxford University Press, 1980.
Dretske, F. 'Laws of Nature', *Philosophy of Science* 44 (1977), 248–68.
Duhem, P. *The Aim and Structure of Physical Theory*, trans. P. Wiener. New York: Atheneum, 1962.
Edwards, P. 'Russell's Doubts about Induction', *Mind* 68 (1949), 141–63.
Ellis, B. 'Causal Laws and Singular Causation', *Philosophy and Phenomenological Research* 61 (2000), 329–51.
—— 'Causal Powers and Laws of Nature', in H. Sankey (ed.), *Causation and Laws of Nature*. Dordrecht: Kluwer 1999, 19–34.
—— and Lierse, C. 'Dispositional Essentialism', *Australasian Journal of Philosophy* 72 (1994), 27–45.

Foster, J. *Ayer*. London: Routledge & Kegan Paul, 1985.
—— 'A Brief Defence of the Cartesian View', in K. Corcoran (ed.), *Soul, Body, and Survival*, 15–29. Ithaca, N.Y.: Cornell University Press, 2001.
—— *The Case for Idealism*. London: Routledge & Kegan Paul, 1982.
—— *The Immaterial Self*. London: Routledge, 1991.
—— 'In *Self*-Defence', in G. Macdonald (ed.) *Perception and Identity*, London: Macmillan, 1979, 161–85.
—— 'Induction, Explanation, and Natural Necessity', *Proceedings of the Aristotelian Society* 83 (1982–3), 87–101.
—— *The Nature of Perception*. Oxford: Oxford University Press, 2000.
—— 'Regularities, Laws of Nature, and The Existence of God', *Proceedings of the Aristotelian Society* 101 (2000–1), 145–61.
Goodman, N. *Fact, Fiction, and Forecast*. 4th edn. Cambridge, Mass.: Harvard University Press, 1983.
Helm, P. *Eternal God*. Oxford: Oxford University Press, 1988.
Hume, D. *Enquiries Concerning Human Understanding and Concerning the Principles of Morals*, ed. L. Selby-Bigge. 3rd edn. revised P. Nidditch. Oxford: Oxford University Press, 1975.
—— *A Treatise of Human Nature*, ed. L. Selby-Bigge. 2nd edn. revised P. Nidditch. Oxford: Oxford University Press, 1978.
Kripke, S. *Naming and Necessity*. Oxford: Basil Blackwell, 1980.
Leslie, J. *Value and Existence*. Oxford: Basil Blackwell, 1979.
Lewis, D. *Counterfactuals*. Oxford: Basil Blackwell, 1973.
Nicod, J. *Foundations of Geometry and Induction*. London: Routledge & Kegan Paul, 1930.
Popper, K. *Conjectures and Refutations*. London: Routledge & Kegan Paul, 1963.
—— *The Logic of Scientific Discovery*. London: Hutchinson, 1959.
—— *Objective Knowledge*. Oxford: Oxford University Press, 1972.
Reichenbach, H. *Experience and Prediction*. Chicago: University of Chicago Press, 1938.
Rice, H. *God and Goodness*. Oxford: Oxford University Press, 2000.
Salmon, W. 'Inductive Inference', in B. Baumrin (ed.), *Philosophy of Science: The Delaware Seminar*, ii. 353–70. New York: Interscience Publishers, 1963.
Shoemaker, S. *Identity, Cause, and Mind*. Cambridge: Cambridge University Press, 1984.
Stove, D. *The Rationality of Induction*. Oxford: Oxford University Press, 1986.
Strawson, G. *The Secret Connexion*. Oxford: Oxford University Press, 1989.
Strawson, P. F. *Introduction to Logical Theory*. London: Methuen, 1952.

Strawson, P. F. 'Universals', in P. French, T. Uehling, and H. Wettstein (eds.), *Midwest Studies in Philosophy* iv. 3–10. Minneapolis: University of Minnesota Press, 1979.

Swinburne, R. *The Christian God.* Oxford: Oxford University Press, 1994.

—— *The Coherence of Theism.* Oxford: Oxford University Press, 1977.

—— *The Existence of God.* Oxford: Oxford University Press, 1979.

—— *Is There a God?* Oxford: Oxford University Press, 1996.

—— (ed.) *The Justification of Induction.* Oxford: Oxford University Press, 1974.

Swoyer, C. 'The Nature of Natural Laws', *Australasian Journal of Philosophy* 60 (1982), 203–23.

Tooley, M. *Causation.* Oxford: Oxford University Press, 1987

van Fraassen, B. 'Armstrong on Laws and Probabilities', *Australasian Journal of Philosophy* 65 (1987), 243–60.

—— *Laws and Symmetry.* Oxford: Oxford University Press, 1989.

—— *The Scientific Image.* Oxford: Oxford University Press, 1980.

Index

Armstrong, D. 1, 94–110, 111–12, 118 n.
Ayer, A. J. 10 n., 15, 22, 30 n., 40–2, 60

Bayes's theorem 23 n.
Black, M. 12 n.
Blackburn, S. 14 n., 80 n.
Braithwaite, R. 12 n.

Carnap, R. 30 n.
Carroll, J. 97 n.
Cartesian view 123–5, 128–9, 131, 139–40, 173–4
Cartwright, N. 37 n.
causation 80, 105–6, 116–18
  between mental subject and body 124–5, 173–4
  compositional relevance 84–5, 94–5
  contravention of laws 84, 178–9
  counterfactuals 40, 93, 158, 162–5
  creation of universe 130–1, 150–5, 161–5, 173–80

Davidson, D. 116 n.
design, argument from 79
determinism 21, 53, 174–6
dispositions 86–8, 114–15, 162–5, 177
Dretske, F. 97
dualism, *see* Cartesian view
Duhem, P. 41 n.

Edwards, P. 13 n.
Ellis, B. 88 n.
embodiment 124–5, 138, 173–4
empiricism 60–1, 80–2, 105, 117–18
explanation 59
  call for in the case of regularities 42–9, 59–69, 112–13, 160, 168

inference to the best 35–6, 41–9,
  and then passim
  nomological 37–56, 69–75, 77–8, 160, 166, 169–72, 181–4
  personal 121–5
  theistic 128–55, 160–84
extrapolation 4–5; *see also* induction

free will 125, 128, 176, 180

General Theory of Relativity 44–5
God 1–2, 78–9, 128–84
  argument for the existence of 1–2, 78–9, 149–50, 160–1
  creator of laws 160–84
  creator of universe 150–5, 161–5, 173–80
  Judaeo-Christian conception of 132–4, 147, 179–80
  sustainer of universe 179–80
  and time 133–4
Goodman N. 5
goodness 120–1, 133, 134, 137, 143–5, 183–4
gravity 37–8, 44–6, 61–3, 69–75, 82–8, 114–15, 157–8, 177–8, 182–3

Harrod, R. 30 n.
Helm, P. 133 n.
Hume, D. 2, 9, 51, 60, 80–2, 105, 116, 123

induction 1–76, 181–4
  attempt to justify by appeal to laws 37–76, 181–4
  attempt to justify by appeal to probability 18–30

induction (cont.):
  attempt to justify by conceptual analysis 13–14
  attempt to justify inductively 12–13
  attempt to justify pragmatically 13
  defined 4–5
  problem of 2–8
  regarded as a basic form of sound reasoning 14–16, 30–6
  scepticism about 6–11, 14–16, 29–30, 52, 69–75, 181–4
inference to the best explanation 35–6, 41–9, and then passim
intelligibility, empiricist criterion of 80–2, 117–18

Judaeo-Christian theism 132–4, 147, 179–80

Kripke, S. 89–90

laws of nature 1–2, 37–56, 69–76, 77–110, 111–12, 116–20, 149–84
  as accounting for natural regularities 37–56, 69–75, 77–8, 166, 169–72, 181–4
  Armstrong's theory of 94–110
  causal account of 155–9
  construed as relations between universals 96–110
  in context of nomological explanatory solution 37–56, 69–75, 77–8, 94–5, 181–4
  contravention of 84, 178–9
  created by God 160–84
  as forms of natural necessity 1–2, 37–49, 71–3, 76, 78, 81; see also kind of necessity involved in
  kind of necessity involved in 82–93, 94–7, 104–8, 111–12, 155–9, 167, 176–80
  ontological nature of 39, 91–2, 155–7
  probabilistic 52–6, 169–72, 175
  problem concerning 2, 77–93, 94–7, 111–12, 155–9, 167
  and reductive accounts of causation 116–18
  scope-restricted 69–75, 115, 181–4
Leslie, J. 120 n.
Lewis, D. 84
Lierse, C. 88 n.
logical necessity 82–4, 88–90

miracles 9, 179
moral goodness 134, 137, 143–5, 183–4
moral ought 144
multiplication principle 22–5

natural laws, see laws of nature
natural necessity 1–2, 37–49, 54, 71–3, 76, 78, 81–97, 111–12, 114–15, 155–9, 167, 176–80, 181–4; see also laws of nature
necessity
  a posteriori 89–90
  logical 82–4, 88–90
  natural, see natural necessity
  strict and non-strict 82–92, 94–7, 111–12, 155–9, 167, 178–9
NES, see nomological-explanatory solution
Newton, I. 37–8, 44–5, 83, 113
Nicod, J. 23 n.
nomic necessity, see natural necessity; laws of nature
nominalism 98
nomological explanation 37–56, 69–75, 77–8, 160, 166, 169–72, 181–4
nomological-explanatory solution (NES) 42–52
  objections to 57–93
  theistic version of 181–4

omnipotence 134, 137–41
omniscience 134, 141–2
Ontological Argument 147–8

personal-agency approach 120–7; see also supernatural personal agent
developed theistically 128–48
Popper, K. 9–11
possible worlds 84–92
probabilistic laws 52–6, 169–72, 175
probability 4, 18–30, 52–6, 64–9, 169–72
 epistemic and natural 19–21
 in attempts to justify induction 22–30

radioactive decay 54–5, 170, 172
randomness 26, 28–30, 171
realism, about universals 97–100
regularities
 attempts to explain naturally but non-nomologically 113–20
 basic and non-basic 53–4, 56, 113–14
 as calling for explanation 42–9, 59–69, 112–13, 160, 168
 nature of 5
 nomological explanation of 37–56, 69–75, 77–8, 160, 166, 169–72, 181–4
 personal-agency explanation of 120–7
 statistical 52–6, 169–72
 theistic explanation of 128–55, 160–84
Reichenbach, H. 13
Relativity, General Theory of 44–5
Rice, H. 120 n.

Salmon, W. 13 n.
sampling, principles of 25–30
sempiternity 133–4, 135–7
Shoemaker, S. 87–8
simplicity, as a criterion of plausibility 129
statistical regularities 52–6, 169–72

Stove, D. 25 n.
Strawson, G. 80 n.
Strawson, P. F. 13 n., 99 n.
strict necessity, see necessity
supernatural personal agent 120–55, 160–84
 causally primitive 131–2
 as characterized by the basic account 129–32
 as characterized by the theistic account 132–48
 creator of human persons 131, 145, 173–4
 creator of laws 160–84
 creator of universe 130–1, 150–5, 161–5, 173–80
 Judaeo-Christian conception of 132–4, 147, 179–80
 perfectly good 134, 143–5, 183–4
 perfectly rational 134, 142–3, 183–4
 a necessary being 147–8
 sempiternal 133–4, 135–7
 unlimited in knowledge 134, 141–2
 unlimited in power 134, 137–41
Swinburne, R. 129 n., 133 n., 134 n.
Swoyer, C. 87 n.

theism, Judaeo-Christian 132–4, 147, 179–80
timelessness 133
Tooley, M. 97, 99 n., 109 n.

uniformity of nature 3, 11, 29, 31, 69–75, 181–4; see also regularities
universalizability, in ethics 75
universals 97–100
 laws as relations between 95–110

Van Fraassen, B. 41 n., 102 n.
verificationism 81–2, 88
virtual probabilistic laws 171–2